Film Narratology

Most modern studies of the narrative tend to focus predominantly on literature, with only passing reference to film. In *Film Narratology*, Peter Verstraten makes film his primary focus, exploring the neglected and essentially different narrative effects that are produced through mise en scène, cinematography, and editing.

Reworking the definitive theory of narration offered by literary scholar Mieke Bal, Verstraten examines cinematic techniques such as external and internal narration, visual and auditive focalization, the narrative force of sound, and the ambiguities caused by voice-overs and flashbacks. He illustrates these with a broad range of examples drawn from avant-garde cinema, golden age Hollywood, blockbusters, and European art cinema. Insightful and comprehensive, *Film Narratology* will surely become the standard reference of cinematic narration for film students and scholars.

PETER VERSTRATEN is a lecturer in Literary Studies at the University of Leiden.

STEFAN VAN DER LECQ is an editor at the Amsterdam School for Cultural Analysis.

FILM NARRATOLOGY

PETER VERSTRATEN

Translated by Stefan van der Lecq

UNIVERSITY OF TORONTO PRESS
Toronto Buffalo London

© University of Toronto Press 2009
Toronto Buffalo London
www.utppublishing.com
Printed in Canada

Reprinted 2010, 2011

ISBN 978-0-8020-9351-6 (cloth)
ISBN 978-0-8020-9505-3 (paper)

Printed on acid-free paper.

Library and Archives Canada Cataloguing in Publication

Verstraten, Peter
  Film narratology / Peter Verstraten ; translated by Stefan van der Lecq.

  Translation of: Handboek Filmnarratologie.
  Includes bibliographical references and index.
  ISBN 978-0-8020-9351-6 (bound)   ISBN 978-0-8020-9505-3 (pbk.)

  1. Narration (Rhetoric).   2. Motion pictures.   I. Lecq, Stefan van der
  II. Title.

  PN1995.V42613 2009   791.43'6   C2009-902853-0

University of Toronto Press acknowledges the financial assistance to its
publishing program of the Canada Council for the Arts and the Ontario
Arts Council.

University of Toronto Press acknowledges the financial support for its
publishing activities of the Government of Canada through the Canada
Book Fund.

Contents

List of Illustrations

Acknowledgments

This book owes its final form to the test readers, whom I would here like to thank for their useful remarks and constructive comments. In order of appearance, they are Ernst Van Alphen, Frans-Willem Korsten, Vincent Meelberg, Mieke Bal, and Bart Vervaeck. Further, I am glad to cooperate with my generous and stimulating colleagues at the Department of Literary Studies in Leiden, who make me experience work as a joyful adventure.

I want to express my gratitude to my parents, who supported me on every occasion. Next I want to thank Chantal Aliet, for always being such a dear friend, and Marieke Buijs, for opening up a portal to the seventh-and-a-half heaven, full of thistle finches.

I dedicate *Film Narratology* to the ultimate darlings, Febe and Bodil, who both adore (film) stories – from *The Gold Rush* to *The Wizard of Oz*, from *E.T.* to *Ja Zuster, Nee Zuster*, and from *Wallace and Gromit* to *Ratatouille*.

Film Narratology

Introduction

When the action-packed blockbuster *Godzilla* (Robert Emmerich, 1998) was released, the tag line was 'Size does matter,' referring to the size of the eponymous monster wreaking havoc in New York. Wittily, sceptics replied, 'Plot does matter, too.' Although it was still possible to make head and tail of the film, it lacked a solid bone structure. It has often been said that big Hollywood productions sacrifice consistent plotlines in favour of spectacle. A decent story is also said to be missing in films such as *Lara Croft: Tomb Raider* (Simon West, 2001) and in European Hollywood imitations like *The Fifth Element* (Luc Besson, 1997). When asked why the digital effects overshadowed the shaky plot of Besson's film, leading man Bruce Willis answered that nobody cares for stories nowadays.[1]

Willis's remark is right insofar as it refers to the classic ways of narrating. These presume that causal relations are consistent, a criterion that has traditionally been considered to be the parameter of plot. We follow a hero in time and space from A to B to C. It is possible for a narration to jump from A to C, but only on the condition that development B is addressed in (for instance) a flashback. If a film starts with development E, A-B-C-D will eventually also be shown. I mean to say that it must always be clear who the hero is, what his or her background is, what his or her aims are, and why the hero does what he or she does. In a classic film, the hero has to overcome obstacles while trying to achieve an aim, for instance because the interests of other characters are in opposition. The hero will normally succeed, but this is not an iron rule.[2]

A narrative logic that is jarring or altogether lacking is primarily the domain of the avant-garde, underground, and independent film, as well as of European art cinema. In Hollywood itself, however, these strict narrative conventions have of course not always been followed with equal rigour. In the musical genre, for example, spectacle triumphs over plot. Storylines are secondary to the song and dance intermezzos, and the logical sequence of causal relations is therefore suspended. From a pattern of parallels and contrasts that is not psychologically motivated, the viewer[3] must ascertain which woman belongs to what man (see Chapter 9). Films in the first phase of New Hollywood cinema (1967–76) often portrayed 'unmotivated' protagonists who strove to achieve few or no specific goals. These films have hardly any intrigue and are often the characterized by inaction rather than action. The hero in *Five Easy Pieces* (Bob Rafelson, 1970), for instance, has almost no other ambition than avoiding his wife.[4] In road movies from this period, the experience of being underway is more important than the journey's destination. The stories in musicals and New Hollywood films can be reduced to reasonably transparent fabulas: generally, it is clear what happens when and where. The point is that musicals and some New Hollywood films present variations on classic Hollywood films by glossing over the motivations for the actions of their main characters.

A more fundamental breach of traditional narrative logic is formed by time-travel films like *The Terminator* (James Cameron, 1984) and *Back to the Future* (Robert Zemeckis, 1985). Even though these films upset temporal developments only mildly, they can still be considered a breaking point with classic storytelling, and their impact has prepared the way for more rigorous variations. In the complex *12 Monkeys* (Terry Gilliam, 1996), a time traveller (played by Bruce Willis) witnesses his own death. What is timeframe A for his youthful self is timeframe E (or F, or G) for his older self. As an eight-year-old, he sees his older self shot as a traveller from the future, causing time to be caught in a loop. *The Terminator* can be seen as a predecessor of the multilayered *Total Recall* (Paul Verhoeven, 1990), in which the protagonist struggles with a permanent crisis of identity that proceeds even beyond the scope of the film. Because his identity is not clearly demarcated, it is difficult to place him on the axes of time and space. The film is unquestionably narrative, but it is impossible to provide the scenes with a clear narrative frame.

According to new media theoretician Peter Lunenfeld, the much-debated crisis of (classic) film narratives has more to do with the sheer quantity of stories in the contemporary information age than with indifference: nowadays, simple references suffice.[5] We can easily jump from A to C while omitting B because the visually literate viewer has already trodden that particular path many times. A tightly structured plot is unnecessary in a blockbuster like *Godzilla*. For the modern-day 'popcorn movie,' intended simply to provide entertainment, the typical, standard elements of a story no longer require elaborate psychological motivations.[6] Characters can be reduced to stable functions: D fights E to save F.[7] In these films the structure of a 'box of bricks' is enough: the stacked bricks do not represent a full development but base their narration on references to overly familiar plot devices. They present a sequence of events that are not explicitly causally related, but the viewer who is familiar with story patterns from other films can usually fill in the gaps.

Apart from these 'box of bricks' films, the last fifteen years have seen the rise of films with a so-called contiguous approach. Films like *Short Cuts* (Robert Altman, 1993), *Magnolia* (Paul Thomas Anderson, 1998), *Amores Perros* (Alejandro González Iñárritu, 2000), and *Crash* (Paul Haggis, 2004) offer a mosaic of widely diverging characters.[8] What connects the characters is often little more than that they (temporarily) reside in the same place, which enables them to cross paths for a short time. These ensemble films are based on a narrative structure that also differs from classic narration in that coincidences now take precedence over causal relations: something might happen out of the blue, and events do not require a thorough introduction. In *Short Cuts* and *Magnolia,* the narrative climax is formed by natural events such as an earthquake and a rain of frogs. These jumbled narratives are surprising and unusual when viewed from the perspective of filmic tradition. Nevertheless, they do adhere to a logic we have come to connect with hypertext, jumping from one link to the next.[9] I want to argue that the altered nature of narration in cinema is an urgent reason to rethink filmic narrativity.[10]

A second reason why a book on film narratology is relevant at this moment has to do with developments in the field of new media studies, which have their impact on academic film culture and vice versa.[11] In their search for a language and grammar of new media, Janet H. Murray, Lev Manovich, and Marsha Kinder, among others, have posed narratological questions. How do digital media, with their database logic and interactive ambitions, relate to narratives, film or otherwise? What are the differences and similarities between the rules of computer games and of narratives? What does the future hold for the narrative in cyberspace, and how does cyberspace in its turn influence cinema? Because the new media have inherited much from cinema, the narratological discussion returns to film studies like a boomerang. This makes a reconsideration of the theory of narrating and narrations essential, especially because the major studies on film narratology are most certainly not without their flaws.

Studies by David Bordwell (1985), Edward Branigan (1984 and 1992), and Seymour Chatman (1990) are acknowledged as authoritative within the field of film studies. Bordwell can nonetheless be faulted for prematurely decapitating his narrative theory, since he insists on a cognitive narrative process that has no specific narrative agent. Partially because the majority of films present themselves as what he calls 'invisible' narrations, he considers the narrator to be first and foremost a projection on the part of the viewer. As a rule, says Bordwell, there is no separate narrator because the film's story is taking place mainly inside the viewer's head.[12] Branigan, on the other hand, unfortunately clings to the idea of a neutral, 'nonfocalized narration' and considers shots to be subjective only when they are justified by the perception of a certain character. That is why he devotes considerable attention to point of view in cinema. Branigan presumes that a narrator can focalize events only if he or she has become a character of sorts and is no longer an invisible agent.[13] Chatman, finally, relies too much on the implied author as the source of textual intention and tends to make the balance shift to the sequence of images or a dominant voice-over in the case of tension or ambiguity.

The flaws of these studies can be grouped under a common denominator. They remain overly faithful to structuralist narrative analyses, whereas the need has risen for a poststructuralist approach to the matter at hand. This especially rings true when one considers the new horizon for cinema created by the new media. In my opinion, Mieke Bal's *Narratology* (1997) offers a starting point for such a film narratology. This might appear odd, since *Narratology* is an English revision of a 1978 study in Dutch that was exclusively focused on literature from a structuralist point of view.[14] However, *Narratology* is partially a poststructuralist adaptation of that study. Bal now has a sharper eye for ideological issues, the role of the reader, and the multivalence of contexts. Furthermore, *Narratology* is the result of her attempts in the intervening years to surpass a simple binary opposition between word and image. Her revised narrative theory offers several possibilities for a visual narratology.[15] Since Bal herself is mainly concerned with the traditional visual arts and less with film, the current book aims to apply her well-established narratological method to the field of film studies.[16]

Filmic Narrator, Visual Narrator, Auditive Narrator

Even though this study has narratology as its starting point, it is essential to realize that the filmic narrator has a different 'identity' from a literary narrator.[17] This causes filmic narration to diverge fundamentally from literary narration. According to Bal, the narrator is an agent – a function – that conveys a story in a specific medium.[18] In literature, this medium is language, in the form of words on paper, and Bal thus gives her chapter on the narrator the title 'Text: Words.' A literary narrator is an agent making linguistic utterances. There can be multiple narrators in a single novel, but because these can be ordered hierarchically their respective statuses can in principle be reconstructed. Every text has either an external narrator who exists completely outside of the fabula, a narrator who refers to himself only on occasion, or a narrator who takes on the identity of one of the characters. The external and internal narrators coincide in the final two examples, but it is nevertheless important to maintain a consistent distinction between the two. An external narrator is the narrative agent that organizes the entire text, whereas an internal narrator signifies a character-bound narration. Within the narration of such a character, another narrator's story may again be embedded ('While travelling I met Peggy, who told me the following story'), and so on. Narratologically speaking, Peggy is accorded the status of an embedded internal narrator of the second level.

Film narratology cannot directly copy this idea of the literary narrator. My work is infused with the understanding that there are, to paraphrase Seymour Chatman, many things that novels can do that film cannot and vice versa. Consequently, a narrative theory for novels has different emphases from a narrative theory for films. Transposing from one medium (or theory) to another does not produce any predictable results because of the distinct nature of each medium.[19] Film, for instance, could be said to be more of a hybrid medium than literature. Apart from a sequence of moving images, film can also contain title cards, spoken words, sounds, music, and so forth. The main function of a filmic narrator is to show moving images (possibly with printed text) and to produce sound (possibly in the guise of spoken text). Since images and sounds can each tell a different story, I propose to divide the filmic narrator into a narrator on the visual track and a narrator on the auditive track. I proceed from the assumption that the narrator on the visual track is essentially deaf to all sounds, just as the narrator on the auditive track is blind to all visual influences. It is up to the filmic narrator to regulate the interaction between both sub-narrators. Because of this specific (and layered) 'identity' of the filmic narrator, the narrative techniques and stylistic procedures in cinema are inevitably fundamentally different from those in literature (or those in comics, music, painting, sculpture, and the theatre, to name but a few).

General Approach

Just as many different types of texts, ranging from novels to newspaper articles, are narrative so scores of films are narrative as well. But to what extent can films be called narrative? Does the narrative nature of cinema have its limits, and if so, how do non-narrative aspects manifest themselves in film? These questions that explore the scope of film narratology will be at stake in Chapter 1. I discuss the criteria that determine the narrative aspects of cinema and argue that narrativity is based on an interaction between the text and its reader or viewer. In this process, the viewer assumes the role of addressee.

In order to equip the viewer properly for his role as addressee, Chapter 2 introduces the basic principles relevant to cinema as well as to narrative texts. These principles – which include story and fabula, space and place, character and focalization – have been introduced by Gérard Genette and were partially revised by Bal. I explore them further in a short analysis of Ian McEwan's novel *The Comfort of Strangers* (1981). Since this book has also been adapted into a film with Paul Schrader as director and Harold Pinter as screenwriter, I introduce the narrative issues in cinema with an example taken from this film in each of the following chapters.

Narration is the representation of a (perceptible) temporal development. For film, this means that showing a moving image may already suffice to create a narration. Imagine, for instance, a one-shot film in which a man carrying a pie slips on a banana skin and, naturally, ends up with his face in the pie. Here, we are dealing with a sequence of events with both a cause (a banana skin that goes unnoticed) and a consequence (a rather awkward fall). Using such an example, we could define filmic narration as showing a moving image with the option of adding either editing or sound.

The showing of moving images concerns a first level of narrativity. It can be considered the primary function of the (external) narrator on the visual track. Filmic showing is never a neutral narrative act, however, but always already an interpretation by the visual narrator. This narrative agent is responsible for choosing who or what can be seen, for locating the characters in a certain space, for positioning the characters with regard to each other, and for determining the kind of lighting in the shot. These issues concerning the mise en scène will be considered in Chapter 3.

Apart from the mise en scène, it is also important to realize how exactly the scene is being shot; this falls under the header of cinematography, the subject of Chapter 4. From what angle (high, low, or eye level) is a certain shot taken and from what distance is the camera filming (close up or long shot)? What lenses are the shots filmed with, and what type of film stock has been used? And is the image perhaps further manipulated by emphasizing certain colours, by superimposing shots, by distorting the image's focus, or by using background projections?

Chapter 5 centres on editing as the second level of narrativity. In an uncut film, we essentially have a continuum of space and time. This continuum can be broken by means of editing. The option of cutting scenes enables the disjuncture of the time of the story and the time of the fabula. On the one hand, I give examples of the ways in which (indeterminate) time leaps can be made. On the other, I discuss how narrative spaces are constructed by means of editing. This requires an elaboration on the theory of suture, which relies heavily on the shot/reverse shot principle.

The first five chapters revolve around the basic principles of narration (1 and 2) and the basic techniques of film (3 to 5). The reader may consider these chapters as an instructive overview of main narratological issues. Progressing from this foundation, it becomes possible to integrate, or, in other words, to analyse, narrative principles in cinema more consistently. Because of the lack of precision in traditional theory, I exchange film studies' deep-rooted suture theory for the concept of focalization as developed by Bal. Since I have not yet treated sound as a filmic category, I will analyse only the way in which focalization manifests itself on the visual track. Through several examples, I explain how external, internal, and ambiguous focalization can be interpreted in cinema; focalization is finally be shown to oscillate between 'correct' perception and hallucination, making it impossible to determine where the balance shifts to eventually. I devote special attention to the option that a shot can show a certain character as the object of focalization while at the same time being an internal focalization of that character itself.

I come to the interaction between the visual and the auditive tracks in Chapter 7, but limit my discussion of the latter track to the (spoken) text of the narrator for the time being, exploring the interface of the voice-over and the images that this off-screen voice accompanies. The visual narrator may assume the role of a police sketch artist, thereby conforming to a character's voice-over. The responsibility of assigning this role lies with the filmic narrator, which, as I indicated before, can be divided into a visual and an auditive narrator. Furthermore, I discuss the flashback that is introduced by a narrating character as well as the principle of the internal narrating voice that is juxtaposed to external or ambiguous focalization on the visual track. I also delve into the remarkable case in which one character narrates by means of a flashback while another character (who is the object of focalization within that same flashback) becomes the subject of focalization nonetheless. This chapter demonstrates the usefulness of a distinction between a visual and an auditive narrator; these two agents can, after all, contradict each other. By dividing the filmic narrator into a visual and an auditive narrator, it becomes possible to articulate this contradiction and to understand how a clash makes sense between word/voice-over on the one hand and image/flashback on the other.

Chapter 8 revolves around the auditive narrator as the external agent that controls all forms of sound – not just voice-overs, but also dialogues, music, clamour, and other noises. In comparison to the previous chapter on visual focalization in flashbacks, the roles can now be reversed: a character can be the object of focalization visually but the subject of focalization on the auditive track. Sound in film has the remarkable characteristic of being able to function as a double track. Extradiegetical sounds (that are being played along with the images, in other words) can, upon closer inspection, turn out to be functioning on the level of the story in the film itself instead, and vice versa. An endless number of different sounds can be stacked together, moreover, and transitions ('cuts') in sound are rather difficult to recognize. Sound that is focalized externally can thus easily intermingle with sound that is focalized internally. In this chapter, I analyse several examples in which sound plays such a manipulative role that we start to perceive the scenes with our ears rather than with our eyes. The process also works the other way around: our perception of sound is partially determined by the way in which we interpret certain situations.

Chapter 9 addresses the problem of intertextuality insofar as it concerns the conventions of and specific types of narration in genres. Generally, a film becomes understandable only when it is related to other films or genres. Many genres are bound to specific narrative conditions. Every new genre film is burdened with these conditions and is continually forced to take an (implicit) stance on its own narrative stipulations. It has become convention, for instance, that the monster in a horror film is usually able to focalize, whereas his counterpart in a science-fiction film generally is not. Furthermore, a cowboy can become a classic hero in Westerns only when he is neither a narrator nor a focalizor. Understanding these narrative principles makes a film belonging to a certain genre or based on the structure of a certain genre more readable. Being aware of the narrative conditions of genres also enables us to recognize any deviations from standard patterns as meaningful interventions.

In Chapter 10, I discuss an issue that, strictly speaking, falls outside of the scope of film narratology but directly relates to it nonetheless. Whenever the stylistic elements of a film seem to be relatively autonomous and do not further the plot or even hinder it, excess ensues. This non-narrative excess can nevertheless be of crucial importance to an analysis of the story because, as I argue, it can serve as an in-built guide for viewing that may be helpful in determining the status of the story. Extravagant stylistic elements can make this status shift, for instance by pointing the viewer in the direction of irony, parody, or persiflage: 'Do not interpret the story of this film according to classic standards, but consider the excessive stylistic elements as a self-reflexive or ironic commentary on a traditional narrative analysis.' Only by properly appreciating such stylistic overkill can the viewer safeguard himself from overly straightforward or naïve readings. The final chapter underlines that the viewer can come a long way by means of a thorough narrative theory, but it also makes clear that narratology is not a magical solution to all interpretative problems. After all, narratology restricts itself to narrative aspects. It does offer a sound foundation, if only the reader of this study realizes that a complete narrative analysis is always 'narratology plus X.'

chapter 1

Is Cinema Essentially Narrative?

In narratological studies, it is customary to work with the triadic set of text, story, and fabula. The literary text encompasses all the words on paper, whereas the filmic text consists of a series of moving images on-screen that are (usually) accompanied by sound. The story concerns the specific way in which plot elements are ordered. The fabula, finally, is the chronological reconstruction of the events according to causal logic. This triad can be condensed into a single formula: 'A says that B sees what C is doing.'[1] A is the narrator on the textual level, B is the focalizor on the level of the story, and C is the actant on the level of the fabula. The term *actant* refers to a relatively abstract role (being a 'helper' or an 'opponent,' for instance) that should be seen in relation to attempts to reach the aim that forms the core of the fabula. Either an actant can decide to take action or an event can happen to the actant. On the level of the story, the role of actant is in effect assumed by one or more characters.[2]

The focalizor is first and foremost, always external, coinciding with the external narrator; there is always an external narrator/focalizer. In a sentence such as 'When the workers opened the sewer, a disgusting smell emerged,' for example, an agent that is not present in the story narrates what it saw and smelled. The focalizor can also be a character, however, in which case this internal, second focalizer is hierarchically lower and embedded in the external focalization. In a sentence like 'Peggy recognized Tosca's perfume and, as she turned around, she indeed saw her friend,' an external agent is narrating and focalizing the scene. Peggy is an internal focalizor and Tosca is the object of her focalization. In this example, the reference to an external narrative agent is a technicality and may seem somewhat redundant, but in Chapter 5

I again use the example of Peggy to show that the reader's awareness of constant external focalization is in fact crucial.

Following Mieke Bal's example, I use the representation of a (perceptible) temporal development as the basic definition of a story. A transition from one situation to another takes place, and that change is brought about by a (non-)act effected by someone or something. If the rain dance of a certain character in a film is followed by a spontaneous downpour, for instance, one may suspect that his act has caused the cloudburst. If the sun breaks through the clouds after the dance, however, this can also be taken as a change caused by the same act. The weather could be interpreted as a reaction to the failure of the dance. But for those who do not believe in the magic effect of the rain dance, the changing weather conditions have nothing at all to do with the dancer's act. If it happens to start raining, the 'event' needs to be attributed to something else: the rain may simply be the result of advancing storm clouds. Generally, *not* conducting a certain act can also be classified as a development. When someone stands by as another person is drowning, his failure to act has consequences for the further development of the fabula. Even if the drowning person is saved after all, a breach of trust might at least be one of the results.

The scope of the term *temporal development* can be debated. Bal claims that temporality can be 'read' in, for instance, paintings. In Rembrandt's work, the depicted scenes often suggest a story by means of the viewing directions and facial expressions of the characters. In *Susanna and the Elders,* for example, we see how Susanna is being watched by the elders while she seems to turn to the viewer for 'protection.' The painting shows a moment 'frozen' in time while simultaneously revealing interaction, both between the characters and between the characters and the viewer.[3] Even non-figurative paintings can be narrative. The wild brush strokes of abstract expressionist action painters like Willem de Kooning and Jackson Pollock 'narrate' the creative process: their fierce painting techniques seem to imply movement.[4] This movement points to a certain temporal order that can be reconstructed by 'reading' the painting.

Essentially, film is the setting in motion of a series of photographic images that pass forward (or occasionally backward) along the temporal axis. Filmic frames are linked moments in time. Because of the emphatic presence of temporality it would not be too big a leap to claim, along with André Gaudreault, that cinema has been equipped with narrative antennae.[5] Concurring with Gaudreault, Seymour Chatman

claims that a novel can give an exhaustive description of the surroundings or of the looks of a certain character – fabula time is then arrested
for a pause in the story – but that film scenes cannot pause and consequently are unable to describe.[6] In his opinion, film cannot withstand
the constant narrative pressure: the projection of moving images on the
temporal axis forcefully drags the story on. Does this narrative pressure
mean film is a machine that, according to Gaudreault, is doomed to tell
stories? This question does not allow for any other answer than a complex 'yes and no.'

Time, Space, Causality

Whoever wants to approach the matter from a strictly historical perspective may be forced to claim, as Sean Cubitt does, that the earliest forms
of cinema were not narrative. Cubitt argues that temporality is not yet
properly directed in the first one-shot films. Originally, cinema was an
endless stream of photo frames.[7] Like waves at sea, this primary state
of cinema is independent of beginnings or endings. In the case of the
Lumière brothers, it was not the things that were shown that gave rise to
fascination but rather that something unprecedented could be shown at
all. The most miraculous effect of cinema was based on pure movement:
this was a cinema of immediate presence, of the here and now, without
past or future.[8] It was straightforwardly sensational and yielded an experience that was not bound to narrative expectations. Having studied
the oldest experiences of the medium, Cubitt cautions that narrativity
is not inherent in cinema. At the moment of its conception, cinema was
neither created nor experienced as a narrative medium.

    According to Cubitt, it is only when the cinematic cut is introduced
that temporality is given a direction.[9] By means of cutting, the length
of shots is shortened and the viewer starts to focus on what exactly is
moving in the image. The cut marks the transition from the experience
to the perception of the filmed object. Cubitt claims that this transition
is comparable to looking at paintings by Camille Pissarro from a distance. When one looks at his canvasses from less than an arm's length,
it seems that the painter has merely applied colourful smudges and
dots. A recognizable image can only be discerned if the viewer increases the distance between himself and the painting.[10]

    Cubitt argues that the viewer becomes sensitive to the composition
and framing of film shots only at the moment he becomes aware of what
he is looking at. This sensitivity generates certain questions. What does

the person at the front have to do with that person in the background? Why have they chosen this setting? The person at the front is looking to her left: what could she be looking at outside this frame? Where will the camera be in the next shot? These questions evince two important principles. First, if the cut encourages the viewer to transform waves of photo frames into 'objects in the world,' the length of the shot is given limits and the moving image becomes located spatially. This transition is marked by the changing attitude of viewers: instead of 'Wow, we are actually seeing a projection of a walking man,' they might now think, 'In the image, a man with a cowboy hat is walking through a wide landscape. Is he going somewhere? How long do we keep following him?'

Second, the filmic space creates causal relations, a typical temporal phenomenon: first this happened, then that happened. A causal link, however, can often be drawn only in retrospect. If we see a shot of a man in a room followed by a shot of a gun in a drawer, questions arise. Does this revolver belong to that man? Why does he have a revolver? Does he feel threatened? If so, by whom? If the man actually uses the revolver later on, the earlier shot of the drawer gains relevance: the weapon was put there for a reason. The showing of the gun turned out to be functional.

I stated that Cubitt gives a strictly historical analysis: cinema has not been narrative from the moment of its conception because true narrativity can only be the product of the possibilities of editing. Speaking against this vision, we could bring in the argument of retrospectivity. With the knowledge of cinema we have now, we can also classify the earliest films as narrative. (And since both visions have their validity, this explains the complex 'yes, and no' answer to the question whether cinema is essentially narrative.)

According to Gaudreault, the short film *La sortie des usines lumière* (Louis and Auguste Lumière, 1895) can be called narrative. In this film, shot with a static camera, the workers do little more than leave a factory. The earliest film of the brothers shows at least part of a certain temporal development: the gates have opened and the workers are walking through it. Therefore, the film can be called a 'micro-narrative.'[11] Gaudreault applies the term *monstration* to these early one-shot films.[12] They are not yet 'narrating' in the proper sense of the word, but by only *showing* they both create a sequence of photographic images and capture movement. This form of showing suffices for Gaudreault as the basic criterion for a (micro-)narrative. He considers monstration to be the first level of narrativity. Whereas Cubitt holds that narrativity comes into the picture only with the advent of editing, Gaudreault believes editing to be a second level of narrativity. The narration is no longer exclusively determined by what is being projected, but mainly by the transitions from one shot to the next. According to Gaudreault, these transitions between images shape narration in cinema.[13] I will discuss this more extensively in Chapter 5, but for now it is sufficient to highlight three important functions of editing. First, it allows time to be manipulated, for instance by omitting a certain time span. Second, space can be framed (time and again). Third, causal relations can take shape because of the way in which images are juxtaposed.

Time, space, and causality are the main principles of narrative cinema. In this type of cinema, multiple storylines can be adroitly combined according to a pattern of causes and consequences; the direct look into the camera has become taboo. If we transpose this to the 'classic' variant of cinema, we would get a formula that says, 'We know, or will soon know, why the characters are where they are and at what time they are there.' The triad of time, space, and causality is therefore a basic ingredient of narratively inclined cinema. Nevertheless, filmmakers have thankfully used the many opportunities to violate these classic conventions. Psychological motivations for someone's actions can remain unexplored, leaving the possibly enigmatic reasons for a certain deed unresolved. In several (European) art films, moreover, it is more or less impossible to fit the pieces concerning time and space together. The clear reconstruction of when what took place is barred. Although these films are a challenge to narrative rules and make it impossible to ascertain a coherent fabula, they are nonetheless narrative.

L'année dernière à Marienbad (Alain Resnais, 1961) is characteristic of the narrative inclinations of 'alternative' films. The title explicitly refers to the classic parameters of time and space: we know when (last year) and where (the health resort Marienbad) the film may be taking place. In the film, a nameless man in an immense baroque hotel is telling a woman about his encounters with her. They are said to have met many times near the balustrade of a garden full of statues in Frederiksbad, or perhaps in Marienbad or Karlsbad. The woman does not have a single memory of their meetings, which generates the impression that the 'events' have sprung from the lover's imagination. The status of the characters is unclear, moreover. We see the woman photographed by a man who is presumably her husband; did this event take place last year, or is it imaginary once again? The fact that the characters in the hotel are moving about like 'statues' and the many references to being dead suggest that possibly the guests are roaming the hotel as ghosts. In the end, the lover claims that the woman has withdrawn with him and away from her husband, but within the context of the film this claim is rather unconvincing. Because of the many uncertainties, it finally becomes impossible to categorize *L'année dernière à Marienbad*: is it an abstract thriller, a love story, or a philosophical puzzle?[14]

Resnais's film violates the traditional use of the basic narrative ingredients, but that in itself is rather unremarkable. However, it makes one wonder whether these ingredients could in fact be lacking altogether. Is non-narrative cinema possible at all? An unequivocal answer sadly cannot be given. I say 'sadly,' because this issue, which I have already touched upon, is one of the most complex matters I intend to discuss. Just as the claim that every film is narrative is not completely correct when one adopts Cubitt's historicizing perspective, the assertion that a genuinely non-narrative film can exist is also hard to defend. Since the debate concerning narrative and non-narrative cinema has not yet wholly crystallized in film theory, the issue demands to be explored more fully.

Freeze-frame and Temps mort

Narrativity is supposed to be innate to cinema because films essentially consist of passing time. An obvious exception to this rule is the technique of the freeze-frame, which literally stops the image and temporarily turns it into a photograph of sorts. A frozen frame, however, does not necessarily cease to be narrative. One of the most famous freeze-frames in film history is the final shot of *Les quatre cents coups* (François Truffaut, 1959). The young Antoine Doinel has escaped from a juvenile institution and is running toward the ocean. The film ends with a 'photographic' portrait of his face in close-up just as he is turning toward the camera. Strictly speaking, the filmic movement is arrested. Nevertheless, the underlying suggestion is narrative. The freeze-frame invites the viewer to complete the story. According to Chatman, the frozen shot does not imply a standstill or a pause, but instead signifies a repetitive pattern: Antoine is trapped in the filmic frame, just as he will remain trapped in an existence made up of failures.[15] All in all, the freeze-frame is the starting point of several sequels about Antoine's life. These sequels, which have in fact been realized, confirm the pattern of struggle already visible in *Les quatre cents coups*.[16]

According to Chatman, the freeze-frame does not escape from the narrative pressure that is supposedly inherent in cinema. He compares the narrative function of a 'dead moment' like the freeze-frame to a taxi meter: even if we are in a traffic jam, the meter is still running.[17] The story continues even when the image stops, if need be with an appeal to the viewers to interpret the freeze-frame for themselves. Like *Les quatre cents coups*, the road movie *Thelma and Louise* (Ridley Scott, 1991) ends with a freeze-frame. A police force has closed in on the heroines and their only option is to drive straight ahead, where a gaping canyon awaits them. Thelma tells her friend to drive on. Louise steers the car toward the abyss. On the level of plot, their kamikaze-like decision equals certain death. As their car is flying through the air, however, the image freezes and dissolves into a bright, white screen: The End. On the one hand, the freeze-frame prevents us from actually seeing the dismal image of the heroines being crushed to death in their car. On the other hand, the choice for a freeze-frame fits in with the drift of the film. Up until that point, Thelma has led a dreary existence as the eternal housewife. Because of her long weekend with Louise, she discovers that she has been a little crazy all along. Surrendering to the police will inevitably prevent her from exploring her newfound freedom any longer, which comes down to her 'symbolic' death. This is the film's message to the viewer: give in to your own folly and experience the unique sensation of an escape from the humdrum everyday. This general idea can live on beyond the credits only on the condition that the film ends in an apparent utopia. By ending *Thelma and Louise* with an eternally hovering moment, we are urged to consider this message as a positive alternative after the film has ended. Because of the freeze-frame, we are given the illusion that the film's ending is not the end but that we can continue it in our heads.

Cinema has in its terminology another technique that implies a standstill: the so-called *temps mort*. This term indicates a scene in which no discernible events take place. In the films of Michelangelo Antonioni, such 'dead time' manifests itself when the camera lingers at a place the characters have already passed. Oddly enough, the absence of the characters within the shot is made all the more palpable by the passing of time: how long will it take for the camera to pick up the characters again? The non-appearance of a character where you would normally expect one to appear is also a form of development, much as a non-act (idly standing by as someone is drowning) is also a form of action.

Tension, Attraction, and Story

With the freeze-frame and *temps mort*, I have discussed the dividing line between narrative and non-narrative on the level of the shot and the scene, respectively. In both cases, the balance shifted to the narrative side. The next step is concerned with the way in which (spectacular) scenes relate to the (main) plot. This step refers back to a debate between historians of the early film about the term *attractions*. This term signifies a type of cinema that was dominant until 1906, a period that preceded the development of the cinema of narrative integration. According to Tom Gunning's famous article 'The Cinema of Attractions,' such early cinema involves an 'exhibitionistic confrontation' with the viewer: look at me performing my tricks.[18] Browsing through old collections, Gunning came to the conclusion that early films were predominantly a display case for a series of circus acts.[19] In the vein of vaudeville theatre, early cinema revolved around unrelated acts that lacked any dramatic unity.

Don Crafton has polemically reduced the difference between attraction and story to a difference between 'pie' and 'chase.' A chase has a cause, shows a linear development, and is only rarely confined to a single space. The throwing of pies in slapstick comedies, on the other hand, seems to be a spectacle staged only for the camera. According to Crafton, such comical actions or gags meet the criterion of a typical attraction: it needs to be a unique, self-sustaining event. If the pie throwing has any cause at all, it disappears in the sheer fun of pies flying through the air. The relation to the main plot is usually irrelevant, which also applies to gags such as comedians' pulling funny faces. Crafton believes there is a fundamentally unbridgeable gap between the gag and the (main) story.[20]

According to Tom Gunning, however, the gag is always integrated into the overarching story of the film. Apart from the fact that the gag already offers a microscopic story in itself, it is only an ornament of the main plot in the first place. Pie scenes may seem to be an end in themselves and to drift away from the film's storyline, but Gunning claims they always have a discernible narrative motivation.[21] A similar tension between story and intermezzo can be found in genres as diverse as the musical, the pornographic film, and the Hollywood action movie. Narrative patterns have been sacrificed for the true attraction of these genres: song and dance, sex scenes, or flashy action sequences. The plot functions mainly as an excuse for or an introduction to these scenes. Eventually, however, these intermezzos are integrated into the plot, no matter how rudimentary it may be.[22]

'Zero Degree' of Narrativity?

The point so far is that specific techniques such as freeze-frames, *temps morts*, and intermezzos become embedded within a larger story. This seems to corroborate Gaudreault's and Chatman's view – that narrativity is inherent in film – but that conclusion remains under dispute. In earlier editions of their handbook *Film Art* (such as the fourth edition of 1990), Bordwell and Thompson dedicated a chapter to 'nonnarrative formal systems'; in it, they suggested the existence of an absolute zero degree of narrativity. It remains to be seen, however, if the 'rhetorical' and 'categorical' films they discuss can be completely disconnected from all narrative structure. The 'rhetorical' documentary *The River* (Pare Lorentz, 1937) has an argumentative structure supported by continual parallels and contrasts, but it also has an undeniable temporal development: in the end, Monument Valley returns to its former tranquil state due to the construction of dams. Leni Riefenstahl's 'categorical' registration of the 1936 Olympics in Berlin is an interaction between narration and rhetoric. In the middle part of *Olympia, 2: Teil, Fest der Schönheit* (1938), the decathlon is covered by focusing on athlete Glen Morris. This particular segment shows the Olympic Games as a competition, composed of elation and disappointment. This is a customary way of narrating sports events: who wins and who loses, who has taken the lead, how he manages to keep ahead, and who is lagging behind. In most of the other sequences, however, there is no competition at all. Only the 'beauty' of sports is revealed as pure attraction, emphasized in shots of anonymous divers exhibiting their skills against the background of a cloudy sky. In these scenes, the usual story of a competition is suppressed and the Games appear to be an event of universal brotherhood in accordance with the slogan 'Participating is more important than winning.' This rhetoric has nothing to do with the competition story in the film itself but is cunningly embedded in the grander story of political propaganda: Look at how we Germans are elevating this grandiose sports event into a feast of beauty for all the citizens of the world.

In the examples of 'rhetorical' documentary and 'categorical' film, similarities and differences between shots and scenes overshadow the temporal developments. Ultimately, however, because they are embedded in an overarching story these developments do not falter. In the seventh edition of *Film Art* (2004), Bordwell and Thompson circumvent the precarious issue of narrative versus non-narrative by transforming the chapter into an account of alternative basic types that are subdivided into documentaries (like *The River* and *Olympia*), experimental films, and animation films. It is predominantly in the category of experimental films, which in turn includes abstract cinema, that narrative integration is almost wholly absent.

Abstract Film

The abstract film *Ballet mécanique* (Dudley Murphy and Fernand Léger, 1924) is based on an argument: rhythmic dancing is done by objects (hats, bottles), whereas people move mechanically.[23] In accordance with Henri Bergson's theory that we laugh each time a person gives the impression of being an automaton, the film opens and closes with an abstract animation of the comedian Charlie Chaplin, whose apparently agile body remains straight as a board while moving and who is consequently notorious for his almost mechanical stiffness. In addition, *Ballet mécanique* predominantly shows rhythmical similarities between objects, shapes, and title cards. The eleven-minute film shows an incredible amount of movement, ranging from objects to human figures, but all of it seems to lack a direction. We repeatedly see a shot of a cleaning lady climbing a stairway, for instance, but the shot cannot be related to a fabula or to a temporal sequence of causes and consequences. The connection with the other shots is graphic and rhythmic: the way in which human bodies move is reminiscent of objects or machine parts.

The abstract form of Murphy's and Léger's 'visual symphony' is suitable to an 'argument' constructed almost entirely by means of metaphorical similarities. In order to reduce human beings to machinery, their psyches need to be as 'empty' as possible. Because of the complete removal of psychological aspects, temporality, causality, and space become irrelevant and narrativity (as a characteristic of the film) is shut out. Similarities grow to be so dominant that the story is suppressed. A film becomes non-narrative by filtering out and suppressing temporality, causality, and space, but consequently turns out to be nothing more than a formal exercise.

One reservation concerning the idea that *Ballet mécanique* is a non-narrative film needs to be made. Psychoanalysis has taught us that the repressed can resurface in a different guise. Even if a film consists of an accumulation of similarities and temporal developments appear to be lacking, the viewer may not be able to resist an inclination toward narrativity. The viewer will possibly try to reorder the endless flow of movements into at least a minimal narrative, a possibility not unlike Bal's idea that the seemingly non-narrative work of action painters can be interpreted narratively if one reads the canvas as expressing movement.[24]

Content, Form

For Bordwell, a narratological analysis revolves around the interaction between narrative tactics and stylistic features. This interaction is analogous to the more familiar distinction between content and form. Content refers to the bare representation of the plot, which is reduced to the question 'What is it about?' Narrative tactics concern the shaping of the content; the order in which events are told, for instance, falls within the story's narrative tactics. Form denotes the furnishing of the content and involves the question 'How and by what means is the content conveyed?' This entails a choice from the entire arsenal of filmic techniques: what camera positions does the director choose, what colours, what type of shot transitions, how does the sound correspond to the images, and so on. Style is a further specification of the formal possibilities. According to Bordwell, style refers to the systematic use of film techniques. He uses the word 'style' when a director or filmic genre can be recognized by the techniques employed. The interaction between content and form, or, in Bordwell's terms, between style and narrative construction, determines how time, space, and narrative logic will be manipulated.

The distinction between form and content is not as strict as it may appear because form is not a neutral conductor. Form is not like a wire that conducts electricity with a burning light bulb as its final 'content.' Formal features inevitably distort the content as well. One could envisage an experiment in which a man is filmed as he is visiting a museum and looking around. If cheerful music accompanied the images, the pleasure of the visit would be emphasized. If ominous music was used, however, the viewer might get the idea that the man is being pursued. Thus, a formal adjustment can greatly influence the content of a film.

Because of the impossibility of a completely neutral form, content is always distorted. I understand this distortion to be 'excess,' a concept I derive from an essay by Kristin Thompson. If a film exhibits 'style for its own sake,' filmic excess ensues.[25] If the style draws too much attention to itself, the story is in danger of dissolving. Excess begins where motivation is lacking, or, in other words, where a stylistic feature does not propel the story or serve a narrative function. In Thompson's view, excess is both 'counternarrative' and 'counterunity'; it prevents the story from creating closure.[26]

According to this point of view, *Ballet mécanique* is an excessive film. Because of the emphatic rhythmic parallels and contradictions, temporal developments become secondary. Bordwell claims that the concept of excess cannot be reconciled with narratology. Excess falls outside the scope of narrative analysis.[27] He blames excess on an exuberant style that is not functional to the story. In Bordwell's view, *Ballet mécanique* is so abstract that the viewer is not invited to read a narrative into the film.

Every film creates a certain measure of excess, but the exact level of excess is determined by the balance between form and content. In the classic film or the average genre film, excess manifests itself where specific stylistic means temporarily short-circuit the story: ostentatiously low-angle or high-angle shots, overly fast shot alterations, very extreme close-ups, sudden subjective shots, and the use of bright or dim lighting are all possibly excessive. Techniques like these can draw attention to themselves in such a way that it distracts you from the story; they can almost make you forget you are watching a film noir or a Western. In the black-and-white Western *Forty Guns* (Sam Fuller, 1957), the camera films the hero almost from beneath his feet, looking up at him (Figure 1.1a). The shot becomes almost an abstract composition. Above the hero's hat, we see a vertical black line. In the next shot, the narrative efficiency of the 'abstract' shot is demonstrated: the line is a rifle, which belongs to a man who is holding the hero at gunpoint from the upper-storey window (Figure 1.1b).

1.1a *Forty Guns* An extremely low angle shows many horizontal lines. The incongruous vertical black stripe above the hero's head …
1.1b … turns out to be a sniper's rifle in the next shot.

It does not seem too big a leap to hypothesize that a classic film with a sound narrative logic can relatively easily absorb excessive elements. Conversely, stylistic excess can less easily be incorporated when a film does not have a tight narrative structure. This hypothesis results in an apparently logical rule of thumb: the less plot or content a film has, the more its style and form move to the foreground. The more strongly form and content diverge, the more excessive the film becomes. This claim can easily be tested against European art cinema. In *L'avventura* (Michelangelo Antonioni, 1960), a group of friends travels to a deserted island. Suddenly, Anna disappears and Sandro and Claudia start a search. Gradually, the cause of the search appears to be forgotten: Anna's disappearance is never solved. In the words of Pascal Bonitzer, 'What happens is that Anna's disappearance itself disappears.'[28] For a film called 'the adventure,' remarkably few exciting events are taking place. As the film progresses and the plotline concerning the missing woman fades away, Antonioni's meticulous style, with its stringently composed black-and-white shots and dead moments, focuses attention on itself to such an extent that L'avventura now seems to be concerned only with its own unorthodox style.

As a rule, no film is unproblematically narrative in its entirety. Storylines are always distorted by formal techniques. The tighter the narrative structure, however, the better this distortion can be concealed. That is why the chance of a disturbed balance between form and content seems greater in avant-garde films and European art cinema than in classic Hollywood films. Nevertheless, this seemingly logical rule requires further specification. Even in films that are exceptionally narrative in nature, the form can be so ostentatious that 'excess' cannot be contained in the end. It would be easy to claim that the issue of excess, strictly speaking, falls outside of the scope of my main subject, narratology in film. However, film analysis is more than analysing narrative aspects – as I said earlier, analysis is 'narratology plus X.' In the final chapter, I discuss this X more closely by studying stylistic conventions in order to broaden the scope of Thompson's definition of excess.

The Film Viewer as Second Person

As a starting point, I asked whether cinema was narrative down to the bone. Earlier, I claimed that no answer is possible other than a complex 'yes and no.' On formal grounds, the majority of films can unproblematically be called narrative. The criterion is whether a narrative agent is conveying a story (or storylines) in which a temporal development takes place. Even when this is not the case, the narrative input can always come from the side of the viewer – an 'abstract' film such as Ballet mécanique, in which metaphorical connections are dominant, can still become narrative if the viewer interprets it as such.

Poststructuralist reception theories hold that the viewer or reader plays a decisive role in the making of meaning. Jonathan Culler claims that the reader can select from myriad conventions when analysing a text. The choice of a reading convention is of key importance to the final interpretation. A reader's interpretation of a sonnet, for instance, will be affected by his assumption that a sonnet should form a 'unity,' or that the second part of the poem should contrast with its beginning.[29] It also makes an essential difference whether a reader approaches a text 'seriously' and literally, or whether he is reading ironically instead. To take up the thread of Bal's example of De Kooning and Pollock once more, the reader can interpret their non-figurative paintings as a type of 'narration' about the creative process because of their brush strokes. The paintings do not represent a definite sequence of events but are themselves a story about the interaction between the viewer and the painting. A precondition for such a narrative reading in the vein of Bal is that we first have to examine how a 'text' (painting, film, novel, and so on) is structured in order to determine the viewer/reader's share of and responsibility for interpretation.[30]

The conclusion to be drawn here is that narrativity in cinema is created by an interaction between the narrative agent and the viewer. In classic cinema, which spells out the developments according to a clear pattern of causes and consequences, the narrative agent is so emphatically directing the story that the viewer need only follow. When this often psychologically motivated pattern becomes less obvious, the viewer can accept the invitation to put in some effort himself. The amount of effort required can vary greatly. In the case of the 'box of bricks' structure of contemporary blockbusters, it is relatively limited. As I mentioned earlier, these films usually omit elements with which the educated viewer has already become sufficiently familiar by means of other films. Complex art films like *L'année dernière à Marienbad*, on the contrary, demand a true exertion on the part of the viewer. There is a fabula to be reconstructed from the scenes, but it remains unclear whether that fabula has actually taken place. On a narrative level, Resnais's film remains ambiguous. *L'éclisse* (Michelangelo Antonioni, 1962) is another fine example. The last five minutes of this film contain shots of the place where the main characters had earlier agreed to meet. They both fail to show up. The five minutes now emphasize the slow passage of time. The film becomes an exercise in patience. Will they show up or not? When the film ends, this question is still not answered. Will they perhaps meet after the film has ended, and if so, what will they say to each other? Even though nothing relevant to the plot happens in the final scene, the narrative issues are simply relegated beyond the scope of the actual film. The narrative agent is putting the story on the viewer's plate, beyond the usual 'The End.'

The viewer can also decline the invitation made by less clearly structured films. In *Germania, Anno Zero* (Roberto Rossellini, 1947), a paedophiliac Nazi teacher tells the young Edmund that the community can thrive only when the strong show no consideration for the weak. When Edmund's father keeps complaining that he is a burden to his family because he has a chronic disease, his young son ends his father's suffering with a poisonous drink. Subsequently, the film shows Edmund hopping and wandering through the ruins of Berlin for minutes. As his name is called and the coffin of his father is carried away, he jumps out of the window of a bullet-torn building. It would be logical to see a causal link between the teacher's advice, his father's death, and Edmund's final suicide. However, Edmund's expressionless face does not reveal anything about his motives for jumping toward his death. His blank expression also does not make clear whether he killed his father out of cruelty, out of love, or because of the supposed command of his teacher. Edmund is such a 'vacant' character that the usual psychological motivations are perhaps best avoided. In the case of *Germania, Anno Zero*, it seems inappropriate to draw any overly firm causal relations.[31]

The examples mentioned above demonstrate that a certain attitude can be expected of the viewer but that there is no pre-set route to be followed. When watching a film, we always set it off against a background of other films. In a movie theatre, we automatically bring an entire visual package as baggage. In short, we always watch intertextually. Concerning this issue, I concur with the view put forward by Julia Kristeva and Maaike Meijer that intertextuality is an interpretative frame that one can choose to employ.[32] Intertextuality is a way of reading or viewing. It does not adhere to a prescribed trajectory and has an impromptu nature. The reason is that the viewer is not a part of the representation but its addressee.

Bordwell does not believe in the idea of the viewer as an addressee. In his *Narration in Fiction Film*, he takes issue with the enunciation theory of the linguist Émile Benveniste, which had a considerable influence in film studies at the time Bordwell was writing. The idea behind this theory is that every model of communication has three agents: 'I,' 'you,' and 'he/she.' This is analogous to a conversation in which a first person (I) is narrating to a second person (you) about a third person (he/she). Supporters of the enunciation theory within film studies make a further distinction between *discours* and *histoire*. Classic cinema can for the most part be classified as *histoire* since the narrative agent in this type of films leaves no trace of itself: because a first person narrator is missing, there seems to be 'invisible' narration. As soon as such a first person narrator is clearly present, the film is classified as a *discours*: a 'speaker' explicitly makes his or her voice heard and the narration reveals itself to be an act on the part of a specific agent. The question is how such an act can make itself manifest. Does this category apply to films that, adhering to the criteria set by the critics of *Cahiers du cinema*,[33] have such an idiosyncratic style that they are recognizable as the 'handwriting' of a certain director, or does the term *discours* have to be reserved for remarkable scenes as in, for instance, the films of Jean-Luc Godard? A voice-over interrupts his *Bande à parte* (1964) to give a summary of the story so far for the moviegoers who came in late. And in *Une femme est une femme* (1961), the movements of the characters are suddenly frozen in order for a short text describing their psychological make-up to be projected into the freeze-frame. In *Pierrot le fou* (1965), finally, Marianne asks Ferdinand, who is looking over her shoulder as well as straight into the camera, who he is talking to. 'To the audience,' is the answer. This is an evident example of Christian Metz's claim that a film is discursive when it exhibits itself and returns the look: 'You are watching me and I am watching you.'[34]

Metz categorizes the films of Godard that reserve a role as second person for the spectator as *discours*. At the same time, he reasons that every film is in fact a form of *discours,* since every film we consider to be *histoire* is actually obscuring its discursive nature: every apparently 'impersonal' narration is inevitably told by a (first person) narrator. In principle, every film has traceable signs of narration, whether plainly visible or concealed. Bordwell's position is diametrically opposed to Metz's. Bordwell drifts completely away from the Benvenistian model of I-you-she/he in the direction of a cognitive approach. In his theory, the viewer determines his own agenda. The viewer interacts with the material at his own discretion and is ultimately in control of its (narrative) meaning. From such a point of view, status as the second person is not advantageous for the viewer since the 'you' is always stuck in an equal yet interdependent relationship with the 'I.'

Bordwell adds that it is feasible a viewer would be directly addressed, which happens for instance on the title cards of *Vampyr* (Carl Theodor Dreyer, 1932), but that a filmic equivalent of Benveniste's 'you' would be possible only if there were a such a thing as a second person *view* in cinema. Is it possible, in other words, that there are traces of the viewer himself in cinema? Bordwell's negative answer to this question is one of the things that leads him to reject the linguistic model as a useful analogy for cinema.[35] Sasha Vojkovic, on the other hand, claims that Bordwell's denial of the second person function in cinema is based on a misreading of Benveniste. The presence of a second person does not necessarily have to be manifest. The second person is automatically a valid option due to the very existence of a first person. Whoever supposes that film can have a first person as narrative agent also assumes an addressee, or second person.

1.2 *Back to the Future* 'Next Saturday night, we will be sending you back to the future,' Doc Brown exclaims and points straight at the camera, indicating both the viewer and the future.

The 'you' does not necessarily have to be an image but can be an experience instead.[36] Within this view, the 'you' is a virtual agent. Vojkovic considers a scene from *Back to the Future* (Robert Zemeckis, 1985) as a concrete realization of the second person in cinema. Marty McFly has travelled thirty years back in time by means of a time machine. Being stuck in the year 1955, he is looking for Doc Brown, who had originally converted a DeLorean into a vehicle for time travel back in 1985; Marty hopes Doc will be able to help him return to his own time. When Doc has completed his plans, he shouts at Marty, 'Next Saturday night, we're sending you back to the future!' Then he swings his arm and points straight at the camera (Figure 1.2). In this way, we, the viewers, are also involved in the story about time travel. First, we are a part of the off-screen space that Doc is looking at. Second, the aim is to send Marty back to a future that coincides with our present: he needs to rejoin our time. The scene is an example of what Vojkovic calls a 'phatic appeal': here, the film attempts to contact us. Even if there is no crystallized image of the viewer, he is implied here as (virtual) second person.[37]

One Viewer, Two Simultaneous Readings
In order to further explain the crucial role of the viewer, I want to

refer to a three-and-a-half-second insert from *Casablanca* (Michael Curtiz, 1942), to which Richard Maltby has dedicated an article. Ilsa Lund and her husband urgently require travel papers in order to be able to escape from Casablanca. Ilsa's former lover, Rick Blaine, has the necessary papers. She attempts to acquire them at gunpoint, but Rick refuses to budge. In tears, she now confesses why she left Rick all those years ago. When Ilsa says 'If you knew how much I loved you, how much I still love you,' the former lovers end up in an intimate embrace. Subsequently, a crossover reveals a shot of an air traffic control tower with flashing lights. After three and a half seconds, we see Rick appear behind the window. He is looking outside while smoking a cigarette. Next, he turns to Ilsa again and asks, 'And then?' After that, Ilsa continues her story.

There are two possible readings of this scene. First, the camera might simply have been somewhere else for three and a half seconds: the shot of the control tower is no more than a short pause in which Rick lights a cigarette before continuing the conversation. The second reading is considerably more suggestive. The few missing seconds may represent a much longer period – after all, the shot transition is made by means of a dissolve, one of the most heavily used techniques to indicate that some time has been skipped. In the omitted interval, the embrace of Rick and Ilsa has developed into a sexual encounter that could not be explicitly visualized because of the strict regulations of the Production Code. Rick's cigarette is actually a moment of relaxation after sex and the tower now becomes a vulgar symbol for the act that has just transpired. According to Slavoj Žižek, who has elaborated upon Maltby's analysis, the viewer will simultaneously activate both readings. He will detect two synchronous possibilities – the explicit and warranted possibility along with the implicit suggestions that trigger the sexual fantasy. The 'innocent' reading is imbued with a suggestive subtext. The codification of the scenes is necessarily double: there is no choice between one reading or the other, but a simultaneous confrontation with both. The suggestive subtext is so powerful precisely because the scene can also be read innocently, and vice versa. The viewer is addressed here in order to make him aware that two 'stories' are being told at the same time. Both the official and the scandalous version make a phatic appeal to the viewer to be decoded.[38]

In *Casablanca*, we encounter an ambiguous story with both a superficial meaning and a sexual subtext. As addressee, the viewer is called upon to make the excessive, functional, and suggestive aspects meaningful. The spectator is a second person who is interacting with the narrative agent. This process is comparable to the famous drawing discussed by Ludwig Wittgenstein. Where one person will recognize a hare, a second person might just as well see a duck; subsequently, they see both animals in the single drawing. Once you have seen both the hare and the duck, you will see them both from that moment on, alternating rapidly between the two possibilities. Never again can you see just a hare or just a duck. It is up to the viewer to continually keep activating both options.

chapter 2

Basic Principles of Narratology

In order to provide the viewer with a set of terms with which to analyse film in the spirit of Bal's *Narratology*, I first need to characterize her
work. This chapter introduces the groundwork of her narrative theory
by analysing *The Comfort of Strangers*, a novel by Ian McEwan. This narratological account will be the starting point for a transition from literature to film.

The Comfort of Strangers is about the unmarried couple, Colin and
Mary, who on their holiday meet bar owner Robert and his disabled
wife, Caroline. These two force their hospitality on the tourists in such
a way that they cannot decline the offer to stay the night and have to
promise to revisit the house soon. When the couple returns, Mary is
secretly drugged with something slipped into her tea. Caroline takes
her to the bedroom, which turns out to be decorated with countless
pictures of Colin. Because of her drowsy condition, Mary cannot warn
her boyfriend in time. Robert cuts the artery in Colin's wrist with a
razor. At the police station, Mary gives a detailed statement of the
events.

This brief summary is the fabula of McEwan's novel. The fabula offers a straightforward and chronological representation of the events
related in *The Comfort of Strangers*. On this level of narration, narratologists speak of Colin, Mary, Robert, and Caroline as 'actants.' They initi-
ate events or get caught up in them. Narratologists make a theoretical
distinction between what is being told – the contents of the plot, a simple series of events – and the form in which the fabula is cast. This form
relates to the specific ordering of the events. Bal considers the story to
be a product of such an ordering.[1] On this second level, Colin, Mary,
Robert, and Caroline are characters: they are either subjects or objects

of sensory perception: sight, hearing, smell, or touch. On the level of the story it is interesting to see who focalizes the events and who plays only a subordinate part as object of perception.

The summary I just gave did not answer the question why. Why is Colin murdered? Tracing the motive is a matter of interpretation. However, there are clues to be found in two substantial secondary fabulas, one told by Robert, the other by Caroline. In the first subfabula, Robert tells Colin and Mary in a café about his authoritarian father and his youth as the only son with four older sisters.[2] The father privileges him, which makes his sisters envious. In an attempt to provoke him, they challenge Robert to violate their father's prohibitions on eating sweets and drinking lemonade. By telling him that only a 'real man' would be able to cram even more, they encourage him to overeat. Later on, when the sisters lock Robert in their father's study, the boy vomits and messes up the entire room. From that moment on, he is out of favour with his father. His mother, however, still dotes on him. Next, Robert tells them about the visit of Caroline, the daughter of the Canadian ambassador. She thinks it sweet when she hears that Robert is allowed to crawl into his mother's bed in his father's absence. Eight years after her visit, Robert marries Caroline.

The subfabula related by Caroline is told exclusively to Mary. The story is about her relationship with Robert.[3] He turns out to be infertile and therefore cannot fulfil his wish to have sons: he is unable to claim fatherhood. That frustration is expressed in increasingly violent forms of lovemaking. Gradually, Caroline finds out that she in fact loves to be tortured. His explicit desire to kill her heightens the intensity of their sexual gratification. Caroline ends up with permanent spinal damage as a result of one of Roberts's aggressive sexual excesses.

These two subfabulas do not provide us with clear-cut evidence concerning the murder of Colin, but they do form the most important indications for outlining the intentions of Robert and Caroline. It is mainly the ordering of the events that causes the motive to remain obscure. The most important ordering principles are sequential ordering, rhythm, frequency, space, character, and focalization. I discuss these aspects in what follows, thereby casting a different light on the narrative agent responsible for the construction of the entire narrative text. It is this agent's manipulative narrative technique that determines to what extent we will be able to ascertain the logic of Robert and Caroline's behaviour. Once I have clarified this technique, I will be better equipped to show how it can be productively employed for analysing film.

Aspects of Ordering

Sequentiality

The first words of the novel are 'Each afternoon' (11). They signify a standard ritual. Colin and Mary have been on holiday for several days and awaken in a similar way every afternoon. The third paragraph begins, 'Each evening ... they had been listening patiently to the other's dreams' (12), followed by an impression of their dreams. These are first dreamed, of course, and told later insofar as they are remembered. A novel rarely develops in exact chronological order.[4] In *The Comfort of Strangers,* this applies, for instance, to the subfabula narrated by Robert, since it refers back to his childhood memories. Strictly speaking, however, the chronology of the text is not tampered with here. The events Robert speaks about may be in the distant past, but the moment of narration is in the present.

The temporal distance to an event may distort its recollection. Robert gives a telling example of this in his story. He recounts how his father referred a request of the daughters to Robert when he was still a little boy. The ten-year-old then proudly and sternly forbids in the name of his father: no, you cannot wear silk stockings; no, your friend will not stay over. Subsequently, Robert adds, 'Perhaps this was only once. To me it could have been every evening of my childhood' (33). A possibly one-time event in the past can have an impact large enough to make it seem as if it occurred many times. The considerable distance between the event(s) and the moment of narration colours the representation of what has taken place.

In almost every other case, the narrated events are far more recent. The second-most distant memory seems to be Mary's longing for the contented feeling she had when she was thirteen years old. Her old habit of checking completed tasks was a comforting activity to her: 'She longed for such comfort now' (19). It is an 'old' feeling she wants to re-experience in the 'present'; in that sense, this retroversion fits within the chronological frame. Next are references to the beginning of the relationship of Colin and Mary, seven years ago. After Colin and Mary's first stay with Robert and Caroline, the external narrator compares the couple's rekindled passion with that of the period when they first met. They congratulate themselves that 'they could still recover such passion ... It meant more than it could have seven years before' (78–9). Here, the past is fitted into Colin and Mary's present as well: the start of their relationship becomes the norm for their newfound affection.

These retroversions have a double status, confirmed by a scene on a terrace that might even have a threefold status. Mary wonders how her children are doing; these children are from a previous marriage. Her question in direct discourse is immediately followed by a text of the external narrator: 'Mary's two children were staying with their father who lived on a rural commune. Three postcards, addressed to them and all written on the first day, still lay on the bedside table in the hotel room, without stamps' (49). The first sentence of this quotation is the narrator's background information to Mary's question. Her children went to stay with their father. Their departure for their father's commune lies in the past and has presumably taken place before Mary herself left to go on vacation, but the stay itself still lasts. Mary's question indicates that her thoughts are with her children at this moment. Consequently, the 'background information' is also the narrator's paraphrasing of Mary's thoughts. The next sentence works in three ways. The narrator refers to the postcards that were written a few days ago (retroversion) but are still lying on the bedside table (present). It may be that Mary, while wondering how her children are doing, all of a sudden remembers that those cards have not been sent: her thought is embedded within the narrator's text. Shortly afterward, Colin remarks that they should have sent the postcards already, making the narrator's text also a paraphrasing of what ran through Colin's head at that very moment.

The examples here are retroversions, or anachronies, but they are somewhat 'false' at the same time. The events have taken place in the past or started a while ago and have lasted to the present. They are 're-thought' or re-expressed within the story's chronology. Anticipations are rarer, but they are nonetheless present too. This one is a clear example: 'Colin and Mary had never left the hotel so late, and Mary was to attribute much of what followed to this fact' (19). We know what will actually follow only when we get to the end of the novel, but the decision to go out late for dinner is marked here as the starting point of an important future occurrence. Sometimes it is unclear whether a certain sentence can be read as an anticipation. At some point, Mary wakes with a start and Colin asks what is wrong. The next sentence reads, 'She shrank away, but her eyes were on him, her look startled and remote, as though witnessing a catastrophe from a hilltop' (85). This sentence can be categorized as a simile, indicated by the words 'as though.' Strictly speaking there is no anticipation here, but the passage still foreshadows a calamity that Mary apparently sees coming. It is noteworthy that the catastrophe hinted at will take place in the future, i.e., onward in time, but that it is perceived as if she is standing on a hilltop – the distance to it is characterized as a spatial one.

The complexity of McEwan's novel does not reside in bizarre temporal deviations. The novel starts with an ordinary vacation day on which the couple meets Robert and the day after that they stay for the night at Robert and Caroline's. The events of the next four days are touched upon only in the passing.[5] On the fifth day, when it is blazingly hot, Colin and Mary go to the beach, make a boat trip, and are finally noticed by Caroline from her balcony, which marks the start of the final (and deadly) visit. The chronology is generally respected, and every anachrony is sufficiently delineated.[6] For example, the narrator first relates how the tourist couple is looking for a place on the beach and subsequently refers back to a moment at breakfast, when Mary mentioned a grainy photograph of Colin that she saw in Robert's house. This is a reversal of time, but is understandable without any difficulty.

Rhythm

Rhythm indicates the relationship between the time of the fabula and the time of the story. The four days following the encounter with Robert and Caroline, for instance, are skimmed over in a few pages. Whereas the time of the fabula is relatively long here, the presentation of that time is rather condensed. If the difference between the time of the fabula and the time of the story were any greater, narratologists would speak of an ellipsis. An ellipsis skips a considerable amount of time, as when A and B have not seen each other for two years and the story picks up again at the moment of their meeting.

In one scene, however, the time of the fabula and the time of the story more or less correspond: the meeting with Robert and the story he tells in the café about his father. Another possibility is that the time of the story exceeds the time of the fabula, in which case we are dealing with a slow down or pause. In a pause, the time of the fabula is arrested in order to extensively describe a character, an object, or a landscape, for instance.

Frequency

The Comfort of Strangers opens with a repetitive pattern: Colin and Mary are woken by the same sound every afternoon. This recurring phenomenon is presented only once in the novel, however.[7] In other words, the event takes place more often in the fabula than in the novel. The fact that the novel starts with 'each afternoon' characterizes the routine that

Colin and Mary are in: their relationship develops according to certain patterns. The meeting with Robert and Caroline breaks the steady rhythm that seems to indicate some kind of seven-year itch: the contact between Colin and Mary is once again the way it was seven years ago, when they first met.

Space

The novel takes place in an unspecified city; we can do no more than guess where Colin and Mary are on holiday. More important than such a guess, however, is the effect that the city has on the two tourists. Narratologists distinguish between place and space. Place indicates the topological position and is an element of the fabula: Colin and Mary are on holiday in the city X (whether or not X actually exists is irrelevant). The way in which place is perceived or experienced is called space. From the beginning, it is clear that the city is a busy one with many narrow streets. A map is required in order not to get lost. Mary's experience of the city is not very positive, but this is also due to her problematic relationship with Colin: they are both upset by the annoying behaviour of the other. Their journey of discovery through the winding alleys of the city causes them to feel 'locked tighter into each other's presence' (15). In other words, the nature of the city makes them feel cast back on themselves. Because their relationship is stuck in a rut, they experience this as a forced burden and a sort of confinement.

When Mary is irritated because she is tired and thirsty, this influences her impression of the city – it becomes 'terribly suffocating' (50). When their relationship has improved somewhat and she is swimming with Colin in open water, she remarks that she loves it 'after those narrow streets' (95). It could be symptomatic that they bump into Robert after they impulsively decide to leave the main streets and wander off into the smaller alleys. They stroll through the intertwining passageways and just before Robert appears, the narrator tells us, 'The street was narrowing and the shops had given way on both sides to high, dark walls, broken at irregular intervals by deeply recessed doorways, and windows, small and square, set high up and criss-crossed with iron bars' (25). Everything seems to point to the fact that the coming meeting with Robert in this specific location – narrow streets, looming walls, prison-like windows – will be disastrous: Colin and Mary become trapped in his web. Robert leads them to a tiny square where six small alleys convene. Using a steep little stairway, they finally descend into a small, overcrowded bar. For Robert, the labyrinthine setting is the ideal location to win the couple's trust: he is the only one who can lead them out of the maze. In this sense, space is a decisive factor in the developing friendship between the tourists and their local guide.

Character

When attempting to typify characters, it is common practice to examine how they are positioned with regard to each other. This applies especially to novels with a clear genre label. If we are dealing with a Western, we wonder who the good guy is and who the bad guy is. This distinction between good and evil is a standard assumption of the Western genre, and typically the difference between the reliable cowboy and the ruthless villain is everywhere recognizable (in their dress, their manner of introduction, or the way they move about). Traditionally, the good guy always defeats the bad guy. The moment the hero loses, it can be taken as a meaningful comment on the genre; additionally, when the difference between good and evil becomes blurred, it may be that (American) heroism is being morally criticized.

The Comfort of Strangers lacks clear markers of genre. It can be considered a psychological novel with an ominous atmosphere, certainly when considering the motto by Cesare Pavese: 'Travelling is a brutality. It forces you to trust strangers and to lose sight of all that familiar comfort of home and friends. You are constantly off balance.' Unlike the Western, which needs cowboys in order to earn the genre label, the psychological novel knows no standardized set of expectations concerning a specific type of character. Our view of the characters is gradually constructed throughout the novel. In an early passage, Mary picks up a travel guide from her nightstand: 'In other parts of the country, according to the photographs, were meadows, mountains, deserted beaches, a pather [sic] that wound through a forest to a lake. Here, in her only free month of the year, the commitment was to museums and restaurants' (15).

The first sentence can still be read as ordinary travel information. The second provides an extra meaning, however, particularly by including the phrase 'the commitment … to.' Either Mary has obliged herself to go on an active and culture-soaked city trip (possibly because she would feel guilty for spending her free month lazily on the beach) or, more likely, Colin has determined their holiday destination – 'one of the eating capitals of the world,' in his own words (25) – and she had to resign herself to his choice. She would rather have avoided the crowds and would have preferred the wide and open feeling of the plains. If we assume that Colin got his way, Mary's acquiescence offers an insight into their relationship. She hopes that the vacation will revive the romance, that Colin's passion for her resurges so that her feelings for him can also be reinvigorated. Her hopes will be realized sooner when he is allowed to go to a place of his own liking. In this way, she is willing to subordinate her holiday pleasure to a serious investment in their relationship.

In *The Comfort of Strangers*, it is particularly relevant to look at the construction of characters in relation to each other. The passion that Colin and Mary had in the old days has faded at the beginning of the novel. After meeting Robert and Caroline, their excitement seems to be rekindled. This encounter has done something to the tourists, possibly because they enjoy the experience of something 'authentic': being foreigners, they feel flattered because of their contact with an 'authentic citizen' (30). Colin and Mary change, then, as a consequence of this friendship and, importantly, their respective transformations seem to correlate. The novel contains a range of indications that there is a strong parallel between the two: 'They often said they found it difficult to remember that the other was a separate person. When they looked at each other they looked into a misted mirror' (18). The first sentence is indirect discourse because of the phrase 'they often said.' The second sentence is the external narrator's text. This passage is taken from the beginning of the novel, when we are told that their relationship has lost its original spark. The fact that they may have become too entangled with one another might be the cause. Their similarity is also suggested more indirectly in the novel: 'Their pace quickened and their footsteps resounded noisily on the cobbles, making the sound of only one pair of shoes' (25). Their gaits are identical to such an extent that their footsteps sound as if they were coming from only one person. The confirmation of the similarity can also originate from a third party. Caroline tells them they are both delicately built, adding 'almost like twins' (67).

The emphasis of these similarities between Colin and Mary paves the way for a major theme in the novel, which is announced by a man who sings in the shower in a house opposite the hotel. Just as on previous nights, he sings a duet from *The Magic Flute*. Although he does not know the complete text, he loudly sings, 'Mann und Weib, und Weib und Mann, Together make a godly span' (13). His 'Mann und Weib, und Weib und Mann' chant is recalled later on (78). Because of their resemblance, Colin and Mary represent a levelling out of gender difference, whereas the other couple, Robert and Caroline, emphatically embodies the contrast between men and women. From the outset it is clear that the 'natives' form a contrast with the foreigners. Immediately after their meeting, when Robert jeers at a feminist placard, Colin remarks to Mary, 'There ... meet the opposition' (28). That they accompany Robert anyway has to do with the circumstances: he can find them a place to eat. When Mary speaks about her past involvement with a women's theatre group, Caroline is very surprised. How can anyone put on a play without men? Nothing will happen! The antithesis is obvious. Colin and Mary support the idea of gender equality, while Robert and Caroline subscribe to an old-fashioned and hierarchically structured division of roles between men and women.

The characters take shape in *The Comfort of Strangers* mainly through similarity (Colin and Mary, who are almost identical) and contrast (Robert and Caroline, who differ immensely from the other couple). The implication in McEwan's novel is that obvious similarities between men and women lead to indolence in the relationship, whereas painstakingly maintained differences rest too much on aggression. The crisis is brought about by the fact that aggression spreads like wildfire between the opposing couples. Robert does not limit his inclination toward violence to his wife, but, supported by Caroline, also chooses Colin as object of aggression. The choice of Colin is not based on his character or background but purely on his looks. Robert had spotted him by chance on the day of his arrival in the city, and both he and Caroline thought him very beautiful. That Caroline is also attracted to Colin may be crucial. In Robert's imagination, Colin can figure as a competitor who threatens his marital bliss. Within this fantasy, moreover, he is a rival with whom Robert is unable and to a degree even unwilling to compete when it comes to looks.

Colin embodies an ideal of beauty that runs counter to Robert's appearance. Robert has thick, tangled hair on the back of his hands, while Colin's legs, for instance, are lean and smooth. In addition, Colin's hair is 'unnaturally fine, like a baby's' and curls on 'his slender, womanly neck' (56). Robert does not exhibit any sign of envy over Colin's boyish or feminine characteristics. But one external characteristic does obsess him: height. Robert's fascination for height stems from certain events in his youth that he himself recounts. He loses his position as daddy's favourite because of the prank pulled by his sisters Eva and Maria, who were much taller than he; moreover, when the sisters locked him in his father's study they taunted him by saying that he was 'big Papa' now (37). But Robert, in his shorts and 'looking like an English schoolboy,' cannot live up to the mockingly bestowed status of 'big Papa.' He introduces the incident as a vital influence on the formation of his identity and his choice of wife. Its impact can be characterized as the loss of his claim to the position of 'big Papa'; he will always be inferior and undersized. His figurative shortcoming also shows itself concretely: 'He was shorter than Colin' (26). Even before Robert has introduced himself, the text states, 'The man filled his lungs with air and appeared to grow an inch or two' (27). And, somewhat later, 'his massive shoulders drooped as he exhaled' (31). Both phrases suggest that Robert tries to seem larger than he is by almost literally inflating himself. If Robert is indeed intrigued by Colin, the simple fact of Colin's height is paramount to that fascination. Because of his baby-like and feminine qualities, Colin is no match for Robert. His height, however, causes him to tower over his host, a fact that might explain the odd blow to the stomach Colin has to take. He has been sitting in a chair and 'as he straightened Robert struck him in the stomach with his fist, a relaxed, easy blow which, had it not instantly expelled all the air from Colin's lungs, might have seemed playful. Colin jack-knifed to the floor at Robert's feet' (73).

Robert hits at the moment that Colin gets up from his chair and literally threatens to oversize him. The blow is playful and vicious at the same time, as if among friends who are competing offhandedly. Colin, folded on the floor, is defeated and literally looked down upon. It will be clear that Robert as a character is completely dependent on others for his self-image. His life story can only be told as a tale about his sisters, his mother, and particularly his father. In the 'present' of the primary fabula, moreover, he constantly positions himself in relation to Colin.

Focalization

From a narratological point of view, the claim that Robert persistently positions himself in relation to Colin needs to be specified further. In the embedded fabula about his relation to his father, mother, and sisters, Robert is a speaker of the second level, but the primary fabula is never presented from his point of view. With the exception of the embedded fabula, Robert never positions himself but is instead positioned. The external narrator constructs his character through a selective choice of words. The narrator's vision of his characters, which is latently or manifestly present in every novel, determines how the readers view them. The narratological term for this vision is *external focalization*. Internal focalization may be present at the same time but is never completely independent; it is always embedded in the external vision. When, in the following, I mention external focalization, I mean to say that there is no indication of any internal focalization. Thus, 'internal' should be taken to mean '(external plus) internal.' Consequently, internal focalization is a case of double focalization. When it cannot be determined whether a character is focalizing along with the external narrator, Bal speaks of ambiguous focalization. I will now examine some examples of internal and/or ambiguous focalization.

Over the course of the few days after the first visit by the tourist couple, Caroline underwent a complete transformation. She now looks like a nurse, dressed in white. She feels more efficient in white, she tells Mary:

> Mary smiled. 'I'm inefficient in any colour.'
> Out of context, it might have been difficult to recognize Caroline. The hair, so tightly drawn back before, was slightly awry; loose strands softened her face which in the intervening days had lost its anonymity. The lips especially, previously so thin and bloodless, were full, almost sensual ...
> Only her skin remained unchanged, without colour, without even pallour, a toneless grey.
> 'You look well,' Mary said. (105–6)

The description of Caroline with her hair awry in soft strands and her full lips may be an interpretation of her metamorphosis by the narrator. The first sentence, however, suggests that the description is not clearly isolated. It is possible that it is part of Mary's realization of how much Caroline's looks have changed. The observations might very well be made from Mary's perspective: in that case, it is she who is analysing the drastic transformation. Mary's final remark can be read as a further argument that internal focalization is indeed (also) taking place here, since it is a sure sign that Mary has been watching Caroline. The transformation is described in predominantly positive terms, seeming to indicate that Mary's compliment is sincere.

The novel abounds in sentences that contain double focalizations. Because Colin and Mary are tourists, they often end up in surroundings that are unfamiliar to them. A description such as 'a number of young men, dressed similarly to Robert, sat on high stools at the bar' (28), for instance, contains a twofold option: it can be a description by the external narrator and/or a depiction by the narrator of how Colin and Mary perceive the place. In such cases, 'and' is more likely than 'or.'

Apart from a consistently double focalization, there may also be an alternation of external and internal focalization. A remarkable case is the scene in which Caroline prepares the tea that will drug Mary. 'Caroline had turned her back on Mary and was putting the lemon slices into the tea. At the clink of a teaspoon Mary added, "No sugar for me"' (107). The question is whether Caroline has turned her back in such a way that Mary is unable to see what she was doing. Hearing the clink of the teaspoon in the next sentence can be attributed to Mary's perception. According to this reading, external focalization is alternated with internal focalization. A second possibility, however, is that Mary does watch Caroline put the lemon slices in the tea. What Caroline is adding in the process, however, is hidden from her sight. In that case, the entire passage is focalized internally with a possible ellipsis. The phrase 'at the clink of' suggests that a short span of time may have elapsed between putting the slices of lemon in and the sound of the teaspoon. We can now say that the external narrator conforms itself to Mary's perception. The narrator does not reveal more than what the character would reasonably be able to perceive. As a result, the quoted passage is optimally ambiguous. Possibly, Mary has not seen anything but only heard something: if that is the case, there is an alternation of external and internal focalization. It is equally possible that Mary has witnessed the act of putting the lemon slices in the cup and then heard something, in which case we are dealing with internal focalization.

A bit more complex is the sentence that follows the drinking of the tea, whereupon Mary's face contracts because of the bitter taste. Caroline has promised to tell Mary about her back injury after the tea. 'They drank in silence, Mary watching Caroline steadily, expectantly, and Caroline glancing up from her lap every so often to smile nervously at Mary' (108). In principle there are three ways of qualifying the status of the word 'nervously.' First, the external narrator may be omniscient enough to be capable of knowing the character's moods. The witty psychological evaluations we are provided with now and then can very well indicate this.[8] The narrator knows that Caroline is nervous and her smile is automatically taken to reflect this. Second, it is possible that the external narrator does not know Caroline's mood but instead observes her smile and interprets it as nervous. Third, it may be Mary who is watching steadily and sees how Caroline glances back. She may be the one taking the smile for a sign of apprehension. We also cannot exclude the possibility that the nervous smile is simply Mary's misinterpretation. It is quite easy to imagine she has a mistrusting nature and suspects that Caroline's nervousness means that she is up to no good. Focalization is always a matter of subjective colouring, an interpretation of (sensory) impressions. Or, to paraphrase the novel, voices can be distorted by the acoustics (43) and the view of a city can be distorted by bluish morning fog (44).

Narratologically speaking, all three options are legitimate. Taking into account the context of the entire novel, however, one can be crossed off the list as less plausible. The external narrator may have the gift of the all-seeing eye, but he nowhere reveals the specific dispositions of Robert or Caroline – only Colin and Mary's inner lives can be glimpsed. Consequently, it is convenient to say that Caroline's smile *comes across* as nervous, and the first option, which presupposes the narrator knows Caroline's mood, is therefore less likely.

Seeing that the narrator cannot penetrate Robert and Caroline's psyche, these characters and their motives remain shadowy. This shadowy quality is even made explicit when Mary sees Caroline for the first time, on the other side of a glass sliding door. While holding her breath, Mary discerns 'a small pale face watching her from the shadows, a disembodied face, for the night sky and the room's reflections in the glass made it impossible to see clothes or hair' (60). The mysteriousness of Robert and Caroline is further enhanced by the fact that they never appear as focalizors. They can be speakers and express themselves, but their thoughts and perceptions are never made (sufficiently) comprehensible. The clearest instance of this procedure is the noise Colin and Mary hear within the mansion when they walk down the stairs and Robert closes the door (76). The focalization is bound to Colin and Mary here, but if we had been allowed to share Robert and Caroline's perspective we would have been able to ascertain what caused the noise.

McEwan's novel owes its disturbing effect mainly to the narrative trick of systematically withholding Robert and Caroline's focalization from the reader. Robert and Caroline can watch, return a glance, and observe, but what exactly they see is never told to us. Their supposed perceptions remain guesses made from the perspective of the tourists. When Colin and Mary are sitting at a terrace, they simultaneously watch the same man standing at a distance of sixty metres with his back toward them. It happens to be Robert and they continue to be enthralled because they are under the impression they see without being seen themselves – they are subject to 'the fascination of seeing without being seen' (52). Only when the mosaic of photos of Colin in the bedroom is revealed retrospectively does it become evident that Robert had in fact been watching them all along. Not being seen appears to have been a complete illusion. At the exact moment that Colin and Mary think Robert has not noticed them he actually already has. This is what makes all the casual descriptions of passers-by seem sinister in retrospect. Early on in the novel, a man in a boat puts his binoculars away in their case and kneels to start the engine (18). When Colin and Mary are standing at a crowded square, about two-thirds of the adult men carry cameras (47). When Mary wakes with a start one early morning and walks toward the open door, footsteps echo away (85). Since the pictures of Colin have been taken from all angles and at impossible times, Robert may have been near them all along.

The Comfort of Strangers has a notable structure so far as focalization is concerned. Colin and Mary are constantly in Robert's field of vision; as a character, Robert almost has a metaperspective. Internal focalization, though, is limited to the unsuspecting tourists. When they actually do believe that Robert is following them, they turn around 'but Robert, of course, was not there' (96). When Colin and Mary are in their company, they do notice Robert and Caroline's continual glances but always attempt to interpret the looks and actions of their hosts from their own perspective. Caroline was staring at Mary 'as though she herself could not be seen' (61). Her face was tense 'as though she expected at any moment a loud explosion' (62). Caroline stared at her hand 'as though it were no longer her own' (67). The repeated use of the words 'as though' underlines the interpretative quality: Mary tries to incorporate Caroline's doings into a larger frame. Colin does the same for Robert. When Robert takes Colin to his bar to take care of some business, words such as 'seemed' and 'appeared' stand out: 'Everyone seemed to know Robert, and he appeared to be choosing a route which would include the maximum of encounters' (101).

The enigmatic host and hostess are focalized by Colin and Mary, and even though external focalization is hierarchically superior, the narrator does not offer extra insights into the motives of Robert and Caroline. As I noted before, the mystery remains partially intact. Mary suddenly understands why all the pictures in the bedroom are there, but that understanding comes at the moment her eyelids close (114). In the tenth and final chapter (116–25), Mary is clearly the internal focalizor of the novel's key event, the murder of Colin. One is inclined to say that this follows directly from the novel's narrative pattern. There is, however, a functional displacement here: during the killing she will fulfil the role of an indispensable witness, forced to be present but passive: 'Caroline was settling Mary in one of the two remaining wooden chairs, arranging it so that she sat facing the men' (116). She cannot produce words or sounds any more but can only watch. Initially, the scene seems almost like a slow-motion film. When Colin enters another room, Robert and Caroline follow, 'blocking her view of him' (118). Gradually, her vision gains clarity: 'And though Mary was watching into the light, and the three figures by the window were silhouetted by the sky behind, she saw with total clarity the obscene precision of every moment, of every nuance of a private fantasy. The intensity of her vision had drained her faculties of speech and movement' (119). The impression that the scene takes place in front of Mary's eyes cannot be rendered more aptly than this: it is almost as if the entire event is staged especially to be seen by her. Her perception is so intense that speech and movement are no longer possible. She then witnesses Colin tear loose and Robert floor him. As he wrestles free, Colin hits Caroline on the lips. Her blood is smeared around his mouth, meticulously reddening his lips. Then, Robert kisses him deeply on the mouth. Mary sees him reach for an object. As she realizes what it is, she attempts to scream but only a whispery breath escapes from her lips. With the razor, Robert slits Colin's wrist and a spurt of blood lands on the floor in front of Mary. After that, she closes her eyes.

Mary's role as witness is fundamental for Robert and Caroline's motive. Where one man competes with another for masculine honour, at least one non-participating bystander is required. The passive witness is then able to testify which man has outclassed his rival and won the competition. An 'average' offender would rather commit his crime in secret; the murderer who kills to achieve honour as a man fights only in front of an audience. The coherent deposition Mary delivers at the police station increases the chance that Robert will be caught, on the one hand, but on the other shows that Robert's masculinity was reinforced at Colin's expense.

The obvious role of Mary would make a reading of *The Comfort of Strangers* as a novel about repressed homosexuality inconsistent.[9] First, Robert attempts to gain not Colin's love but his trust. A remarkable incident occurs during the visit to the café, where Robert has apparently spread the rumour that Colin is his lover: 'I told them that you are my lover, that Caroline is very jealous, and that we are coming here to drink and forget about her' (103). On the one hand, this statement betrays Robert's misogynistic outlook and his contempt for his own wife: look how easily we can exclude women! On the other hand, this 'declaration of love' can be seen as an attempt to provoke Colin, who does not speak the local language. In the presence of others, Robert has declared Colin 'his possession' without the latter being able to have a say in the matter.

Second, if Robert is indeed a closeted homosexual and secretly adores Colin as the 'beautiful' man he claims him to be, it is crucial that his attraction should *not* be seen. Repressed homosexuality can play itself out only in the shadows and is usually not showcased in front of others. In the key scene Mary is positioned in such a way that she can perfectly observe the scene. Moreover, after being manipulated by Caroline, Mary's vision is so clear that all her other senses disappear into the background. Because she is drugged, it could be said that the scene is similar in nature to a razor-sharp hallucination. There is a very strong impression that Caroline has drugged her in order to make her a better witness than she normally would be. It deepens her crucial role as witness of Robert's masculine victory.

Story: Fabula

Earlier, I wrote that according to narratologists, the story is the product of the way in which the strict content or series of events is ordered. The fabula progresses from a crisis that works toward a solution by way of a number of events. According to Sasha Vojkovic in her study on New Hollywood cinema, such a solution ideally confirms a known world view. If that is the case, then the fabula is the carrier of an ideological convention or conventions. Vojkovic claims that the crisis in several seminal New Hollywood films is brought about by an alarming character flaw of the father. A film like *Back to the Future* (Robert Zemeckis, 1985) is symptomatic. Marty's father is constantly bullied by his boss, and the son wishes his father would cast off his submissive demeanour. The son returns thirty years into the past and teaches his young father to stand up for himself before he even becomes a father. Back in the present, he notices with satisfaction how his father expresses himself more forcefully. The traces of the son's intervention in time have been erased in order to make the father's authority seem natural. The close of the story now coincides with the patriarchal myth that the father always remains superior to the son. The promising prospect of the future is that the latter will follow in his father's footsteps.

Both McEwan's *The Comfort of Strangers* and Schrader's screen adaptation deviate from this pattern because the story and the myth of masculinity never coincide. The conventional ideological motif that the novel refers to is the homosocial oscillation between rivalry and friendship.[10] A group of friends often has an (implicitly) acknowledged leader whose authority is challenged in a way that may or may not be playful. Murderous competition is usually reserved for men who fight openly; this is a model accounted for in countless Westerns. The story of *The Comfort of Strangers* offers an improper exaggeration of this ideological convention for three reasons. First, Robert does not play fair because he feigns friendship in order to violently outdo Colin. Second, Colin's death is a kill-or-cure remedy for Robert to make love to his own wife, Caroline. Third, the homosocial pattern that usually remains implicit is put under a magnifying glass. For these reasons, *The Comfort of Strangers* is too excessive to make the story and the fabula coincide. This excessiveness is precisely why the reader is encouraged to reflect on the question asked by the character of Marge in *The Talented Mr Ripley* (Anthony Minghella, 1999): 'Why is that when men play, they always play at killing each other?' McEwan's novel suggests an unsettling answer: instead of valuing companionship, it may be more important for the homosocial man to aggressively outclass his friend in order to affirm his own masculinity.

The focus of my reading of *The Comfort of Strangers* has been on the level of the story; I discussed the level of the fabula only to some extent. An analysis of the story was necessary in order to provide a motive for the fabula. Consequently, I paid attention to terms that have to do with ordering, such as space, character, and focalization. These are ordering principles that are also relevant for a narratological approach to film. I discussed the narrative agent insofar as it 'manipulated' the story. I have not, however, touched upon the identity of this agent, for the simple reason that the literary narrator is characterologically different from its filmic counterpart. A narrator in a novel communicates the story with words, whereas in film the communication is accomplished by images combined with sounds.

This statement provokes a set of questions that I deal with in the coming chapters by referring to the cinematic adaptation of McEwan's novel. Does the level of monstration imply a method of narration that fundamentally distinguishes cinema from literature (Chapters 3 and 4)? In what ways does film separate story and fabula (Chapter 5)? Does the separation of image and sound in cinema mean that there are multiple external narrators, in contrast to the single agent of novels (Chapter 6)? And what is the relation between the internal narrator and the images shown (Chapter 7)? Does the nature of film also mean that focalization can occur both visually and auditively (Chapter 8)? What intertextual codes and genre conventions lie behind filmic images and sounds (Chapter 9)? And finally, as a supplement, in what way does film express the excessive nature of the narration (Chapter 10)?

chapter 3

The Narrative Impact of the Mise en Scène

The meeting of Colin and Mary with Robert is the starting point of the dramatic developments in *The Comfort of Strangers*. As the two tourists are making their way to a restaurant, their path is blocked by a short man (Robert), who is described more extensively somewhat later on:

> He was shorter than Colin, but his arms were exceptionally long and muscular. His hands were too large, the backs covered with matted hair. He wore a tight-fitting black shirt, of an artificial, semi-transparent material, unbuttoned in a neat V almost to his waist. On a chain round his neck hung a gold imitation razor-blade which lay slightly askew on a thick pelt of chest hair. Over his shoulder he carried a camera. A cloying sweet scent of aftershave filled the narrow street. (26)

As I pointed out in the previous chapter, the status of a descriptive fragment like this is twofold. On the one hand, the external narrator pauses the story in order to describe the strange man whom the reader does not yet know. Specific sentences are devoted to his arms, hands, shirt, and chest hair. Such an explicit description can interrupt the story if the flow of the fabula time is arrested. On the other hand, it could be said that descriptions serve the narrative. Although there is no direct indication of internal focalization here, it is possible that we see Robert through the eyes of Colin and/or Mary.[1] Their path has just been blocked and it is not inconceivable that they would examine the unknown man.

If the description of Robert occurs by means of the perception of at least one of the two tourists, it becomes plausible to assume that the description is embedded in the temporal flow of the fabula. Colin and/or Mary take their time to observe him – from his arms, their eyes go to his hands, his V-necked shirt, his chest, and his shoulder. Finally, they smell his aftershave. Note that the fragment reveals details of Robert only between his neck and his waist: further impressions of his face or hairstyle are missing.

What is the visual equivalent of the fragment quoted above in Schrader's film *The Comfort of Strangers*? Colin and Mary wander through the narrow streets while the camera moves with them. Mary says, 'I think we're on the right track,' to which an unknown voice replies, 'So do I.' Colin and Mary halt, whereas the camera moves farther to the right. The couple ends up in the left of the frame while looking at a man framed between pillars, who is visible from top to toe. His hair is combed back and he is dressed in a splendidly white suit with a tie – his chest is not bared (Figure 3.1). That this Robert does not match the description

3.1 *The Comfort of Strangers* Looking along with Colin and Mary, we see a
     man in a white suit.

of Robert in the novel is of little consequence. It is far more essential that the composition of the shot creates a certain analogy to the literary fragment. On the left, relatively close to the camera, are Colin and Mary. Their looks are fixed on the figure standing to the right, farther away from the camera. The camera is looking past the figures of Colin and Mary at the man in the white suit. By means of this composition, our eyes follow the viewing direction of the two tourists and Robert becomes the focal point of our attention. Colin and Mary's perception is not 'autonomous' but is embedded in the viewpoint of the camera. There is, in other words, external focalization here. The filmic narrator on the visual track shows us Robert while at the same time mediating his appearance through the eyes of Colin and Mary.

Showing

Before, I argued that the composition of the shot created a 'certain' analogy to the quotation from the novel. A complete analogy is impossible because of the insurmountable differences between the two media. A narrative agent in literature expresses itself through language. Situations are communicated in either shortened or extended form. A compression of events can be recognized in a phrase such as 'Even though they had met only half an hour ago, Peggy was already telling Tosca about her youth and marriage.' A period of thirty minutes is abridged in a single sentence. A temporally extended effect would be achieved by a sentence such as 'A spoke with a softened voice, carefully choosing his words while his face tensed as if he were expecting a loud explosion any minute: [followed by his actual words].' The quoted words are an addition to what A in fact says; they are the narrator's impression characterizing A's way of speaking.

Monstration

Unlike the literary narrator, the main function of the narrator in film is to show moving images. In the early one-shot films, such as those by the brothers Lumière, the mini-plot is represented by the moving image that develops in front of a static camera: a baby is being fed; a boy fools the gardener by putting his foot on the hose. According to Gaudreault, this type of film has a first level of narrativity in which showing is the exclusive form of telling. The narrator on this first level – termed 'monstrator' by Gaudreault – is an agent that simply projects images on to the screen in a number of frames per second from an unchanging position. Here, cinema is literally no more than a moving picture, a display of a sequence of photographic signs. Gaudreault's analysis that we are dealing with a *first* level of narrativity implies that this level is structurally present in film. In its naked essence, cinema always encompasses monstration: film is like a continuous showing of photographic frames that usually connect in a fluent rhythm.[2] Showing is a primary but not necessarily paramount form of narration within cinema. The fact that story time and fabula time coincide and that the monstrator shows 'in the present tense' is characteristic of this form of narration.

Showing Overspecific and Selective Framing

In and of itself, the shot from *The Comfort of Strangers* I mentioned earlier can be analysed on the first level of showing. What stands out in the shot is that we immediately get a full impression of Robert: we see him from top to toe. But how detailed is that full impression? Chatman has claimed that a literary description can demonstrate precision and exhaustive meticulousness, whereas cinema is always 'overspecific.'

Even though the scene from Schrader's film already shows us a complete shot of Robert, a close-up of his face would have been overly detailed as well. A close-up of a man's face inevitably shows us his sideburns, glasses, the mole on his left cheek, and the drooped corners of his mouth, for instance. Since an average shot immediately reveals a whole range of details, cinema always involves implicit description: it reveals but does not explicitly describe. Unless we are dealing with an unusual experiment – the film *Blue* (Derek Jarman, 1993), for instance, which entirely consists of blue screen – film cannot be visually vague. A logical objection to the overspecific nature of cinema would be the well-known convention in horror films to withhold the sight of the monster from the viewer. The gruesomeness of the monster is expressed only through the facial expressions of the characters, but the customary reverse shot is omitted. Even though such horror films are visually vague about the monster's appearance, they do overspecify the impact the creature has. In the end this convention, too, confirms Chatman's general rule that film cannot refrain from describing.[3]

Descriptions attribute certain qualities to characters or objects. In film, this implicit process generally occurs in one of two ways. In the opening scene of *Rear Window* (Alfred Hitchcock, 1954), the camera wanders about the courtyard of an apartment complex. This scene is disconnected from the perception of the main character, who is still asleep. The opening is a matter of showing things overspecifically: the scene offers an impression of the general ambiance without highlighting details. The viewer, however, has the option to select fragments from the shot and single out types of flowers, the colour of the bricks, the shining drops of sweat on a forehead that indicate summer heat, and so forth. From myriad visual impressions, the viewer 'edits' his own description.

A second means by which cinema can attribute certain qualities to characters or objects is called selective framing. This is no hard criterion, though, because all shots are essentially manipulative. Every shot unavoidably limits the image and creates an off-screen space. However, some shots direct the viewer's attention more strongly than others. If a man steps out of his car when the camera is at eye level, the viewer might notice that he is rather corpulent. If a low angle near the car door had been chosen in the same scene, however, the size of the man's paunch would automatically have been accentuated. Although cinema usually relies on showing overspecifically (a shot customarily shows an excessive number of details, too many to notice), certain filmic techniques can be applied to emphasize particular aspects. Apart from camera operations, framing, and different angles, shots can be manipulated by the use of particular lenses, the workings of light and dark, adding colour, and other techniques. A general rule is that the more the image has been modified, the more explicitly the viewer's attention is being directed. A red jacket will stand out in grey surroundings.

Filmic Description through Focalization

In an eminent case study, Chatman has indicated how the principle of focalization in film can be employed as an alternative to an explicitly descriptive literary passage. In a short story by Guy de Maupassant, the external narrator portrays Mademoiselle Dufour as an extremely attractive young woman. According to the narrator, she also embodies a certain innocence because she is never aware of her sex appeal. The filmic 'translation' of this passage by Jean Renoir in the eponymous film *Partie de campagne* (1944) is not accomplished by a voice-over that recites the narrator's text and provides appropriate images. Neither does the camera scan the body of Mademoiselle Dufour: that would reveal her attractiveness but would also destroy her innocence. Renoir's trick is to offer impressions of her beauty and erotic naïveté by means of so-called reaction shots. The reactions of the bystanders indicate how we should see her. A man with a striped shirt is watching her from behind open shutters (Figure 3.2a), a group of seminarians passes behind her back (Figure 3.2b and c) and a couple of boys spy on her while hiding behind a wall. The men are outside Mademoiselle Dufour's field of vision, so she has no idea she is being watched. Moreover, she is absorbed in swaying back and forth on a swing and is not looking around her (Figure 3.2d). By adding the watching men Renoir's adaptation does not attempt to render de Maupassant's text literally, but this addition approaches the descriptive effect of the short story. The looks of the men reveal her beauty, and her ignorance implies her innocence. The textual description of the young woman is structured as follows: (the narrator describes that) she was a young lady who behaved in such and such a way. The filmic equivalent is structured somewhat differently: (the visual narrator shows that) the men watching her saw a young lady who behaved in such and such a way.

Explicit descriptions can take place in literature unproblematically, but the expository nature of cinema causes filmic descriptions to remain implicit – except where voice-over is used. Moreover, as the example of de Maupassant versus Renoir shows, film tends to entwine

3.2a *Partie de campagne* The man on the left has opened the shutters to 'enjoy the view.'
3.2b Mademoiselle Dufour is filmed from the back, in long shot.
3.2c In retrospect, 3.2b seems to be a focalization of the passing seminarians. Some of them cast meaningful glances in the young girl's direction.
3.2d The camera matches the ecstatic swinging movements of Mademoiselle Dufour.

descriptions with the plot more than literature does. At first, the young woman is described 'silently' by showing her, but the descriptive impression is manipulated further by the looks of the bystanders. In other words, she is described by means of male focalization.

The Implicit versus the Specific

Literature's 'handicap' is that it requires many lines to give a complete impression of a character. The impression of Robert in *The Comfort of Strangers* remains incomplete and initially focuses on peculiar characteristics (shortness, arms, chest hair, razor, camera, aftershave). A novel demands an active attitude from its readers in that they need to form a mental image of a character on the basis of a sketchy outline only. A quality of McEwan's novel is that the selective mentioning of details automatically creates distinctive accents. These details have great narrative import retrospectively because they are clues for tracing the motive behind Robert's actions. Robert's shortness compared to Colin is mentioned first and consequently receives emphasis.

The overspecific nature of cinema automatically fleshes out mental images: the appearance of characters is immediately clear. With a glance, the viewer can determine how Colin, Mary, and Robert look in the film. It also becomes clear that Rupert Everett, who plays Colin in *The Comfort of Strangers*, is indeed taller than Christopher Walken (Robert), especially in the scenes that show them both in a two-shot (Figure 3.3). Because this difference in height is emphasized nowhere, it is a detail that might stand out to the attentive viewer – perhaps because he has read McEwan's novel – but it also might easily slip from the viewer's attention. A defining characteristic of cinema is to show much, but the narrative function of this overspecific showing tends to remain implicit. In the novel, conversely, Robert's facial features are extensively specified. When Colin and Mary are sitting in the bar, they look at him with their full attention for the first time. They notice how Robert seems older than he did on the street. Furthermore, their glances apparently focus on the geometrical lines in his face, the parallel lines across his forehead, and a deep fold over the bridge of his nose (31). This perception of the tourists is so specific that it could only be reproduced on-screen by overly artificial and extreme close-ups. Even then, however, the chance remains that the shot stays so overspecific (and implicit) that other facial characteristics, such as the eyebrows, again start diverting attention from the lines and folds.

The implicit filmic description characterizes itself by such an excess of visual details that the specific qualities of those details are in danger of going unnoticed. It can also be seen as an invitation to the viewer to create his own emphasis. Employing many shot changes makes it difficult to 'read' the filmic image with care, however. The famous French film theoretician André Bazin showed himself a major proponent of an expository cinema in his essays from the 1940s and 1950s. He preferred films with lengthy shots and different levels of depth (i.e., the presence of clear foregrounds and backgrounds in a shot). By means of this so-called deep focus, the viewer was manipulated only to a minor extent

3.3 *The Comfort of Strangers* An example of visual overspecificity. It is evident
that Colin is taller than Robert, although the difference in height is not
accentuated.

and was also encouraged to actively distil his own 'story' from the shot
or to attribute qualities to characters or objects. Bazin was taken with
the idea of a cinema dominated by a monstrator, a narrator showing
moving images from an unchanging camera position. As was indicated
before, monstration indicates a first level of narrativity and limits the
level of narration to the so-called framed image or shot. This framed
image can be divided into two techniques: mise en scène and cinematography. I discuss the first technique here and the second in the following chapter.

Mise en Scène

The first level of narration concerns every filmic means that is theoretically relevant for a single shot (but that is almost never limited to a
single shot in practice). A twofold question can be asked concerning the
first level of narration: who or what is being shown and how are they
being shown? This 'who or what' question relates to the mise en scène,
whereas the question 'how' is about the cinematographic characteristics. Although I treat them separately here, mise en scène and cinematography are hardly strictly distinct aspects of film in practice: on the
contrary, they are continually linked. In other words, what we see can
never be detached from how we see it.

In Chapters 5 and 6 of their *Film Art,* Bordwell and Thompson have
discussed the techniques of mise en scène and cinematography, respectively. The description is a bit dull and formalistic, but nonetheless very
thorough and extensive: Bordwell and Thompson at their best. They
indicate, for instance, which three sources of light are employed in clas-

sic Hollywood cinema and from what direction they need to shine in order to illuminate a character clearly. Also, they discuss different kinds of film strips with their respective light sensitivities and all possible screen formats. This chapter and the following one are in no way meant to be as exhaustive as Bordwell and Thompson's account of all these technical aspects. I concern myself primarily with the narrative effects of mise en scène and cinematography. By means of rudimentary and diverse examples I want to outline their possible narrative impact.

Choice of Actors

Mise en scène encompasses everything that has been constructed within the image frame, such as the choice of actors, their acting style and position in front of the camera, costumes and make-up, the scenery, the location, the lighting, and the colours. The casting director is tasked with finding the right actor for the right role. Sergei Eisenstein had a tendency to exaggerate during his casting process. Acting qualities were less important than the actor's physical appearance. It was of paramount importance whether someone looked like a doctor or a peasant when such a role was needed: a classic case of 'typage,' or typecasting.[4] In many films, and especially in genre films, actors are cast because their physiques already suggest certain character traits. For a romantic but tough hero, one is more likely to choose a type such as Sean Connery than Klaus Kinski; for their respective roles as movie monster, both Max Schreck, with his hollow eye sockets and aquiline nose (*Nosferatu*, F.W. Murnau, 1922), and Boris Karloff, with his massive forehead (*Frankenstein*, James Whale, 1931), had the appropriate facial features.

In these cases, casting has a narrative impact: physical features correspond to the character traits of those the actors are to portray. When directors deviate from this general rule, casting is often part of a specific cultural commentary. In *Hairspray* (1988), cult director John Waters parodies the ideal of feminine beauty. The film's heroine is the chubby Ricki Lake, who plays the role of Tracy Turnblad. Despite her not quite elegant dance moves, she gets the most close-ups in a television show, is popular with the boys and, to the utter dismay of her main rival, the slim, blonde Amber von Tussle, she has a huge fan base. At the end of the movie, she gains the title of dancing queen and ascends her throne – in a cockroach dress. With the unorthodox casting of Lake as a diva, the film shows that when characters look at her as a dancing queen everybody will start believing she actually is one: beauty is in the eye of the beholder. In 1990s horror films, there is a clear propensity to cast well-known stars in the role of the monster: Johnny Depp in *Edward Scissorhands* (Tim Burton, 1990), Gary Oldman in *Bram Stoker's Dracula* (Francis Ford Coppola, 1992), and Brad Pitt, Tom Cruise, and Antonio Banderas in *Interview with the Vampire* (Neil Jordan, 1994). In this way, the monster is presented as sexually attractive and the dividing line between good and evil becomes blurred.

A meaningful choice of actors is characteristic of *La Strategia del Ragno* (Bernardo Bertolucci, 1969), which is analysed by Bordwell in *Narration in the Fiction Film*. The son of a supposed hero of the Resistance becomes caught up in the investigation of his own father's murder in 1936, allegedly committed by the fascists. The film consists of flashbacks, with the actor playing the son in the present and the father in the past. This double role is motivated by the similarities in appearance between father and son. However, other characters (Athos Magnani's mistress and his three friends) are also played by the same actors in the present and the past; although over thirty years have passed, there is no significant attempt at aging their appearance. This approach to casting seems to indicate that the past still has a deep influence on all those involved.

Acting Styles

Acting styles have gained importance in achieving narrative aims. Method acting, which involves a far-reaching identification with the part in order to portray the character in as true a way as possible, has been held in high esteem since the early days of cinema. It needs to be taken into account, however, that what was considered realistic in the 1950s looks artificial by current standards. Moreover, method acting is not a suitable style for every role. For her part in *Sunset Boulevard* (Billy Wilder, 1950), Gloria Swanson had to overact in an out-of-date fashion because she is playing an aging actress whose heydays were in the 1920s. Before 1927 the majority of films were silent, necessitating an exaggerated acting style that would be considered theatrical nowadays. Ostentatious gesticulation expressed what could not yet be said. At the beginning of *Nosferatu* (F.W. Murnau, 1922), the actor playing Thomas Hutter exaggerates in his acting to such an extent that it becomes toe curling for a modern viewer, but his acting style is nonetheless functional. In this way, he immediately displays his childishness, sexual immaturity, and hidden relief for leaving his young wife, Ellen. An 'uneasy' acting style was effective not only in the early days of cinema. *Starship Troopers* (Paul Verhoeven, 1997) has been criticized for its featherweight protagonists. That argument was reason enough to discard the film in its entirety: empty characters means empty film. If the film is read as a satire of American foreign policy and its 'silly' propaganda, however, the fact that the characters appear to be nitwits is consistent. Intelligent characters are supposed to be able to see through the bombastic political advertising, which would have resulted in a completely different film.

Positioning the Characters

In an early scene from *La pianiste* (Michael Haneke, 2001), a film about the sado-masochistic fascinations of piano teacher Erika Kohut, Erika climbs a flight of stairs with her mother.[5] The two walk in the direction of the camera, and looking over their shoulders, we see a man coming in through the door behind them. His contours are unfocused. As the door closes, mother and daughter have reached the top of the stairs and turn right (left for the viewer). Erika looks behind her, but her mother pushes her forward. 'Aided' by a slight tilt of the camera (which is a cinematographic element, strictly speaking), the mother moves in such a way that she blocks our view of the person who has just entered. In this way, she positions herself between her daughter and the 'pursuer.' This positioning already concisely captures the psychological dimension of the story. As soon as someone attempts to break the symbiosis between mother and daughter – when he enters, the man has 'come between them' visually – the mother will resist the intrusion. The characters are repositioned in such a way that the mother forces herself into the centre of the frame and becomes a physical obstacle between her daughter and the 'intruding' stranger. The positioning of the characters in this shot already makes clear that the domineering mother has cast a shadow over Erika's relationships to others and will continue to do so.

Another fine example of the narrative positioning of characters can be found in *All That Heaven Allows* (Douglas Sirk, 1955). Cary Scott's two children cannot accept their mother's affair with the young gardener, Ron Kirby. They announce that the coming Christmas will be the last they spend at their mother's house. Then, the children's Christmas present for their mother arrives: a brand new television, so she will not feel so alone. The message behind this gift is painful: if she would only watch enough TV she would not miss her children and no longer need the company of her gardener. This message is underlined by the positioning of the characters. We see Cary with her holiday entourage, surrounded by her children, but the television screen reflects only the image of the mother. The screen's reflection shows the threat of the near future: without Ron and with her children gone to live on their own, she will wither away.

In his analysis of *Morocco* (Josef von Sternberg, 1930), Ambro Van Oosterhout indicates how the positioning of characters in front of the mirror reveals who is the true love of cabaret star Amy Jolly. The wealthy La Bessière is in the dressing room where Amy prepares for her act. Although he is standing close to her, he is not reflected in the mirror on the wall. Only Amy can be seen in the mirror (Figure 3.4a). When the soldier Tom Brown enters Amy's dressing room in the next scene, we do not see him in the shot. The camera is positioned to reflect them both, however, thereby showing them as a couple (Figure 3.4b).[6] In the end, Amy will not see through her planned engagement to La Bessière and will start looking for the soldier instead. This turn of events is already foreshadowed in the mirror.

3.4a   *Morocco* The respectable La Bessière is standing next to the mirror, but his image is not reflected in it.

3.4b   The American soldier Tom Brown is outside the shot, but his reflection can be seen next to Amy Jolly in the mirror.

Costumes

Clothing is another element of the mise en scène with a narrative impact. In the beginning of *Now, Voyager* (Irving Rapper, 1942), Charlotte Vale is still the ugly duckling her mother makes her out to be because of her unattractive dress and shoes, but during the film she slowly transforms into a stunning beauty with increasingly chic outfits and expensive pumps. Costumes can be extremely extravagant and largely determine the identity of the characters, as in the transvestite film *The Adventures of Priscilla, Queen of the Desert* (Stephan Elliott, 1994). The man with the most fabulous attire will gain the title of 'queen.' However, costumes can also be noteworthy because of their strategic inconspicuousness. The surveillance expert Harry Caul in *The Conversation* (Francis Ford Coppola, 1974) has a professional need to blend into the masses. His interest in looking unremarkable legitimates his nondescript outfit and dreary raincoat.

The cowboy can choose a sand-coloured outfit to serve as camouflage in the space between wilderness and civilization, but he nonetheless often shows off some catchy accessories. *Shane* (George Stevens, 1953) is a good example. In order to remain a 'real man,' however, a cowboy cannot dress excessively. In *Man without a Star* (King Vidor, 1955), the inexperienced young man Jeff Jimson is very impressed by the appearance of the tough Dempsey Rae. We see Jeff walking into the saloon in a brand new costume, with garish colours, huge leather chaps, and a rope in his hands. To the hilarity of the onlookers in the saloon, Dempsey 'startles' and jumps into the arms of a woman. The feigned panic of the experienced cowboy invites one to read the exact opposite of the desired effect: the boy commands no respect at all. A cowboy makes an impression by nonchalantly wearing clothes that fit his surroundings perfectly. Jeff's costume makes his desire to achieve 'true' masculinity so obvious that he is immediately disqualified as a 'real man.' His failed attempt displays a lack of insight into the way in which dress codes work.

Probably the best-known dress code in Westerns is a convention from B movies in the 1930s and 1940s: costumes make clear who the 'good guy' is and who the 'bad guy' is. According to this historically determined convention, the man with the smooth-shaven face and handsome suit is automatically positioned as a morally just character; and the scruffy, hairy man can only be up to no good. Appearances indicate to the viewer who has the right to triumph, and the neatly dressed cowboy will always win. Altering this code by giving the villain saintly looks would thus always be a narratively meaningful modification.

Props

A cowboy is recognized not only by his costume but also by his six gun, whereas a detective has his magnifying glass and Charlie Chaplin always carries his walking cane. Props are an unmistakable part of the image of a character and can aid in finding solutions to dilemmas. Alfred Hitchcock was a master in using props to guide or even reverse the story. In *Strangers on a Train* (1951), Bruno Anthony comes up with a 'brilliant' plan when he meets famous tennis player Guy Haines on the train. Bruno has learned from the newspapers that his travelling companion wants to divorce his wife, Miriam, because he is having an affair with Ann Morton, but he also knows that Guy's wife is stalling the procedure in hopes of ample financial compensation. Bruno, for his part, wishes his father dead. He proposes to swap murders. They are, after all, strangers to each other and Bruno has no more motive for killing Miriam than Guy has for murdering Bruno's father. Instead of rejecting the ridiculous idea straight away, Guy reacts ironically. His response, however, is interpreted as consent by Bruno. Then Guy accidentally forgets his lighter with the inscription 'from A. to G.' This prop has several functions. After killing Miriam, Bruno shows the lighter to Guy as proof that he has fulfilled his part of the 'bargain.' When Guy then refuses to do away with Bruno's father, the lighter becomes a means of blackmail. The inscription 'from A[nn] to G[uy]' proves that Bruno and Guy are no strangers to each other. As soon as Bruno realizes that Guy's refusal is final, he wants to return the lighter to the scene of Miriam's murder in order to incriminate Guy.

The symbolic function of the lighter is paired with another meaningful object in Hitchcock's film: glasses with strong lenses. As Bruno is strangling Miriam, her glasses fall on the ground, and the act is then filmed through one of the distorting lenses. In the rest of the film, Bruno becomes upset only when he sees the sister of Guy's mistress, Ann. This girl, Barbara, has glasses identical to Miriam's; whenever Bruno looks at her, he sees the murder scene reflected in Barbara's spectacles. The glasses are thus what I would characterize as a 'stubborn object.' When Ann finally understands why Bruno seems to get so upset whenever he meets Barbara, she becomes convinced of Guy's innocence and realizes how the murder actually took place. In *Strangers on a Train*, both the lighter and the glasses are crucial for propelling the plot.

Location

The showdown in Westerns usually takes place in the scorching sun, near the saloon on the dusty main street of a small town. As soon as a cowboy ends up in a snowy landscape, as in *McCabe and Mrs Miller* (Robert Altman, 1971), for instance, we as viewers should be prepared for his pending doom. Situate a cowboy in New York and his unfamiliarity with city culture creates a 'crisis' in itself. A film like *Midnight Cowboy* (John Schlesinger, 1969) shows that the cowboy can hardly ever contain such a crisis. He initially thinks that his tough appearance will win over anyone he meets, but in the eyes of the city dwellers he always stands out. The only ones who embrace him are those who think of him as an interesting rarity, but he is too naïve to see through this irony.

The examples mentioned above are based on the idea that certain genres demand certain locations. When a film deviates from those stan-dards, the choice automatically has consequences for the course of the narrative. The choice of a specific *kind* of location, however, can also be narratively embedded in an aesthetic or cinematically artistic vision. The postwar neorealist movement in Italy strove to chart the state of the country and created cinema that was filmed on location with a semi-documentary approach. To achieve an optimal 'neorealistic' effect, the strict causal logic of conventional film narratives had to be broken.

Classic Hollywood cinema always presents a sequence of events that is clearly motivated: event A is the cause and event B is its logical con-sequence. The outcome of a search is the sum of all sorts of discover-ies and clues. In *Paisà* (Roberto Rossellini, 1946), however, a woman is looking for the resistance fighter 'Wolf.' When she looks after a dying soldier on the way, she accidentally learns from his mumbled words, not intended for her, that Wolf has died. She discovers his fate unex-pectedly in passing, therefore, rather than by way of causality.

According to neorealists, this chance knowledge accords far better with everyday reality than do the narrative compositions of Hollywood cinema. They considered their approach more 'natural' and therefore more 'realistic' than the classic modes of narration. In neorealist film the setting, as well, cannot be said to determine or fill in the story, but a frequent choice of outside locations synchronizes with their suppos-edly 'natural' mode of narration.

Setting

Where naturalness is concerned, German Expressionism is located at the other end of the spectrum. More artificial sets than those in *Das Kabinett des Dr Caligari* (Robert Weine, 1920), which was heavily influ-enced by Expressionist painting, is hardly conceivable. They are geo-metrically absurd and have an ambiguous narrative function in this film. On the one hand, they express the twisted fantasies of the charac-ter Francis, who narrates the story of Dr Caligari. On the other hand, the sets may represent the split and manipulative mind of the hypnotist Dr Caligari, dressed as a showman at a fair. In the latter case, the sets are a visual support for the narrating character's vision of Caligari as having an ominously dark side to him.

The setting can also carry intertextual connotations. In McEwan's novel, the touristy city is never explicitly named. The novel gives only a sketchy description of a city full of water and with labyrinthine alleys. The spatial ambiguity contributes to the disorientation of the charac-ters.[7] The film adaptation does make the location explicit: Venice. This could be taken as a reference to two of the most famous films that also take place in Venice: *Morte a Venezia* (Luchino Visconti, 1971) and *Don't Look Now* (Nicholas Roeg, 1973). In both films, the male protagonist meets an untimely death. The choice of Venice creates expectations concerning Colin's fate, and those expectations are met.

Lighting

The 15 April 2004 edition of the Dutch newspaper *de Volkskrant* contained a beautiful passage on *La passion de Jeanne d'Arc* (Carl Theodor Dreyer, 1928), a silent film with title cards:

> Whoever looks into the eyes of Jeanne and her judges can see the director's lighting design in the reflections of their pupils. Facing Jeanne, there is a battery of lamps that do not let any expression go unnoticed but that also make her face appear smooth and pure. The men that persecute her, however, are all lit by a single spotlight. The sharp light accentuates the wrinkles of their eyes and the folds around their mouths with shadows in order to underline their malicious intentions.[8]

This fragment from an article by David Sneek emphasizes the workings of light. The lighting creates a sharp contrast between Jeanne as a pure (and consequently good) character and her interrogators as lined (and consequently evil) figures. The lighting morally typifies the characters, and this moral quality is emphasized all the more when the light becomes increasingly 'unmotivated' (and, as a result, less realistic).[9]

In *Léon* (Luc Besson, 1994), the title character is introduced as a skilled assassin. He lives in the apartment next to the eleven-year-old Mathilda and her family: father, mother, stepsister, and four-year-old brother. The father is receiving death threats over a stash of drugs from a gang led by a criminal psychopath When Mathilda is out grocery shopping, the account is violently settled. When she returns home, she sees a man on the lookout at the door and overhears someone saying, 'You killed a four-year-old kid! Did you really have to do that?' She decides to ring her neighbour's doorbell and desperately hopes he will answer. Léon has observed the scene and is in doubt. While we see Mathilda waiting in a medium shot, she is suddenly bathed in light. Léon has opened the door and the excessive glow suggests that the light must be coming from a 'good' source. In other words, the ruthless murderer from the opening scenes can only be a 'warm' character. The rest of the film will show that this impression was the right one: Léon will look after Mathilda.

In the infamous interrogation scene from *Basic Instinct* (Paul Verhoeven, 1992), Catherine Trammell, superbly dressed in white, is sitting opposite a number of male police officers. The lighting in the scene causes horizontal stripes to fall over the men, apparently by shining through the grating above their heads. Visually, they are 'imprisoned.' This reverses the actual situation, because Catherine, as a suspect, would logically have to be disadvantaged. During interrogation, however, Catherine assumes such a provocative attitude and gives such forward answers that the men slowly start to feel that she is toying with them. This gradual reversal of roles was already prefigured by the lighting.

Colour

The use of colour and colour contrasts forms the best proof that mise en scène and cinematography are difficult to distinguish. On the one hand, colour belongs to the category of the mise en scène simply because actors, costumes, and sets have colour; those colours are self-evidently not without meaning. The impression that Pippi Longstocking is a headstrong girl with an inborn disregard for authority is conveyed not only by her cheerful facial expression but by her red and green stockings, oversized black shoes, colourful clothes, red hair, and freckles.

Colour cannot be disconnected from the setting as well. We have only to think of a phrase such as 'grey surroundings.' If the second half of a film takes place against a more colourful backdrop, that may be an indication of a narrative turning point. In *Play Time* (Jacques Tati, 1967), for instance, we see Monsieur Hulot getting caught up in an ultramodern building of glass and steel. In this setting, dominated by sombre tints of grey, brown, and black, the interaction between characters is problematic. In the second half of the film, however, Royal Garden becomes the most important setting. As the vivacity of the place increases, a broader spectrum of colours is used and the characters interact more spontaneously.[10]

Special colour tints and effects can also be the result of using a certain type of film stock or of manipulating the images. In those cases, colour has to be categorized under the heading of cinematography. Cinematography is the technical and artistic way in which a scene is photographed. It encompasses matters such as how we record the scene (on what material and at what speed); from what angle we film the scene and with what lenses; what optical effects we apply and how long we hold the shots.

chapter 4

The Narrative Impact of Cinematography

After only a few minutes, the viewer of *The Comfort of Strangers* notices that Colin and Mary are being photographed without their knowledge. As the camera moves backward at the same speed at which they are calmly strolling through Venice, we hear the sound of a photo shutter. From a reverse angle we see the couple in a black-and-white freeze-frame (Figure 4.1a). The image has noticeably been manipulated in two ways here: the movement is frozen and the shot is decolourized. This manipulation is a part of the cinematography – 'filmic writing' – and concerns the way in which recorded scenes are shown.

The choice for a freeze-frame in *The Comfort of Strangers* first and foremost provides information about the plot. Unlike the reader of the novel, the viewer already suspects at an early stage that the couple is being photographed, although it remains unclear why. The first freeze-frame is followed by a countershot, in which the camera lingers on the spot Mary and Colin have just passed. Suddenly, a man in a white suit appears in the alcove across the water. He is presumably the one who has been taking the pictures (Figure 4.1b). At the same time, the plot device has greater impact if we consider the composition of the photograph. In the first photo, we see Colin from his right, in the middle of the frame, blocking our view of Mary somewhat. In the second black-and-white freeze-frame – a few minutes later, when the couple has entered a square – Colin is again in the centre of the frame. His face is clearly visible in profile, whereas Mary's head disappears behind her curly hair. Both freeze-frames are structured in such a way that Colin is featured more prominently. Later on, it will become clear that the pictures are indeed taken because of Colin and that Mary is only extra. The photographing of Colin foreshadows the ominous course the film will take.

4.1a *The Comfort of Strangers* A black-and-white freeze-frame of Colin and
Mary.
4.1b The camera holds position after Colin and Mary have passed. A man in a
white suit has appeared in the alcove to the left.

In *Camera Lucida*, Roland Barthes has argued that the magic quality
of photography is that it renders a past reality present. A picture showing your image is an indication that you have in fact been somewhere,
even if you no longer remember it yourself. For Barthes, photography
is related to long-gone events: 'Look, here's the proof that it actually
happened once.' Being photographed captures you in a motionless
pose, regardless of whether you posed for the picture or not. The living
'object' becomes immobile and is forever anchored in the past, frozen
in a single position. For Barthes, this reveals a fundamental difference
between photography and cinema. The motionless pose that characterizes photography is cancelled in film by the relentless progression
of images. Film can always summon the illusion of a permanent present, whereas a photograph is always defeated by time. For this reason,
Barthes defines photography as a catastrophe that has always already
happened. In a manner of speaking, the motionless pose becomes the
object's death mask. Pictures are like a chronicle of a death foretold.
The past of the pose – a 'that has been' – correlates for Barthes with the
coming death of the photographed object – a 'this will be.'[1] Keeping
this theory in mind, it could be said that the freeze-frame of Colin is a
cinematographic manipulation that prefigures his pending fate.[2]

Cinematographic Choices

Colour
A first cinematic consideration can be whether to record the film in co-

lour or in black and white. When making a film about the Second World War with a 'realistic' look, black and white is a viable option. Since documentaries made in that period were always shot in black and white, the convention of historical images prescribes that black and white is the best option in such a case. It is possible to alternate colour and black and white as well. The war scenes in *Schindler's List* (Steven Spielberg, 1993), for instance, are black and white, but the scenes in the present are in colour. The most famous example of the alternation between colour and black and white is *The Wizard of Oz* (Victor Fleming, 1939). Dorothy's home, Kansas, is filmed in black and white and presents a rather miserable sight. The girl fantasizes about a world beyond the rainbow, which is exactly where she ends up after a tornado. This fantasy world named Oz is brightly coloured and commands our admiration. The development Dorothy goes through, however, results in a renewed appraisal of her black-and-white house back in Kansas: 'There is no place like home.' The colourful world of Oz is only make-believe; in the end, it is no more pleasant than Kansas, which seemed so 'dull' before.

I claimed earlier that where colour is the result of a manipulation of the image, it falls under the heading of cinematography. Such a manipulation is usually imbued with meaning. A fine example can be found in a scene from *Out of Sight* (Steven Soderbergh, 1998), in which prison escapee Jack Foley and police officer Karen Sisco end up in the trunk of a car together because of a bizarre turn of events. Awkwardly positioned in the barely lit trunk, they kill time with idle chit-chat about Faye Dunaway movies. Karen mentions *Three Days of the Condor* (Sidney Pollack, 1975) and claims it is rather implausible that Dunaway falls in love with Robert Redford that quickly. At the exact moment she refers to the film, an intense red glow shines on both their faces. The red light – which is far too obvious for the dark and narrow trunk – is an ironic signal that the con man and the officer will fall in love even faster than the couple in *Three Days of the Condor* or, rather, that they have already fallen in love. Our acceptance of this 'incredible' scenario is due to Karen's self-conscious reference to Pollack's film – love at first sight is possible only on the condition that we express its impossibility.

Film Stock

What film stock is chosen partially determines the texture of the cinematic image. The most important distinction between different kinds of black-and-white film stocks is between 'slow' and 'fast.' A slow film stock is characterized by a detailed texture and smooth contrasts, which makes it suitable for the more contemplative cinema of Michelangelo Antonioni and Andrei Tarkovski, in which time seems to pass slowly. A fast film stock is more sensitive to light, which results in a grainier image with sharper contrasts. The kind of film stock used depends on the sort of atmosphere the texture of the images should evoke. If a film should have bright colours (because it is a musical, for instance), Technicolor, which was used frequently during the mid-1930s and the 1940s, is a suitable choice. In his (anti-) Western *McCabe and Mrs Miller* (1971), Robert Altman strove for the opposite effect. He wanted his images to be as ashen as possible in order to create a look akin to old sepia pictures taken in the period in which the film is set.[3] Today, digital cameras are used more and more often because of the ease and reduced cost. These cameras miss the density and focus of the superior film stock, even though the quality of digital films has increased exponentially since the mid-1990s. The first two Dogme 95 films, for instance, stand out because of the deliberately grainy texture that was partially created by the digital camera.

The success of *Festen* (Thomas Vinterberg, 1998) and *Idioterne* (Lars von Trier, 1997) was due to the fact that the 'messy,' grainy image was legitimated by the storyline. *Festen* records the celebration of the sixtieth birthday of a pater familias, but the festivities soon get out of hand when the eldest son reveals that the father used to abuse him and his younger sister, who has recently committed suicide. The son uncovers this horrible truth in a speech to his father, in the presence of all the latter's guests. Formally the speech confirms exactly to the ritual of the eulogy, from the choice of words ('Dad, do you remember when you used to bathe us?') to the tone of voice in which it is delivered. Precisely by adhering to the conventions of the eulogy, the shock of the revelation is reinforced. This radical divergence of form and content greatly confuses the guests; one of them even starts to applaud because that is the custom after a speech and is met with disapproving glances. The speech is paradigmatic for the tension between form and content: everything looks festive, but the mood is ruined. Nevertheless, the debutant master of ceremonies continues to do his best to make everything look like a party. Because of the stubbornness of most of the guests in continuing to adhere to party rituals, it is consistent that the film does not have the polished look of a professional motion picture but the amateurish guise of a home movie made by an obliging uncle instead.

More or less the same applies to *Idioterne*. A group of people have decided to act as if they are complete lunatics while they visit a factory, a restaurant, and a swimming pool. Hence, they feel excused to display obnoxious behaviour. In their attempt to bring out the idiot in themselves as well as in each other, it is appropriate that the desired idiocy is reflected in a deviant film style and texture. Just as the characters act out their insanity because of a wild desire to experiment, the film looks like the product of someone who completely ignores the conventions of a well-produced picture.

Framing

Every shot is demarcated by the frame: who or what fits in the image, and who or what falls outside of it? The importance of off-screen space cannot be underestimated. A character who is constantly discussed but who does not appear clearly on the screen might take on mythical proportions. Think, for instance, of the mysterious Keyser Söze in *The Usual Suspects* (Bryan Singer, 1995). The final suggestion that the ordinary-looking 'Verbal' Kint, with his halting limp, might be Keyser Söze is met with surprise because of the evident contrast. Stories about the unknown Keyser Söze have made him out to be such a colossal figure that he hardly can be embodied at all any more, let alone by such an apparently uninteresting figure as Verbal Kint.

The matter of what to show is an exponent of the way in which actors are grouped in front of the camera, which is an element of the mise en scène. Framing can be distinguished from this positioning of characters because it focuses mainly on how much is shown within a shot. This already comes into play when the frame format is chosen. The widescreen format is much larger than the so-called Academy ratio of 1:1.33 (the old-fashioned television ratio, in other words, which was the predominant format used in classic Hollywood movies). In the widescreen format, much more can be shown in a single shot, and shot alterations do not have to take place as rapidly.

In slapstick films there is a well-known procedure of telling jokes by showing actions taking place outside of the characters' line of sight in long shots. In *The General* (Buster Keaton, 1927), northern troops have hijacked a number of train wagons, with Annabelle Lee, the lover of Johnny Gray, still on board. He pursues the troops in his locomotive, but becomes so occupied with wood for the engine that he initially does not notice the advancing northern troops that we see passing in great numbers in the background. The joke in *The General* is that we already see what is going on behind Johnny's back because of the precise framing, whereas he is still immersed in other business.[4] For the progression of the plot, however, it is crucial that his awareness of being behind enemy lines on his own comes too late and that he has to come up with a ruse to return to safety with Annabelle Lee.

The question of camera angles is intimately bound up with the matter of framing. Earlier on, I claimed that characters being filmed from below literally appeared 'fattened.' A low angle can also make a character seem impressive or arrogant, however, because he or she has been elevated far above us. The idea of self-importance can be confirmed if that same character stumbles rather clumsily, for instance by tripping over his or her own feet a moment after their appearance. The effect of the chosen perspective always remains a matter of interpretation.

The distance between camera and character has to be taken into account as well. A character who often appears in close-up tends to build up narrative 'credit': there is a good chance that his or her vision will become known to the viewer. However, the reverse is also possible. Isabel Archer appears in close-up extremely often in *The Portrait of a Lady* (Jane Campion, 1996): the film might have been called '*Portrait of the Head of a Lady.*' Nonetheless, the character gives rise to irritation for two different reasons. First, we often see her so close up that it is hard to determine how exactly she relates to her surroundings. Second, the camera seems to be stuck on her face to such an extent that it seems we can see inside her head – yet, we get hardly any reasons why she does not abandon the sluggish and authoritarian Gilbert Osmond other than that she refuses to go back where she came from. A clue that we do not really gain access to Isabel's psyche is also provided by the framing. We often see somewhat tilted shots, which might be a sign that Isabel's world is slightly twisted.

Depth and Focus

Camera lenses can also be used to distort perspectives. The lenses that create the strongest effects are the telephoto lens and the wide-angle lens. When a character or object is filmed from a great distance with a telephoto lens, they appear close. The space in the shot seems flatter than it actually is and characters are seemingly close to each other even though they are in fact separated by quite some distance. The wide-angle lens has the reverse effect: it exaggerates the depth of the image. Objects close to the camera in the middle of the image become extra large; objects placed at the fringes of the screen quickly seem smaller because the wide-angle seems to hide the outer edges. In *The Trial* (Orson Welles, 1963), the wide-angle lens is put to effective use. Josef K.

enters a nightmare when he is arrested without a clear charge and starts to lose his grip on daily reality. This loss is signified by the fact that the world he inhabits has literally been jerked out of perspective by means of wide-angle lenses. Josef seems disproportionately small when facing his enlarged opponents, and the distance between them appears to be enormous. Only at the end of the film, when Josef K. finally understands that there is a 'dirty conspiracy' going on, is the world restored to its proper dimensions, but this comes too late to prevent his eventual elimination.

Lenses also determine the level of focus in the image. If both foreground and background can be seen, the focus is either on both (deep focus), or on one (shallow focus), or it shifts from one to the other (rack focus).[5] André Bazin has a marked preference for deep focus because this technique – like widescreen – can show much in a single frame and necessitates fewer shot changes. As such, the viewer can make his own selection from what is being offered. The possibilities of shallow focus, however, are at least as interesting. In *La Strategia del Ragno* we see a flashback in which Athos Magnani and three of his friends discuss a plan for an attempt on the life of Il Duce, Mussolini. Athos is sitting in the background and is slightly out of focus compared to the other three. This shallow focus prefigures Athos's fate. The assault will indeed take place, but Athos himself will be its victim (which, incidentally, is partially his own doing).

Shallow focus was meaningfully employed in French Impressionist Cinema in order to show mental absence. When a character's thoughts drifted in the midst of a company of people, his image became unfocused. This method is also used in a scene from *The Pledge* (Sean Penn, 2001), in which Jerry Black is surprised with a party in honour of his early retirement as homicide detective. In a short speech he claims to be deeply moved. Shortly after, there is a shot in which the movements of the party guests are slowed. In the foreground, we see Jerry's head in close-up and out of focus. Such a shot suggests that the festivities are passing him by, as if he experiences the party under the influence of alcohol or drugs. The people around him seem to be dancing in slow motion. Judging by their faces, however, the party is not exactly dull. Consequently, the slowed effect can be attributed only to Jerry's perception: the situation seems to move him so much that he can no longer see clearly.

Narratologically speaking, the scene from *The Pledge* is paradoxical. It would be logical to show Jerry's hazy perception in a shot that coincides with his point of view, making him an internal focalizor. In this scene, however, Jerry himself is out of focus. Even though he is the (outward) object of focalization, the shot cannot be interpreted other than as a representation of his (inner) state of mind. This split, in which a character is internal focalizor and object of external focalization at the same time, is hardly unique. The principle will recur in Chapter 6, where I discuss films such as *Fight Club*, *Marnie*, and *Il Deserto Rosso*.

Superimposition, Iris, Background Projection
Apart from shallow focus, superimposition is a common optical effect. Two or more images are superimposed in a single shot; in other words, they are double printed. A character may be so tormented by a certain thought, memory, or desire that we see its content projected across his brooding face.

Another functional optical effect is the iris-in, in which the focus moves in from the edges of the frame to leave only a small image in the centre. In *Jules et Jim* (François Truffaut, 1961), for example, the title characters meet a wily woman named Catherine. The scene ends with an iris-in, as if we were peeping through a keyhole. In the circle we see Jules and Catherine, an effect that foreshadows their imminent liaison.

At the height of the studio age in Hollywood, in the 1930s and 1940s, financial considerations often necessitated background projections. Two characters having a dialogue in a car can be shot far more cheaply in a studio. In the background, shots of shifting landscapes are projected. The final image creates the illusion that the car is passing through these landscapes. In his film *Europa* (1991), Lars von Trier uses this technique of background projection as a narrative element. Leopold, the protagonist, is an idealist whose focalization conveys events during the rebuilding of postwar Germany. Crucial clues appear in background projections to show that he lacks the insight to see through the politically corrupt games he gets caught up in. The things that appear in the projections occur outside of Leopold's sight and are all cases of external focalization. The viewer thus gains more accurate knowledge of the murkiness of the situation than does the protagonist himself. The number of projections decreases as he begins to understand how critical his position actually is. At the exact moment he realizes he is being used, an extreme close-up of his own face and glasses appears as projection. His own widened eyes are a sign that he casts off his gullibility and understands the situation, or, in other words, that he has gained the same level of insight as the external focalizor. Only now can he come to his final act: he causes the train he is on to explode and ultimately drowns.

Camera Operations

So far I have discussed mainly the framing of static shots, but of course the camera can also move about in all directions. It is relevant to ask what causes camera movements. Is there a narrative necessity for the camera to move toward or away from a certain character?

Imagine, for example, a man walking toward the camera. If his countenance seems friendly, the camera might move forward in order to approach the man. If he looks threatening, on the other hand, one might be inclined to recoil from him. If the camera does indeed move away from the man, the narrator/external focalizor acknowledges the threat. Now imagine that the same man were to approach an internally focalizing character in a menacing way. If the camera moves backward but the character remains on his spot, then we get an over-the-shoulder shot that illustrates the character's resolve. Conversely, if the camera remains rooted and the character withdraws, he is revealed to be a coward. The shot becomes more ambiguous when both the external narrator/focalizor and the character stand their ground and face the threat. Does the character refuse to be intimidated, is the menace little more than bluff, or does the narrating agent remain loyal to the character (if he does not recoil, neither will the narrator)? The reverse is true when both the narrating agent and the character give in to the threat. Can the menace be considered real or are both narrative agents in fact cowards? In all of these cases, the external narrator/focalizor determines the nature of the situation (friendly, menacing, bluff). If and how the camera moves now becomes a reaction that might also reveal the steadfast or fearful nature of an internal focalizor.

In the case mentioned above, the narrative motivation for a camera movement can be found primarily on the level of the actions (and consequently on the level of the fabula): how to react to a concrete threat? Camera movements might also primarily concern the level of focalization. A much-used method is to have the camera move toward the face of a character (dolly forward) when he or she is looking intently at some object or when he or she has made a major discovery. The camera might also advance to draw attention to the internal object of focalization. A famous forward tracking shot occurs in the tennis scene in Hitchcock's *Strangers on a Train*. Guy is waiting in a chair for a tennis match to end so that he can start his own game. Coincidentally, he surveys the audience. Then the camera speeds forward to reveal that all the heads of the spectators are moving back and forth to follow the match – all except one, that is, whose head is the focal point of the shot. The eyes of Bruno are fixed on Guy. The quick tracking shot accentuates Guy's dismay that Bruno is tirelessly pursuing him. In this case, the camera movement is linked to internal focalization.

The camera can also move – or refrain from moving – in order to focalize externally. Imagine a character who does not take well to being fired by his superior. As he is taking it out on his boss, the external narrator/focalizor can distance itself from him. The camera moves backward to show that the angry outburst is excessive. Conversely, if the camera remains close to the fired employee, the external focalizor remains in solidarity with the character, and his actions can be interpreted as justified. The final interpretation remains dependent on the exact context. In the Western *High Noon* (Fred Zinnemann, 1952), Marshal Kane is determined to fight a villain who has just been released from prison. All the citizens bail out on him and he is forced to face the four shady individuals who oppose him alone. Right before the confrontation, the camera swings upward and shows him as a small figure in an abandoned street. On the one hand, this camera movement emphasizes how the marshal has been let down by the citizens and commands admiration for his steadfastness. On the other, the camera 'leaves' him as well. Nevertheless, the marshal will finally gain an unexpected triumph.[6]

Taxi Driver (Martin Scorsese, 1976) contains scenes in which the external focalizor comments on the actions of characters by means of certain camera movements. In a famous scene the character Travis Bickle makes a telephone call while the camera pans on in the direction of an empty wall. Equally well known is the scene in which Travis enters a room and walks to the viewer's right while the camera circles to the left until it picks up Travis again. In both scenes nothing in the story motivates disengagement from the character. The fact that the camera floats free of the character without any narrative reason seems to indicate that the external narrator/focalizor distances itself from Travis. By doing this, the visual narrator criticizes the moral mission of the taxi driver, who is planning to deal with all sorts of scum. By having the camera move away from Travis at certain moments, the narrator expresses the suspect nature of the protagonist's mission. The viewer gets a (short) breathing space in which it becomes possible to distance himself from Travis as model for identification or moral guide.

A camera can also mark the turning point in a fabula, as André

Waardenburg makes clear in the case of *The Killing* (Stanley Kubrick, 1956). With the help of a small group of accomplices, Johnny Clay has thoroughly and systematically prepared a robbery and appears to be getting away with his crime. Throughout the film, Waardenburg observes, the camera moves predominantly to the right, across the surfaces of walls and through rooms. This movement seems natural because it corresponds to our direction of reading and writing, from left to right.[7] At the airport, however, Johnny loses control over his bold plan. He cannot bring his suitcase full of money on board as hand luggage. He watches anxiously as the suitcase is being transported to the plane on a luggage trolley. At that moment, a dog escapes from the arms of its owner and the camera suddenly moves to the left to trace the animal. The airport chauffeur has to jerk the wheel to avoid the animal, the suitcase falls off the trolley and springs open, and the money is blown away in the turbulence of the plane's engine. In other words, 'as fate intervenes, the camera moves in the opposite direction, in breach of the intuitively acquired movement.'[8] The reversed and contravening camera movement synchs in with the change for the worse the fate of the story's protagonist undergoes.

A camera movement can also be combined with adjusting the focus. The pan-and-zoom technique is meaningfully employed in *The Damned* (Luchino Visconti, 1969). The camera revolves horizontally around its own axis without changing position, while at the same time focusing on important objects or faces that appear in front of the camera. When Roberto Rossellini uses a technique such as this, the seeming impassiveness of characters immediately stands out: the camera may focus on a face, but the shot never reveals a character's motivation. In *The Damned*, the pan-and-zoom is used to show a succession of faces. They are the faces of the German family Von Essenbeck, listening intently to the cello playing of Gunther, one of the nephews. In this way, the camera uncovers how this well-to-do family remains completely turned in on itself during the rise of Hitler.[9] The external narrator reveals that their blank faces are sign of indifference. The German bourgeoisie is so passive that the Nazis can easily have their way.

One of the most unorthodox camera movements can be found in *Le Mépris* (Jean-Luc Godard, 1963). Paul has noticed that his wife's passion for him has diminished and wants to talk to her. Initially, the camera is aimed at Paul, but then it moves to the right toward Camille. The camera continues to move slowly from right to left, as if a sluggish version of the already rather slow 1980s computer game *Pong* is being acted out. Moving back and forth regardless of who is speaking, the camera operates independently of the dialogue. In this way, the camera suggests that it matters little who speaks and what is being said.

Since a meeting between Camille and the pompous producer Jeremy Prokosch, Paul has been trying to find out why his wife despises him. There are some clues to her contempt, but these remain speculative. As Camille does not explain the cause of her disdain, Paul remains in the dark. A possible answer is contained in the formal characteristics controlled by the external narrator, such as the aforementioned camera movement. In its 'indifferent' steadiness it puts the tediousness of the conversation on display. Moreover, the camera continually passes by a huge lamp standing between Paul and Camille, which is repeatedly turned on and off. This particular mise en scène, combined with the camera movement, turns the lamp into an obstacle that prevents a meaningful exchange of thought. Now they understand each other, now they don't: on, off. The strategically placed lamp and the indifferent camera movement show that the love affair of Paul and Camille is in a blind alley. The filmic style, in other words, reveals the bankruptcy of their relationship.

In Chapters 3 and 4, on mise en scène and cinematography, the central issue was the framed image, which Gaudreault considers to be the first level of narrativity. Editing can be seen as the second level. In its most basic guise, editing concerns the 'suturing' of two shots recorded from different camera angles, on different times and/or on different locations. The joining of separate shots makes it possible to depart from spatial and temporal continuity, thereby creating all sorts of new narrative possibilities for an editor.

chapter 5

Story and Fabula Disconnected through Editing

The first images of *The Comfort of Strangers* offer little support for the plot. While we are hearing an unknown male voice, the camera wanders through an immense palazzo. In a next scene we see shots of Colin and Mary, both in their hotel room and as they are strolling through Venice. Just after a tourist has taken a photograph of the couple at their own request, we see an inserted shot: a man who has not yet been introduced is giving a backrub to a woman we do not yet know. Outside, it is dark. The male voice continues the story that was broken off some eight minutes ago. Then, the film returns to Colin and Mary again. The inserted shot is hard to place temporally. In all probability, considerable time has passed between the insert and the shots of Colin and Mary that preceded it. Possibly the shot is taking place at the same time as the following shot, in which Colin and Mary are drinking wine on a terrace at night. In that the case, the temporal sequence might be as follows: 'While a man is giving a backrub to a woman in a palazzo, the two tourists are drinking wine somewhere else in the city.' However, we are not given any certainty. It also remains unclear how the insert is related to the opening images of the camera wandering through the palazzo. The story is told by a male voice at the beginning of the film before we see Colin and Mary, and the same voice continues the story at the moment that the shot of the massage is inserted. Does the voice prove that the insert is a direct continuation of the opening, turning the scenes of Colin and Mary into an intermezzo? Is the man repeatedly telling this story, making it possible that hours have past between the opening and the insert? Or is the voice-over of the man simply not synchronous with the image we are seeing?

These considerations make clear that the inserted shot cannot be placed chronologically. What the insert does show, however, is that editing can make time and space diverge. In an uncut film – which, consequently, makes use only of monstration – story and fabula are ordered according to an identical chronology. An uncut shot narrates in the present tense and temporality cannot be manipulated in any way other than by altering the image, for instance by slowing or accelerating the take (on the level of the framed image) or by showing the images backward. A cut, however, marks the length of a shot and makes it possible to revise the order of shots. Moreover, the frequency can be increased: a single shot can be repeated as often as necessary and a single event can be approached from all sorts of different angles. These options make it possible to cut to a shot of another space, a technique that forms the basis of cross-cutting: 'meanwhile, at the same time, somewhere else.' A cut can also transfer us to another temporal slot: 'at the same place, some hours earlier/later.' Finally, of course, a cut can do both: 'at another location, some hours earlier/later.' Editing allows time and space to be manipulated, thereby disconnecting the story from the fabula. This chapter discusses some editing principles ranging from cross-cutting to the shot/reverse shot principle. It is precisely this last mechanism that has become such a strong convention that it prevents Schrader from straightforwardly transposing to his film Mary's crucial role as focalizor in the novel.

Editing

In the early single-shot films, there are no temporal leaps. Moreover, the space is fully determined as soon as a camera angle has been chosen. In the case of the early 'chase' films, this mechanism remains largely intact despite the presence of editing. We see, for instance, a group of men run to the left as their pursuers appear to right, somewhat out of focus and in the background. The shot continues until both the front group and the pursuers have moved off-screen. Then, the camera picks up the frontrunners again from the moment they re-enter the frame. This second shot shows a situation that is chronologically continuous to the previous shot and takes place in a neighbouring room. Despite the fact that cuts are made, early chase films such as these never interrupt the temporal continuity or spatial contiguity.[1]

Cross-cutting
With the advent of chase films made by, for example, D.W. Griffith from

1908 on, the pattern of continuous time and contiguous space altered. Cross-cutting has become a much-used technique to increase tension, brilliantly employed in the race against the clock of Bruno and Guy in Hitchcock's *Strangers on a Train*. When Bruno realizes that Guy has no intention of murdering the father of his 'partner in crime,' he decides to put pressure on Guy. As I already mentioned, Guy has a lighter with the inscription 'from A. to G.' He is determined to place the lighter at the spot where he has strangled Miriam. Although Guy is aware of the danger, he first has to play a tennis match in front of a large crowd before he can start to pursue Bruno. The shots of the game are alternated with shots of Bruno's long journey to the crime scene: first by cab, then by train, and finally on foot, he travels to a fairground. When Guy receives a setback, losing the third set and thereby making the match last longer, we cut back to Bruno, who is also delayed: the lighter has fallen down a sewer drain. After we see how he has only just managed to reach the lighter with his fingertips, we hear the spectators of the tennis match applaud: Guy has won the match in four sets. In a great hurry, he leaves the court in an attempt to intercept Bruno.

Cross-cutting creates a different way of conceiving temporal and spatial segments. Unlike in the early chase films, the action no longer takes place in adjacent locations but in separate spaces. Moreover, time is no longer necessarily continuous because the option of simultaneity is added. Narratively, the development of intercutting has been crucial as a filmic counterpart of a standard literary construction such as 'While this was taking place there, that happened here.' A narrator switches from one scene to the other, temporarily interrupting the progress of the first scene and postponing its continuation to a later moment. Hence, cross-cutting is the visual equivalent of the idea expressed by 'meanwhile.'[2]

Apart from a dramatic, tension-building effect, editing as used by Griffith can also create ironic contrasts or parallels. The alternation of scenes starts to function as a moral commentary rather than solely as a way to indicate simultaneity. In *A Corner in Wheat* (1909), shots of a speculator at an expensive party are intercut with shots of exhausted wheat farmers and of city dwellers who cannot afford to pay the steep price of bread. Gunning notes that these three narrative threads never converge. Whereas the distance between characters is always bridged in chase films or 'race to rescue' films (in which one character is looking for another and eventually meets the person), the sequence of scenes remains strictly separate in this case. The causal relation is motivated only economically: the speculator is making exorbitant profits at the expense of the farmers and the citizens. In *A Corner in Wheat*, editing is used to create a painful antithesis.

When the editing pattern does not suggest simultaneity but establishes parallels or contrasts, it is customary to speak of parallel editing. The contrast in Griffith's film functions as an incentive to interpret class differences morally. The transition of shots serves the story, but first and foremost it serves a social argument. The suggestion that the speculator's attitude is outrageous is clearly emphasized by the contrasting shots. It seems to be an act of poetic justice that the speculator coincidentally ends up in a wheat pit that is just being filled.[3]

In his films Eisenstein has taken the principle of parallel editing to a different level. In *October* (1928), a film about the days of the Russian Revolution in 1917, we see Prime Minister Kerensky waiting impatiently in front of a closed door. This is followed by a shot of a peacock's head, an image that has no direct link to the plot. Then, we switch back to the edgy Kerensky, after which we see another shot of the peacock. By now, the bird has spread out its tail feathers. The alternating shots invite us to associate their content, partially because a direct narrative relation seems to be lacking. Since the peacock is the archetypal symbol of vanity, this character trait is now attributed to Kerensky as well. When it turns out that the bird is actually an automated part of some type of clockwork, the alternation of shots also emphasizes the inhumane character of the regime that Kerensky heads. As the peacock starts turning around, the next shot reveals that the door still remains closed to the prime minister, thereby accentuating how ineffectively his government is functioning. In this sequence, in short, Eisenstein encourages the viewer to make comparisons and track differences. Its meaning cannot be construed by simply adding up the different shots but is determined by the transitions from one shot to another. Cutting from one image to the next and back again leads us to think in metaphorical terms: 'X is as ... as Y,' or 'with respect to ..., X is diametrically opposed to Y.'

Earlier, I claimed that the absence of editing did not stop Gaudreault from classifying one-shot films as narratives; instead, the possibility of montage adds a second level to the first narrative level formed by the principle of monstration. In the case of editing, a narrative agent intervenes visibly. Both a change of camera positions and the shifting of a scene are examples of such undeniable interventions. In my viewing, filmic narration can be defined as 'showing' with the option to edit. (I am conveniently leaving out the possibility of sound here; see Chapter 8.) I use the word 'option' because cutting from scene to scene is not an absolute criterion for a narration. A film like *Russian Ark* (Aleksandr Sokurov, 2002) consists entirely of one take, which is a deliberate choice rather than a technical imperfection. Quite the opposite: recording a film in one take is a technical test of quality that demands careful preparation. *Russian Ark* might have had a shot transition at any moment, but the choice was made to do away with editing completely. In this case, not cutting is also a form of cutting.

Editing within the Frame and Découpage

Due to new technical possibilities, *Russian Ark* is the rigorous version of the early films that, by making use of the improved depth focus of lenses, resisted the temptation to cut scenes into little parts. Some scenes in *La règle du jeu* (Jean Renoir, 1939) and *Citizen Kane* (Orson Welles, 1941), for example, are shown in one take where partition into separate shots would have been the standard choice. In *La règle du jeu*, Lisette falls for the charms of the new servant Marceau, which of course infuriates her husband, the hunting supervisor Schumacher. In the castle of his employer, Schumacher starts chasing his wife's love interest. After getting tired of all the running through the castle, where a ball is taking place at the same time, he catches his breath in the kitchen. As Lisette is distracting her husband, we see how Marceau attempts to sneak away behind his pursuer's back (Figure 5.1a). Unfortunately, he accidentally knocks a stack of plates off the table. The noise makes Schumacher jump up and chase his rival through the kitchen (Figure 5.1b). All this is filmed in the same shot. As long as the characters remain in the frame, Renoir's camera does not change positions during the chase.

With this type of camera configuration, the shots are relatively lengthy. When the action in *La règle du jeu* transfers to the background, a shot transition is not necessary because the background is almost as much in focus as the foreground. The principle of deep focus is diametrically opposed to montage in a narrow sense because shot transitions are relatively few. Consequently, deep focus can be considered a form of 'montage within the frame': the viewer can divide the space however he deems fit. Whereas deep focus is a figurative form of 'montage within the frame,' it is also possible actually to edit within the frame. When I discussed cinematography in the previous chapter I briefly referred to the technique of superimposition, or double printing. If a character is brooding, we may for instance see the content of her thoughts projected

5.1a *La règle du jeu* Marceau sneaks away in the background …
5.1b … and Schumacher pursues him. All of this is shown in one lengthy
shot.

across a close-up of her face. In principle, editing is a temporal procedure. Here, however, the mental content does not precede or follow the
shot of the face but is simultaneously shown on top of it. There is also
montage within the frame in the case of a split screen, which divides a
single frame into two or more parts. In order to convey the connection
between three characters at separate locations in *The Grifters* (Stephen
Frears, 1991), we see them simultaneously in a split screen shot while
they are looking over their shoulders in a more or less identical way.

It is important to realize that an uncut scene does not automatically tell more or less than a scene with shot transitions. If we imagine
the scene from Renoir's *La règle du jeu* as if it were made according to
the classic rules of *découpage,* the space would have been divided into
smaller parts. The camera would have shown the lover sneaking away
in a medium shot, followed by a shot of the husband talking, and then
it would have focused on the lover again as he knocked the plates off
the table with his arm. The scene would have possessed about the same
level of understandability, which makes the difference between deep
focus and classic *découpage* mainly a matter of distinct ways of telling:
neither of the two is necessarily superior to the other.

A classic *découpage* draws attention to crucial details we might otherwise easily miss. On the one hand, the spectator is able to gather the
same amount of information as an observant character in this way. In
The Lady Vanishes (Alfred Hitchcock, 1938), for instance, Iris Henderson

and the musician Gilbert are looking for Miss Froy, who has mysterious-
ly gone missing during a long journey by train. They open a compart-
ment door and find a nun watching over a coffin. Before Gilbert closes
the door again, we see Iris looking with heightened attention. In the
hallway of the train, Iris remarks that nuns do not normally wear high
heels. Gilbert opens the door again, after which the camera tilts down to
her high-heeled shoes. An important detail that Iris had already focused
on and that neither Gilbert nor the viewer can afford to miss is zoomed
in on. The shot of the high heels gives both Gilbert and the viewer a new
chance to be as alert as Iris.

On the other hand, the spectator might gain more insight than a character can by means of classic *découpage*. In *Twentieth Century* (Howard
Hawks, 1934), theatre producer Oscar Jaffe wants to turn the hopeless
squeaking of actress Lily Garland into a proper horrid scream. During
rehearsals, he sends director Oliver Webb to the farthest row to test if
her scream can be heard at the back of the theatre. Slightly bored, Oliver
complies with the urgent request. This makes him the spectator of the
scene, so that he now functions as a stand-in for the viewer. Oscar is on
stage with Lily, but in an extreme close-up we also see that he is holding a needle in his hand. After Oscar has pricked Lily with the needle,
Oliver drowsily reports that the scream could be heard in the back. If
this scene had been filmed like the scene from *La règle du jeu*, we would
have missed Oscar's cunning trick. Like Oliver, we would simply not
have noticed it from such a great distance.

The example from *Twentieth Century* has a strict chronological order,
and all the acts take place in a single location. The reason why editing
and narration are so strongly associated with one another is that editing
creates the possibility of breaching the spatial and temporal continuum.
If a scene shifts from one location to another, classic methods can mark
the transition. Shots of a street sign, of a shop window with a store
name on it, or of any other location marker can be inserted in order to
inform us where the characters are at the moment. An interior scene
can also be preceded by an establishing shot showing the location from
the outside. The more clearly the locations are differentiated from each
other, the easier it is to keep track of the story and to reconstruct the
fabula.

Breaching the Temporal Continuum

A time span can be conventionally abridged by a shot of a clock (whether anxiously watched by a character or not) or by a shot showing the

fluttering sheets of a calendar. What applies to space also applies to time: the better temporal 'gaps' are filled and the more scenes are put in a chronological sequence, the clearer the story and the fabula become. Take a film such as *Memento* (Christopher Nolan, 2000), which presents its scenes in reverse order: once you see through the principle of telling a story 'backward,' the right chronological order can be established regardless. Some signs indicating temporal breaches have become a part of the classic film idiom. A dissolve, for instance, is conventionally used to indicate a temporal ellipsis.[4] If we see a man sitting on a bench in shot A and a dissolve reveals the same man still sitting on the same bench in shot B, we recognize that as a signal that the man has been waiting for an indeterminate amount of time. The speed and frequency of the dissolve might even lengthen the time the man is waiting. The transition can also be marked by a 'fade-in, fade-out,' in which the shot grows gradually darker and then brightens up again.

There are myriad examples of a breached temporal continuum to be found in the history of film. I will mention only four. The first is the much-quoted breakfast scene from *Citizen Kane* (Orson Welles, 1941). In flashback, Jedediah Leland talks about Charles Kane's first marriage, to Emily Norton, which developed 'just like any other marriage.' In the flashback we see a two-shot of Charles and Emily at the breakfast table, where he professes to worship her. Then, there is a transition by means of a so-called flash pan. This is a horizontal camera movement in which the camera seems to be spinning so fast that the images become recognizable. The short flash pan functions as a sign of a temporal ellipsis. Instead of a two-shot, we now see a couple of shot/reverse shots alternately showing husband and wife separately. She complains about his tendency to work late. Another flash pan follows. Now she complains about his negative reports on the president, who is her uncle. Yet again we see a flash pan. The conversation at the table is reduced to a minimum. She begins, 'People think,' and he completes her sentence, 'what I tell them to think.' Finally, after another flash pan, we see the couple breakfasting silently, each of them engrossed in a newspaper. The camera moves back in order for them both to appear in the frame. Husband and wife are at opposites end of the table in order to illustrate their estrangement. In this sequence, time leaps are made by means of flash pans that continually return to the same camera position. The increasingly formal clothes, the shortening conversations, and the growing distance instantly show the decline of the marriage.

Whereas the scene from *Citizen Kane* is an example of efficient and compact storytelling with recognizable temporal leaps, the finale of *Invasion of the Body Snatchers* (Philip Kaufman, 1977) contains an extremely uncanny transition. In this remake of the 1956 Don Siegel film, alien pods hatch in order to become a perfect copy of a human body. The pods duplicate in the bodies of the 'elected' look-alikes while the latter are asleep. In this way, people transform into mechanical and emotionless creatures. The protagonist, Matthew, has escaped this fate so far, but during the night he is pursued by an entire crowd of alien creatures. While he is hiding, he overhears a voice saying that he cannot stay awake forever. Then, the screen becomes white a moment before we see Matthew walking on the street again by day. There is no clue how much time may have passed. Is this the next morning, or is it perhaps two days later? Has Matthew slept in the meantime or has he stayed awake? We see him return to work, where he carefully watches his colleagues. His facial expressions are cool and unpleasant, but he might simply be looking tired because of his attempts to stay awake. He might also have heeded the advice to show as little emotion as possible in order to avoid attention. He joins his colleagues as they are lining up. He goes for a walk outside, where he is approached by Nancy, a good friend who is apparently still 'human.' As she is walking toward him, Matthew points at her. He opens his eyes and mouth wide and we hear a horrible droning sound. The camera zooms in on Matthew and 'disappears' into his gaping mouth: the end. The few seconds in which the screen was completely white turn out to have marked a time span during which Matthew fell asleep and turned into a duplicate himself.

In *Le Mépris*, playwright Paul Javal is hired to redraft a film script about Homer's *Odyssey*. Producer Jeremy Prokosch theorizes that Odysseus takes such a long detour because he is reluctant to return home, knowing that his wife, Penelope, had scorned him. This is precisely the fate that awaits Paul. At some point he notices his wife's sudden contempt for him, but he does not know why or when it started. The analogy between Odysseus and Paul is further emphasized by a remarkable insert.[5] Paul's wife, Camille, joins Prokosch in his flashy red car, and Paul follows on foot. As he sets out (Figure 5.2a), we get an inserted shot of a Poseidon statue (Figure 5.2b). In *The Odyssey*, Poseidon is the archrival intent on preventing Odysseus from ever getting home. After this insert, we see how Paul arrives at the house by cab. When he joins Prokosch and Camille, he is confronted by a sulking wife: 'What kept you so long?' Paul answers by telling a complicated story about a cab accident and the search for a replacement car.

5.2a *Le Mépris* Paul's walk is interrupted by …
5.2b … a shot of the sea god Poseidon.

In all of the three exampled mentioned above, an ellipsis took place. The antithetical counterpart of 'omitted' time is the technique of so-called overlapping editing. These repeating shots occur in Eisenstein's films, and also in the art house hit *The Usual Suspects,* which was already discussed in the previous chapter and is my fourth example here. At the end of the film, Detective Dave Kujan is reading the clippings on the board across from his desk while drinking his coffee. Suddenly, he startles and lets his mug slide out of his hand. In order to underline the shocking effect of his discovery, we see the same mug crash on to the floor in slow motion no fewer than three times. Here, the principle is reversed – an event that takes place rather quickly is extended by repeating (overlapping) and delaying the shot. The clippings make Kujan realize that the witness, Verbal Kint, has made up all sorts of details, picking the names of the people and places in his story from the clippings on board. When we see the shattered mug on the floor, we can read the final crucial name from the witness's story: Kobayashi, who was supposedly the right hand of the mysterious gangster Keyser Söze, is only a name on the inside of a coffee mug.

Suture Theory

Because of editing, the identification process in film can progress according to a three-part plan. First, the camera 'looks' at someone or something. Second, the spectator watches the film. These two steps are characteristic for the early 'cinema of attractions.'[6] The transition to the cinema of narrative integration, which was initiated by D.W. Griffith in the second decade of the twentieth century, is marked by the third step. Each of the characters in the film is looking at other characters and things: this is the diegetic level.[7] The linking of two shots by means of the eyeline match, in which the reverse shot either shows the character looking or the thing he is looking at, is crucial for the filmic process of narrativization. In this way, the character can function as a stand-in for the viewer who seeks to identify with him or her.

Theoretically, this identification process has been justified by introducing the Lacanian concept of suture into the field of film studies. As soon as a subject gains access to an entire field of meaning, it necessarily must sacrifice its untranslatable 'being' in the process. It is now addressed by a proper name, but that name does not correspond to the subject's essential core. The name is only a random signifier that does not refer to any specific characteristics. Lacanian psychoanalysis therefore presupposes a fundamental lack: 'being' always falls outside the scope of symbolic representation. This lack forms the basis of desire in us all. The impossible desire of the subject is to symbolically recuperate the lost 'being.' However, every satisfaction in the end turns out to be a substitute for the original desire. The subject is permanently characterized by a *manque à être*, a lack of 'being.'[8] A fulfilled wish is no more than a mirage and offers only a transient and false euphoria of wholeness. Suture signifies the process of 'attachment' in which a fulfilled wish masks itself as a satisfaction of the desire. Because this guise eventually turns out to be false, suture needs to be repeated continually in order to suppress the permanent void at the core of every subject.

What does this psychoanalytic intermezzo have to do with cinema? Take, for instance, the classic opening of the Western *Shane* (George Stevens, 1953). We see an extreme long shot of a rider on horseback in a wide landscape against a backdrop of mountains. No matter how wide this panoramic view might be, it nevertheless confronts the viewer with the limitation of the frame that is characteristic of all shots. The camera cannot register anything but a limited view. By means of a pan it can record that which is to the left and right of the initial shot, and by means of a tilt it can move up or down, but the biggest 'gap' remains in the area directly behind the camera. Reverse shots can show what is lacking from our current perspective.[9] In this case, we see that there is a boy on his father's ranch who is fixedly gazing into the distance. Because this shot is juxtaposed with the panoramic shot, we can reasonably assume that this boy is watching the rider's approach – the principle of the eyeline match holds that the content of the first shot corresponds to the perspective of the character in the second. Since the late 1960s, film theoreticians have used the term *suture* to indicate that the limited frame of a shot is cancelled out by a reverse shot that considerably widens the camera's range.[10] While the panoramic shot resulted in the absence of a viewing area, however, the compensating shot of the boy again creates such an absence. Every attachment of a shot to its reverse shot compensates for an absence but at the same time evokes the void it is trying to fill once again. Another reverse shot is required: now, the viewer wants to see what the boy is looking at. Suture refers to the on-going process of supplementation in which each reverse shot presents itself as the answer to a missing perspective while at the same time summoning a new absence. In this way, films becomes an endless chain of images that can end only with the rather arbitrary statements like 'the end,' 'fin,' or similar closing words.

Since Lev Kuleshov's experiment, it is well known that a story can integrate scenes.[11] When shown two separate shots back to back, the viewer tends to assume there is a narrative relation between those two shots. When you show a bowl of soup followed by a shot of a man's face, as Kuleshov did, a connection is almost automatically made: it looks as if this person might be hungry. When Kuleshov showed the identical shot of the face along with a coffin, the inference was that the person was mourning.[12] In the case of *Shane*, the cowboy on horseback in combination with a boy who is gazing upward gives the impression that the boy's look is a sign of admiration.

Conversely, it is also true that suture makes the story. In *Screening Cowboys*, I argued that the gaze of the boy is a precondition for the forcefulness of cowboy Shane's actions. He demonstrates strength and composure only if the boy, who is an outspoken fan of his, is present as a witness. Without the focalizing child, the cowboy is not pushed into action and there is no eventful story.[13]

Kaja Silverman has indicated that we are desperate for suture. In *Psycho* (1960), Hitchcock has cunningly exploited this urge. The 'scandal' of this film is that we lose our protagonist, Marion, after the first thirty minutes, when she is stabbed to death under the shower. Norman Bates, the motel clerk, then starts to clean the bathroom and wants to dispose of the body. He puts Marion's corpse in the trunk of a car he plans to sink into the swamp. In a medium close-up, we see Norman anxiously watching the vehicle sink. Shortly afterward, the sinking stops: the car is still partially sticking out of the swamp. We notice the shocked expression on Norman's face. Fortunately, the next shot shows the car sinking again after all. I have used the word 'fortunately' because it perfectly demonstrates how the principle of suture manipulates us. Norman cannot be trusted since Marion has been killed in his motel, but nonetheless we share his hope that the car will disappear completely into the swamp. The medium close-ups of his face are important to gain our willingness to identify with him. We need to attach ourselves to a character that functions as our stand-in in the story. For lack of a better alternative after Marion's death, we are even willing to grant that role to Norman.[14]

Visual Pleasure

The idea of suture is also fundamental to perhaps the most cited article on film theory ever, namely Laura Mulvey's 1975 piece, 'Visual Pleasure and Narrative Cinema.' Films are pleasing when viewers can identify with the male 'bearer of the look.' Mulvey associates visual pleasure with narrative films that legitimate a voyeuristic attitude on the level of the story, for instance by letting a woman perform as a dancer on a stage. Such scenes contain an invitation to the viewer: like the (male) spectators in the audience, 'you' can sneak a peak as well. These spectators mediate and justify our position as peeping Toms. In a film such as *Blue Velvet* (David Lynch, 1986), this principle becomes even more explicit. The young Jeffrey Beaumont is forced to hide in the closet of nightclub singer Dorothy Vallens. Unable to run away, Jeffrey is 'condemned' to witness a bizarre rape scene. The specific tension in this case is that Jeffrey runs the risk of being discovered as a voyeur, but the viewer can safely indulge his thrill because he experiences the tension through Jeffrey.[15]

Subjective Shot and Interest Focus

Like Mulvey's essay, Nick Browne's crucial article 'The Spectator-in-the-Text' was published in 1975. His article can be read as a warning against an overly rigid opposition between the carrier and the object of the look. He creates a distinction between a perceptual, or literal, point of view and an 'interest-focus.' Literal point of view is largely identical to the idea of suture. We are 'literally' looking along with a character since we see the events more or less from his or her viewing direction and position. Logically, such a character has a privileged position: we feel sympathy for his or her vision or situation. However, Browne analyses a scene from *Stagecoach* (John Ford, 1939) that contradicts this logic. We see seven characters travelling by stagecoach who must share a lodging. The visual composition of the shots creates a clear division. Within the group of seven, the elegant lady Lucy Mallory considers two of them to be outsiders. The prostitute Dallas and the escaped convict Ringo are usually shown in two-shot and in this way become separated from the rest. The shot that most closely approaches a subjective one is the that in which Ringo offers Dallas a chair before taking place next to her; in it the camera slowly moves forward (Figure 5.3a). In the subsequent shot, we see a medium close-up of Lucy, who is looking at the duo with a disgruntled expression on her face. This makes her the focalizor of the previous shot (Figure 5.3b), in which the forward movement of the camera was a sign of her heightened attention. In a third shot, we see Dallas looking past the camera lens in Lucy's direction. Her expression shows she is aware of Lucy's disapproving look. In Lucy's eyes, Dallas does not have the social standing to be in her company.

5.3a *Stagecoach* The two outsiders, Dallas and Ringo Kid, are eyed by ...
5.3b ... a sullen-looking Lucy.

Anyone looking at the scene in isolation might agree with Lucy. The camera position shares her point her view, which forces us to accept her attitude. Normally, subjective shots are used to make us identify with the focalizing characters. A subjective vision can nevertheless be neutralized, or even overturned. According to Browne, we can also identify with the *position* of a character in a certain situation.[16] Earlier scenes have shown how unjustly Dallas was treated in the town she fled from. This narrative context may cause us to feel sympathy for Dallas instead of for the focalizing subject. Such a context can alter the scene under discussion completely: strictly speaking we are invited to share Lucy's position, but the narrative context urges us to disagree with it. Browne claims that we also weigh the interests of characters: we are not willing to accept the repeated unfair treatment of Dallas.

Browne's analysis of literal point of view, or internal focalization, can very easily be compared with interest focus. This can be demonstrated by returning to the scene from *Partie de campagne* I discussed earlier. I indicated how Mademoiselle Dufour is being watched by all sorts of male bystanders. This principle indicates that she is an attractive young woman. She retains her innocence because she is unaware of her admirers. Rodolphe spies on her from behind a shutter, some boys are watching her from behind a wall, and seminarians are passing behind her back. The scene intercuts this series of male looks with close shots of the swing. The camera follows the swinging motion while showing Mademoiselle Dufour's happy face (Figure 3.2d, p. 54). These shots of her do not represent the perspective of a specific character but reveal her ecstatic emotions: while she is on the swing, she does not have a care in the world. Strictly speaking, the shots are not in the least subjective but instead represent her interest, or, a better term in this case, her experience.[17]

I would like to conclude the section on the distinction between internal focalization and 'interest' by referring to *Basic Instinct* (Paul Verhoeven, 1992). The representation of Catherine Trammell as a devious heroine is almost entirely mediated by the vision of Detective Nick Curran. She shows herself to be so evil that she comes to embody both the detective's worst fear and his ultimate fantasy. According to a 'strict' narratological analysis, Catherine is mainly the object of Nick's focalization – the standard pattern, according to Mulvey. Once again, we are presented with a male vision of a woman. Apart from this structure, however, there is also a 'loose' vision. After all, Catherine is the epitome of taunting independence. Her character comes down to the fact that she does not allow herself to be contained by either a man or a certain vision. She constantly turns out to be a step ahead psychologically, and her prediction to Nick is certainly no bluff: 'Pretty soon I know you better than you know yourself.' Her ways are thus beyond understanding. After all, Verhoeven's film ends with a scene in which Nick believes he has won her over but does not know that there is an ice pick lying under her bed, which was the murder weapon used at the beginning of the film. On the one hand, *Basic Instinct* constantly judges Catherine by the standards of male fantasy (thereby serving a male 'interest'). On the other hand, there are many clues that her character is 'excessive': she cannot be captured by the male imagination. She is more familiar with the psychology of men than men themselves are, enabling her to exploit all their weaknesses. First and foremost, this serves a (vengeful) 'female' interest, which is based on the notion that she has a surplus of knowledge that provides her with a vastly superior position.[18]

Mary as Crucial Witness versus Stand-in for the Viewer

The role of Mary in Schrader's *The Comfort of Strangers* differs from her role in McEwan's novel in that she does not give a witness statement at the end of the film. If faithfulness to the source were used as a standard to judge the film by, one might conclude that it falls short. Faithfulness is a dubious criterion, however, because it automatically privileges the original over the adapted version: the standard assessment is that 'the book was better than the film.' A more interesting issue is whether changes from novel to film have something to do with the nature of the two media.

Schrader's film contains several series of shots and reverse shots that indicate Colin and Mary are being followed. When they are walking about, the camera moves forward in their direction and through the curtain of a glassblower's workshop. There is a cut to a medium shot of Colin, who suddenly turns around. The following shot, filmed from the opposite angle, is an eyeline match: because the reverse shot is explicitly connected to Colin's act of looking, its content would logically be his perception. He sees 'the distorted figure of a man in a white suit' slip away between the curtains.[19] In retrospect, it becomes likely that the earlier shot with the forward camera movement was a subjective shot of the person who Colin now sees hurrying away.

The most prevalent sign giving rise to the impression that Colin is being spied on is the freeze-frame, as I discussed in the introduction to Chapter 4. Contrary to the novel, the film constantly prepares us for the fact that a man in a white suit is continually watching Colin and Mary and taking their picture. By emphasizing that some shots are voyeuristic early on in the film, both the script and the film quickly reveal that Colin and Mary are being watched everywhere. McEwan's novel also contains possible clues that the couple is being spied upon, but they are so implicit and subtle that only a rereading brings them to light. In the beginning, for instance, a man quickly puts down a pair of binoculars (18). This seems to be a completely incidental observation that serves merely as a characterization of the surroundings. (Pinter's scenario has a man with binoculars watching Colin from a vaporetto.) Whereas the film has shots that can be interpreted as the focalizations of a man in a white suit, *The Comfort of Strangers* lacks clear suggestions that an unknown man is spying on the couple.

Earlier, I indicated that the motif of Colin's height disappears in the film because the specific nature of narration is embedded within the overspecific nature of monstration. The most decisive reason why the impact of the film does not equal that of the novel, however, resides in another characteristic that differentiates the media. In the narratological analysis of *The Comfort of Strangers*, I pointed out Mary's crucial role as witness of the key event. Caroline rearranges the chairs so that Mary can clearly see the upcoming event, whereas the script merely places her in a chair: 'Caroline seats Mary.'[20] The film does not make clear that she is consciously being positioned in a place from which she can perfectly witness what is happening. Moreover, Mary's role in the novel was paired with an 'intensity of vision' that temporarily pushes all other senses to the background. The figures of Caroline, Robert, and Colin at the moment of the murder are presented as silhouettes in the novel, but the thing Mary sees perfectly is the 'obscene precision of every movement, of every nuance of a private fantasy' (119). Earlier on the narrator noted that Mary suddenly knew the answer to the question why (114), which leads us to the impression that she understands the act she is watching. She seems to realize what drives Robert, which makes her the perfect witness. She can give a coherent report in her statement. It is in her 'interest' to report Robert, and it is in his 'interest' that she recognizes his masculinity by doing so.

Logically, the emphasis in the film shifts way from that of the novel. What narrative tricks are used to manifest Mary's heightened sense of perception and her eventual understanding of Robert's particular fantasy? This psychological development is too abstract to be visualized. After Robert's 'I'll show you,' Schrader's film shows a medium close-up of Mary's drowsy face in order to emphasize her inability to avert the danger. When the reverse shot reveals how Robert grabs the defenceless Colin by the hair, it becomes clear that the latter is a dead man. Robert's final act – cutting Colin's throat, whereas the novel makes clear that it is Colin's wrist that is slashed – is filmed from a position that does not coincide with the distance and perspective of Mary. Then, the camera moves backward into a high angle, away from the scene. Only one more shot more or less coincides with Mary's perspective. The camera exclusively focuses on the bloody and slouched body of Colin, after which Caroline and Robert pass in front of him without their heads being shown.

The narrative effect of *The Comfort of Strangers* is first and foremost sadistic. Mary is 'allowed' to watch her boyfriend die without being able to intervene. The novel, however, turns her into a witness of Robert's actions rather than Colin's fate. In McEwan's novel, the importance of looks is prominently emphasized by means of all sorts of formulas of perception: 'she saw,' 'she watched,' 'in front of her eyes.' The filmic equivalent of these formulas is the eyeline match: a shot of a certain character is followed by a shot of his perception, or vice versa. However, this procedure is so ordinary in cinema that it has become difficult to highlight its use. The visual mechanism of the eyeline match has pervaded cinema to such an extent as a basic principle of suture that it can hardly be made more specific. The fact that Mary is watching as she does in the novel has less to do with her role as witness than with the filmic need for suture: she represents the absent area from where the scene is perceived. She is the stand-in for the viewer, who legitimizes that we are also watching the horrors as they happen. Such a necessary stand-in is characteristic of cinema but no requirement in literature.

Because shot and reverse shot form a ground rule of editing, the use of this procedure is not very remarkable. Suture is such a familiar mechanism in cinema that Mary's role as witness does not appear to be important. The device of a character whose look mediates ours adheres to filmic conventions. Such internal mediation is known in literature, but it is not a traditional element in all novels. For this reason, the continual reminders of Mary's focalization in McEwan's novel transform her perception into a true act of looking. That Mary's testimony is of the utmost importance in the novel, whereas she is 'only' a witness in the film, has to do with the nature of both media. One could even say that the strength of McEwan's novel resides in the consistent way he has adapted the shot/reverse shot principle of films.

In the next chapter, I argue that *The Comfort of Strangers* offers an alternative to suture that, on closer inspection, gives the film an unsuspected sense of impending danger.

chapter 6

The Visual Narrator and Visual Focalization

The beginning of *The Comfort of Strangers* is highly indeterminate and deviates markedly from the novel. Schrader's film opens with a camera moving forward past the artefacts of a monumental palazzo. After some time, we hear a voice-over of a man who later turns out to be Robert. The camera position may be subjective: it may coincide with the eyes of character and it is likely (but not necessary) that those eyes belong to the character whose voice we are hearing. The script mentions that a hand belonging to a man appears in the frame in order to put on a gramophone record, although in the film we see only a gramophone that is already playing.

The opening of *The Comfort of Strangers* consists either of an impersonal tracking shot or of a classic point-of-view shot. Consequently, there are two options: the camera may be showing us the interior of a stylish apartment, or it may represent the look of a character walking through the apartment. Since the reverse shot is categorically lacking, there is no way to decide between possibilities. The paramount importance of the reverse shot in cinema is demonstrated by *The Lady in the Lake* (Robert Montgomery, 1946), both a film noir and the most notorious experiment with a subjective camera. The protagonist is a detective whom we see only briefly in the introduction and at the end of the film. Between the opening and the finale, the camera coincides with his eyes; the only time he appears on screen during this interval is when he looks at himself in a mirror. The entire story is developed by means of subjective shots. The film has limited itself by not showing any shots that are not also point-of-view shots. In Žižek's view, *The Lady in the Lake* has a paranoid effect. Every object is potentially threatening because we are not able to see anything beyond the detective's viewpoint. Every character approaching the detective is walking directly toward the camera, which, according to Žižek, is experienced as an aggressive violation of our privacy. We are trapped in the 'glass cage' of the detective's perspective, as it were.[1]

The only way to break out from this confinement is by way of a shot showing the detective from an external point of view, but this escape is continually withheld. Normally there is some distance between the character and the viewer, making the character into a stand-in with whom it is safe to identify. *The Lady in the Lake* evaporates this distance, condemning the viewer to the role of stand-in. Because of the permanent use of internal focalization, the detective himself is visible only in the mirror. Consequently, it remains unclear how the main character is situated in the larger 'frame' of the film.[2] The fact that Montgomery's film makes ample use of an explanatory voice-over by the detective does not entirely compensate for this lack of a visual anchor.

In classic cinema, there is no 'prohibition' on subjective camera positions as long as the rule that every point-of-view shot requires a reverse shot is adhered to.[3] Nevertheless, this pattern has some inventive variations, some of which I discuss below. After that, I expound on the importance of the shot/reverse shot principle for the construction of narrative space in cinema. Yet however fundamental this principle may be, its drawback is a lack of accuracy, although it can be neutralized by making a strict distinction between internal and external focalization.

Reverse Shot Variations

Postponed Reverse Shot
At the beginning of *Mildred Pierce* (Michael Curtiz, 1945), we see an establishing shot and hear a gun blast. The next shot shows a man, Monte, looking straight at the camera while bullets are fired at him. When he falls, the shot pans downward and a gun is thrown next to his body from behind the camera. The next shot is a medium close-up of Monte's face from a slightly different angle. We hear him mutter 'Mildred,' after which the camera moves toward a door. Subsequently, we see an extreme long shot of the room where the murder has taken place. The corpse is left lying on the floor.

In the course of Curtiz's film, we are presented with a number of clues that the murder was committed by the woman whose name we heard from the dying man's lips and who is also the protagonist of the story: Mildred. That same night she considers drowning herself, but eventually makes a statement during an interrogation. Only at the close of the film do we understand that it is in fact not she who was the murderer, but her daughter, Veda. Mildred has known this all along, but intentionally brings the suspicion on herself; all her life, she has disregarded her own interests for the extremely spoilt Veda. *Mildred Pierce* is a whodunnit propelled by the question what the reverse shot after the murder should have been. The solution to the murder mystery is finally revealed in the actual reverse shot, which has been suspended for over a hundred minutes: the shooting is eventually shown again, but this time we see Veda pulling the trigger.[4]

Absent Reverse Shot

A reverse shot can also be withheld in a more 'convenient' way, which happens in a crucial scene from *Dark Passage* (Delmer Daves, 1947).[5] Vincent Parry has escaped from prison and is picked up by a woman who advises him to have plastic surgery.[6] Despite his changed appearance, he remains afraid of being discovered. When he learns that the police are about to be warned, he decides to flee over the roof of the apartment block where he has been hiding. He has no choice but to take the endlessly long stairs of the fire escape. His descent is filmed from a relatively low angle, leading the viewer to suspect that a character is watching Vincent as he climbs down the stairs. But a reverse shot revealing such a character never follows. All we get is dissolves showing the descending Vincent. By the time he reaches the bottom of the stairs we hear police sirens and the sound of people crowding in the street, but no one seems to notice Vincent. Vincent has been hiding the entire film, fearing discovery. He has, moreover, just killed a person who did indeed know his past, but as he crawls down the fire escape on the street side of the building he seems more 'invisible' than ever. The low angle is after all not accompanied by a reverse shot.[7]

God's Eye as Reverse Shot

That a reverse shot can also make our previous view of a character shift is demonstrated by the final image of *Breaking the Waves* (Lars von Trier, 1995). The deeply religious Bess McNeill is blissfully happy with her husband, Jan, whom she married recently. She constantly has conversations with God as she sits in church and thanks Him for all she has received. Also, she prays that Jan may be home more often. When Jan has a severe accident shortly afterward, making it impossible for him to return to work on an oil platform, Bess believes her prayers have been 'answered' and considers herself guilty of Jan's dismal fate. During her 'dialogue' with God, she asks him what she is to do. By impersonating the figure of the Father with a low voice and closed eyes, it is Bess herself, however, who provides the answers. In a reproaching tone, she charges herself to do penance so that Jan may recover. When his situation fails to improve, 'God' commands her to chastise herself even more. The ritual conversations with God hold a deep truth for Bess, but demonstrate her naïveté to us. Bess firmly believes in a connection between her penance and Jan's recuperation. 'God' tells her, 'Prove that you love him and I will let him live.'

Bess finally makes a sacrifice so large that she loses her own life in the process. Her death runs almost parallel to Jan's miraculous recovery. At the end of the film, we suddenly hear church bells. The chiming comes as a surprise, since the community is so orthodox that festive things such as church bells are strictly prohibited. Jan and his friends go outside and look up (Figure 6.1a). Logically, we should be seeing a reverse shot that more or less matches the point of view of the men. However, the final shot shows us a perspective from above the clouds with two chiming church bells in view (Figure 6.1b). The concluding image can be taken as an internal focalization of the supreme being. Because of its position in combination with the bells, the shot may be interpreted as God's 'answer,' implying that God has indeed intervened from above. When Bess was still alive, her upward glances were never answered visually by a returning look from the 'other party' of the conversation. We as viewers assumed that the counsel 'from above' was only a projection by Bess herself. The medical indication that she might have been psychotic and the idea that she was at least naïve did not seem unjusti-

6.1a *Breaking the Waves* As we hear the chiming of the bells, Jan and his friends look up.

6.1b Instead of their focalization, the final shot shows the chiming bells from the perspective of 'God's eye.'

fied. Because of the belated reverse shot from God's perspective, however, this impression needs to be adjusted. Perhaps, the saintly Bess has been right all along and Jan's recovery is indeed the result of her willingness to sacrifice herself for him.

Establishing Shots of a Voyeur?

Unlike the examples of reverse shots that are either lacking (*Dark Passage*) or postponed (*Mildred Pierce, Breaking the Waves*), *The Comfort of Strangers* seems to operate entirely within the shot/reverse shot convention. At an early stage, the film already 'reveals' who has made the first picture and who is following the tourists into the glassblower's workshop. In the reverse shots, we see, respectively, a man in a white suit appear from a niche and the same man attempting to sneak away quickly. Nonetheless, the shot in which Robert appears from the niche is a case of strictly external focalization and takes place behind Colin and Mary's backs. At that moment, they are completely unaware of being spied on. The reader of McEwan's novel has about the same information as Colin and Mary, since every important scene conforms itself to the focalization of the two tourists. Conversely, the viewer of Schrader's film is significantly more informed than the characters because the external focalization transcends their limited internal perspective. Crucial shots that lie outside the perception of Colin and Mary are shown to us.

By quickly revealing the spying Robert, the film version seems to give itself away prematurely. At the same time, however, a disturbing side effect is created. Schrader's film has many 'standard' shots that cannot be thought of as subjective in any way. I am referring here mainly to the establishing shots that situate Colin and Mary spatially when scenes shift. Considering that the viewer may now suspect that these shots are in fact subjective shots by Robert, which do not expose their subjective status, the scenes may retrospectively give rise to some discomfort.

In an 'average' film, establishing shots serve an introductory purpose. They are intended primarily to position characters within a certain space. When characters change position, a re-establishing shot often follows in order to redefine the spatial relations. In Schrader's film, (re-) establishing shots have a similar purpose, but every such shot also offers a vantage point from which Colin and Mary may unwittingly be watched by the quietly observing Robert. A reverse shot might confirm the suspicion that Robert is spying on the two tourists. The viewer now remains in limbo over the status of the establishing shots: does this shot position the characters within a certain space or is this an unmarked vantage point? Cinema is thought to be a manifestation of narrative pleasure as soon as a voyeuristic way of watching is legitimized. The reasons for the behaviour of the 'peeping Tom' have to be clear and/or the circumstances should give rise to it. Seeing that neither of these criteria is met in *The Comfort of Strangers*, the possibly voyeuristic nature of the establishing shots is obscured. This potentially secretive nature, however, generates apprehension and creates a desire for reverse shots that reveal whether or not Robert is indeed a voyeur here.

Schrader's film taps into the viewers' desire for suture, especially in wide-angle shots that usually do not require any. Some of these are straightforward 'touristic' pictures of Venice as a picturesque locale. Within the context of the story, however, there is a shift from place to space. In its narratological sense, 'space' refers to a specific place that is bound to a certain focalization. The city becomes a space because of the way in which its scenic backdrop is transformed into a threatening one. The alarming effect is mainly created by the persistent option that the 'picturesque' images are in fact subjective shots of a sinister character.

External and Internal Focalization on the Visual Track

Apart from framing the space outside the filmic image, the traditional rules of continuity in classic cinema also served to uphold the idea of a spatial unity.[8] For both aims, the looks of characters are useful interlocutors. When a character is looking around in shot A, shot B 'demands' that the space he resides in be defined and that the object of his look revealed. If it turns out that the character is in a museum and looking at a painting, our initial curiosity is sufficiently satisfied. This principle is strongly established, as is demonstrated by the Kuleshov experiment (see Chapter 5) and emphasized by a scene from *Nosferatu* (F.W. Murnau, 1922).

In the far reaches of Transylvania, Thomas Hutter spends the night in the castle of the vampire, Count Orlok. As Orlok approaches his guest menacingly, Thomas's wife, Ellen, starts sleepwalking in her home at Wisborg, near Bremen. As the shadow of the vampire falls across Thomas in Transylvania, Ellen, who has returned to her bed, sits bolt upright. In an inserted title card, we see that she is calling her husband's name. In the next shot, we see the vampire's shadow shrink as the creature looks over its shoulder. Logically, the next shot should show the 'content' of his gaze, but it again reveals Ellen, after which we see the count withdraw. Ellen sinks back on the bed with relief. The shots are juxtaposed in such a way that Thomas's wife and the count seem to react to each other directly, despite the enormous physical distance. It is as if Ellen 'saw' the danger in store for her husband, and as if the count 'heard' her fearful cry before deciding to withdraw. The editing pattern suggests a deep connection between the woman and the vampire.

Criticism of the Suture Theory

The desire for suture is so deeply embedded in filmic grammar that it matters little whether shot B is filmed from the exact position of, and at an equal distance to, the character in shot A. If this is not the case, shot B is not a 'literal' subjective shot but an 'approximate' subjective shot. It is also thinkable that shot A reveals a painting on a wall and that we look along with a character in next shot, B, which shows the painting from behind the character's shoulder. The difference between the approximate subjective shot and the over-the-shoulder shot is not accounted for by the suture theory. According to Sasha Vojkovic in her analysis of *E.T. the Extra Terrestrial* (Steven Spielberg, 1982), the disregard of that distinction causes an important narratological nuance to disappear from view.

Vojkovic argues that the status of the alien creature E.T. is split. Either the creature has actually landed in a space ship, or the arrival of the extraterrestrial has sprung from the imagination of the boy Elliott. A remarkable indication of the possibly imaginary status of E.T. can be found in the scene in which the space creature is pointing upward with its finger while saying the word 'home,' as the shadow of its index finger falls precisely on the middle of Elliott's forehead. E.T. may be the product of Elliott's brain, in other words. The interpretation of an imaginary E.T. means that the creature's presence is dependent on Elliott: the boy's mind has brought the extraterrestrial to life. By means of a close analysis of some scenes, Vojkovic discovers a remarkable shot/reverse shot structure. E.T. does focalize Elliott when the two meet, but the reverse is not true. A shot of Elliott can be (more or less) subjective, but a shot of E.T. is always external focalization and often an over-the-shoulder shot taken from behind Elliott's back. On the level of the fabula, E.T. is not a qualified subject since the possibility that he exists only as a part of Elliott's imagination is still open. In his turn, however, Elliott is not a qualified subject on the level of the story; unlike E.T., he cannot focalize 'independently' 'as his vision is always embedded in that of a superior narrative agent. This leads to the paradox that E.T. on the one hand, possibly as the product of Elliott's imagination, is able to see the boy, but that Elliott, on the other, cannot perceive his own projection independently.[9]

Elliott has the idea that no one appreciates him for his own qualities: neither his older brother nor his mother has much regard for him, and his father has left the family. This lack of confidence expresses itself in Elliott's inability to represent his point of view in subjective shots; his look is always embedded in the vision of the external narrator. It is only with the arrival of the government agent 'Keys' at the end of the film that Elliott's subjectivity can be recuperated and that he is able to look E.T. straight in the eyes. The solution of the crisis in the film runs parallel to the shift from over-the-shoulder shots to subjective shots: first Elliott was only partially in the frame whenever he was looking at E.T., but later the camera finally coincides with his point of view. The point made by Vojkovic is that the suture theory trivializes the subtle distinction between over-the-shoulder shots and subjective shots. Suture theory is therefore ill equipped to articulate the development in *E.T.* on the level of the shots.

Vojkovic proposes to replace the theory of suture with the narratological set of terms employed by Bal. The paramount benefit of the latter is the strictly maintained distinction between internal and external focalization. Since I restrict myself to the moving image in this chapter and am not considering text and sound, the visual narrator takes up the central position as external focalizor. Internal focalization occurs in subjective shots: the perception of the character coincides with that of the visual narrator. An over-the-shoulder shot distinguishes itself from a subjective shot because internal focalization has now become embedded in external focalization.

Kill Bill, Vol. 1 (Quentin Tarantino, 2003) contains a good example of a shift from a presumed subjective shot to an over-the-shoulder shot. In a pickup truck she took possession of earlier, the Bride arrives at Vernita Green's house. Chronologically, Green is the second name on her list of targets, but on the level of the story she is the first victim (the execution of target number one is shown only much later). We see the Bride look in the direction of the house, and in the next shot, we see the house itself. This shot seems to be focalized by the Bride, but that illusion is shattered when she walks into the frame from the left. It seemed as though the Bride was the focalizor, but on closer inspection it becomes clear her focalization is embedded: we are not looking 'through' the Bride's eyes but along with her through the eyes of the external focalizor. The remainder of this chapter further specifies the relation between the focalizing characters and the visual narrator (in its capacity as external focalizor by building gradually from seemingly clear-cut to ambiguous instances of that relation.

From a Child's Perspective

A classic example of a novel about focalization is Henry James's *What Maisie Knew* (1897), in which a little girl is the main focalizor of the events. Because of her lack of knowledge where 'adult' matters such as the bitter feud between her divorced parents are concerned, she interprets affairs in an innocent and consequently unorthodox fashion. This makes the reader aware of the great divide between the naïve register of impressions of the child and the actual nature of the venomous conflict. In a similar way, the second half of *La Vita è Bella* (Roberto Benigni, 1997) is a film about focalization. The Italian Guido, who is of Jewish descent, is transported to a concentration camp together with his son, Giosué. The father attempts to conceal the real horror of the enforced incarceration from his son at all costs. He makes the boy believe that the entire setting has only been staged for a game in which the first man to collect a thousand points wins a state of the art tank.[10]

The most poignant scene occurs when the war is almost at an end and Guido has found his son an ideal hiding place, from which the boy will be able to survey the entire courtyard through a small opening. As Giosué hides, Guido is arrested while attempting to find his wife, Dora. The visual narrator shows us how a German soldier transports Guido to a covert place in order to be executed. On the way, Guido must pass the courtyard that his son is looking out on. Suddenly, the father halts and winks in Giosué's direction. We see a shot of the boy in his hideout (Figure 6.2a). Then, we see a subjective shot from Giosué's point of view. Through the opening he watches his father marching down the courtyard in slapstick fashion (Figure 6.2b), thereby infuriating the German soldier: 'Was zum Teufel machst du?' This subjective shot demonstrates once more the painful discrepancy between the image that Giosué has of his father and the grave circumstances they actually find themselves in. Guido is the clown who continually tries to uphold the illusion of the game he thought up for his son, but as soon as he is out of Giosué's view he once again becomes a man who can hardly stand the forced labour, is desperately looking for his wife, and will soon be executed. Whether or not his son is looking at him determines Guido's attitude and behaviour. *La Vita è Bella* operates on two tracks. On the one hand, the visual narrator shows us how grave the situation actually is. On the other hand, the extravagant behaviour of the father is exclusively staged for the eyes of his son. The final words, spoken by an adult voice-over, make clear that the latter has only understood this discrepancy many years later: 'This is my story. This is the sacrifice that my father made.'

6.2a   *La Vita è Bella* Through a small opening in the door of his hideout, Giosué watches ...

6.2b   ... and sees his father perform a 'silly walk.'

From the Perspective of an Object

Whereas Benigni's film has a character fulfil a central function as internal focalizor, *Amadeus* (Milos Forman, 1984) has an 'object' focalizing in a crucial way. In *Amadeus,* the serious but supposedly mediocre composer Antonio Salieri makes a lengthy confession about his rivalry with the 'obscene giggler,' Wolfgang Amadeus Mozart. As musical prodigy, the latter is the centre of attention at the imperial court in Vienna. This causes Salieri's jealousy. Despite his successes, however, Mozart's life is certainly not carefree. Salieri narrates how the brilliant composer begins to weaken physically after the death of his ever-demanding father, Leopold. Even though the film centres on the doubtful part Salieri may have played in Mozart's early demise, the many shots of one particular painting in the young composer's apartment are striking. This painting shows Wolfgang's father, depicted with glaring eyes (Figure 6.3a). The continuous gaze of the portrayed man pressures Mozart into anxiously stressful labour. When his father was still alive he could at least attempt to impress him with brilliant compositions, but against this unrelentingly harsh, dead look he stands no chance. As a result, he resorts to drinking and drug abuse.

   Although both the boy and the painting play a decisive part as focalizors in *La Vita è Bella* and *Amadeus*, respectively, the focalization is
of a different quality in each. The behaviour of the father in the death
camp is essentially split. The way in which he manifests himself – either
jokingly or seriously – depends on only one thing: is his son able to see
him or not? This dependence is emphasized in subjective shots: shots
in which the visual narrator is looking through the boy's eyes. First, the
subjective shots frame the point of view of the boy. Second, they underline the importance of the son's perception of his father in determining
the father's slapstick-like behaviour.

   In Forman's film, on the contrary, the focalization by the painting is
always embedded: there are no subjective shots through the 'eyes' of
the depicted father figure. The pattern here is predominantly structured
as follows. A shot of the painting fills the filmic frame. A reverse shot
shows Wolfgang in crisis, either working frantically or, in one scene,
making taunting gestures at the painting (Figure 6.3b). The scenes are
edited in such a way that the inserted shots of the painting suggest that
Wolfgang finds himself in his father's field of vision. This is effective
in rendering the impact of the painting on Wolfgang, since the portrait
gives him the feeling that his father is constantly watching him. The
crisis has gone through since his father's death, however, has nothing
to do with whether he is in fact near the painting. If that were the case,
the solution would be simple: get rid of the painting or simply turn it
around. The painting is only the material manifestation of the omni-
present 'gaze' of the father. Because of this ubiquity, the field of vision
does not have to be framed, and subjective shots are unnecessary.

6.3a   *Amadeus* A shot of the portrait of Wolfgang's father with piercing eyes …
6.3b   … is followed by the son's hysterical cackle.

Focalization by Means of Colour

The shots of the painting are unnecessary to the development of the
plot in *Amadeus*, but they are essential for fleshing out the story. The vi-

sual narrator strategically inserts the shots at moments when Wolfgang is in crisis. This implies that the visual narrator plays a decisive role in tracing focalization. In *Narratology,* Bal attempts to explore the relation between the visual narrator and internal focalization by referring to *Schindler's List* (Steven Spielberg, 1993).[11] In this film, Oskar Schindler, an average Nazi, transforms into someone who tries to save a number of Jews from certain death. His change of heart takes place at the moment he starts *seeing* Jews as individuals. Bal asks how this 'seeing' is rendered visually. Or, to be more specific, how can the visual narrator show what 'seeing' Jews as individuals does to Schindler?

The key fragment occurs when Schindler is out riding with his mistress and reaches the top of a hill. Beneath them, a pogrom is just commencing in a Polish ghetto. We follow some characters amid the chaos, oppressive anxiety, and brutish cruelty of the pogrom. After a few minutes, the camera returns to a medium close-up of Schindler, who is still on top of the hill. Then, we get a shot whose angle and distance coincide with his perspective for the first time. Between the branches and houses, we see an uncontrolled mass of people. In the middle of the shot a lone girl walks across the wet cobblestones. Suddenly, we see and hear that a man is being shot just behind her. At that moment we see Schindler's mistress in medium close-up, as she turns her face to her companion. The camera pans to Schindler, who is gazing intently in medium shot. Again, there is the same extreme long shot of the ghetto. The girl is still trying to find her way through the chaotically moving masses. Next, we see a medium close-up of Schindler, who is now slightly frowning. In the next shot, the camera is at the level of the ghetto rather than the hilltop, and an impression we got earlier is now confirmed. Spielberg's film is in black and white, but from the hilltop the girl's coat seemed to be red. The colour red is now more clearly visible. Shortly afterward, we get another shot of Schindler and we see how his horse is becoming restless. In a following high-angle shot we see the girl appear behind the rooftops, but now she is moving from left to right instead of the other way around. We get another shot of Schindler's mistress, who turns around and with a quivering voice begs her companion to leave with her: 'Oh, please, let's go.' Schindler remains to watch and finally sees how the girl slips past a queue of people in order to enter a door. We get a shot from within the house, through the thick woodwork of a balustrade. The girl, whose jacket is still red, is climbing up the stairs. After that, we are shown how Schindler turns his horse around and leaves the site. Once more, we return to the girl: as she hides under the bed, the jacket is black and white, just like her surroundings.

An airy children's choir can be heard from the moment we see the medium shot of Schindler in which he is looking on. It supports the use of colour in this scene, but for now, I will disregard the singing in my analysis; the role of sound will be explored in Chapter 8. Here, I concern myself with the fact that the girl's jacket is red during this short time span. The manner of editing corresponds to classic principles, but it is very likely that the red is an indication of Schindler's sharpened perception or otherwise heightened attention.[12] Furthermore, the colour is a sign that Schindler is moved by what he sees (and precisely this was what interested Bal). The shot in which the girl appears was, after all, explicitly linked to his subjective vision. Her jacket only 'decolourizes' when Schindler turns away from the scene. According to Bal, this is the visual narrator's way of showing that the protagonist is no longer unaffected by the horrors taking place. In this fragment, he gets an emotional 'injection.' The visual narrator shows this 'injection' by means of the colour red and in this way visually motivates Schindler's change of heart.

To summarize: by tracing the shot/reverse shot pattern, we can interpret the shots of the ghetto as the focalization of the character Schindler. At the same time, the visual narrator intervenes by means of an optical effect. This narrator on the visual track applies a colour marking *on behalf of* the main character. In this scene, the visual narrator conforms itself to the way in which Schindler interprets and emotionally experiences the pogrom.

In a colour film, the camera could have possibly zoomed in on her to show that Schindler is looking specifically at her. In that case, the crowds around her might have disappeared, at least momentarily. However, even when the camera is filming her at the level of the ghetto she is not close enough to be clearly distinguished from the other people. Nevertheless, this shot is problematic if the idea of the eyeline match is interpreted strictly. The camera chooses an angle and a position that cannot correspond to Schindler's eyes; this criterion was met only by the earlier shots in which Schindler was gazing down on the ghetto from the hilltop. The shot from the ground is, strictly speaking, an external focalization of that belongs exclusively to visual narrator – yet the jacket is still red.

The narrative status of this shot can be interpreted variously. First, the preceding shots have prepared us for Schindler's focalization. He is concentrating so intently that this shot shares his perspective in the manner of showing, not literally, but figuratively. The shot does not coincide with his gaze but with his vision and interpretation of the scene. The close camera position is justified by his extremely thoughtful look. Technically speaking it is external focalization, but within the context of the scene the close shot represents internal focalization. It does not coincide with his perception but becomes a sign of his heightened attention because of its position. The same principle applies to the shot in which the girl climbs the stairs after slipping into the house. Here, she cannot be seen by Schindler. The red is a sign that all of his thoughts are still with her. Only after he turns away does the jacket revert to black and white. The second option is that the visual narrator is watching with the same 'eyes' as the main character: the narrator is moved by this scene as well, and therefore allows the jacket to remain red.

The colour red in Spielberg's black-and-white film is an optical effect functioning as an interpretation of the scene by the visual narrator on behalf of a character. The fact that focalization is never neutral but always 'coloured' is demonstrated quite literally here. The nature of this 'colouring' is clearer in some cases then in others. Whereas one film might clearly indicate that a certain scene is a representation of the (confused) imagination of a character, other films have few markers – or none at all. Below is a series of examples in which it becomes increasingly difficult to determine whether a character is hallucinating or whether the visual narrator is in fact presenting its own vision.

Evident Hallucination

The Dutch film *Ja Zuster, Nee Zuster* ('Yes Nurse, No Nurse,' Pieter Kramer, 2002) contains a court scene in which Barend Boordevol accuses an engineer living in the neighbouring rest home of Nurse Klivia of poisoning his cat. The engineer has tested some pills on the cat, which has now become so docile that she refuses even to eat mice. During his lengthy complaint, Boordevol suffers a coughing fit and reaches for his medicine. What he does not know, however, is that his pills have been replaced by the very same pills his cat ate earlier. In a split second, Boordevol changes from a bitter old man into a loving, relaxed person. This shift of character is shown in the following way: behind the judge in the court where Boordevol brings his complaint is a painting of the previous Dutch queen, Juliana (the film is set in 1968). After a medium close-up of Boordevol, we see a shot of the painting. The painted queen suddenly winks. We also hear the chiming of a cheerful bell, but I will leave sound aside for now. The wink does obviously not occur in the film's diegetic reality but can be attributed exclusively to Boordevol's perception. A possible 'literary' translation is, 'Only Boordevol saw the queen on the painting wink at him.' In this example, the visual narrator has completely subordinated itself to the perception of Boordevol. The narrator on the visual track has only the intermediary: 'I do not show what I, the narrator, am seeing, but I conform to the imagination of the character instead.'

The shot of the winking queen is a clear example of focalization by Boordevol, the angry neighbour, since the framing of this shot corresponds to the position and viewing direction of this character. Moreover, the hallucination is narratively motivated by the pills the character has taken. The scene from *Ja Zuster, Nee Zuster* can therefore be related to the famous chicken scene from *The Gold Rush* (Charlie Chaplin, 1925). Big Jim McKay, a gold hunter, is taking shelter in a snowed-in cottage, along with the Lone Prospector, played by Charlie Chaplin in his Little Tramp persona. Jim is ravenously hungry. In a long shot in which we see both Jim and the 'Lone Prospector '(Figure 6.4a), the latter is transformed into a human-sized chicken by means of a dissolve (Figure 6.4b). As soon as the feathered creature sits down, however, it turns back into the 'Little Tramp.' In a medium close-up, we see the starving Big Jim shake his head and let out a burst of laughter. A title card gives us his line, 'I thought you was a chicken.' Shortly afterward, we see the Little Tramp take on the guise of a chicken again. This time, Big Jim jumps for his knife and his rifle. He chases the beast into the snow until it turns into the Little Tramp once more. The next title card reads, 'I'm sorry. I must be crazy.'

The long shots in which we see both Big Jim and the tramp-turned-chicken in the same image are an example of strictly external focalization, since the shots are not linked to the point of view of a certain character. The figure of the chicken as such, however, as an element *within* the shot, cannot be thought of as anything else than internal focalization. The appearance of the giant creature is evidently an hallucination sprung from Jim's mind and motivated by his hunger, as represented in an earlier title card as 'Food! Food!' Moreover, Big Jim himself indicated that he might be going mad because he thought he saw a chicken. Although this shot sequence is focalized only externally, the appearance of the chicken must be taken as the internal focalization of a character who is emphatically present in the frame at the same time.

6.4a *The Gold Rush* In the presence of the hungry Big Jim, the little tramp transforms ...

6.4b ... into a man-sized chicken. The external focalizor conforms itself to Big Jim's hallucination.

The undeniable status of the chicken as hallucination creates a difference with the so-called motive shot, a term coined by Gunning in his study of the cinema of D.W. Griffith. In *A Plain Song* (1910), the psychological motivation of a character is suggested visually.[13] A girl leaves her elderly parents. During her escape, she sees a group of seniors being transported to the poorhouse. Then, we see a shot of the girl's old father and mother at home. We return to the motionless girl, who now decides to go back home. The inserted shot of her aged parents can be interpreted as a standard case of cross-cutting: while the girl is trying to escape, they are sitting quietly at home. Her choice to return is an impulse without a clear cause. However, the insert can also be taken as a 'mental' shot: she imagines what her parents are doing and fears that the poorhouse will be their lot as well. She returns home to give them better prospects. If the insert is read as a mental shot, it can represent the thought that motivates her decision. The use of motive shots has proliferated in classic narrative cinema; it is frequently used in the psychological thriller, for example.

Possible Hallucination

Whereas the inserts in *A Plain Song* can provide a mental motive as well as representing the visual narrator's way of characterizing the situation, a scene from the psychological horror film *Dressed to Kill* (Brian de Palma, 1980) takes narrative uncertainty one step further. Liz Blake flees into a subway station because she believes she is being followed by a person with dark glasses and blond hair. A sequence of subjective shots characterizes the scene: the camera films from her point of view and moves at the same speed as she does. Liz is paying attention only to her stalker and suddenly finds herself surrounded by a rowdy group with a ghetto blaster. The men intimidate her, and she decides to jump into a subway train that has just halted on the track beside her. Liz approaches the conductor and reports that she is being chased by a couple of punks. In a medium close-up, we see him and Liz look in the direction from which she has just come: the eyeline match, however, reveals only an empty platform and a single person getting on board the train. Because the shot that is being focalized by both Liz and the conductor does not confirm the presence of a group of assailants, we are alerted to the possibility that Liz is only imagining that she is being chased. As soon as someone looks with her, the assailants disappear. The moment she and the conductor look away, however, we see a shady group of figures hurry into the train in the background. When the conductor gets off a few stops later, the men appear in Liz's carriage. She crosses several carriages in order to get away from them, disturbing her fellow passengers with her panicked behaviour. Some travellers also respond with annoyance to the ruckus of the punks who are chasing her, but these shots are always subjective: they are focalized by Liz as she is looking over her shoulder. In this way, it remains unclear whether the punks are real or imaginary.

The scene from *Dressed to Kill* illustrates the potentially thin dividing line between the exclusive vision of the narrator and ambiguous focalization. In the first case, the visual narrator show the situation as it actually 'is,' whereas in the second case the narrator adds the option that the scene is a representation of how the character experiences the situation. This problematic distinction makes the difference between an actual threat and paranoia, but that dilemma is not solved here. As a consequence of this ambiguity, the scene keeps shifting from one option to the other: is Liz being chased or does she suffer from an 'overactive imagination,' as is suggested explicitly in the film? It remains uncertain whether the threat is real. This has a possibly double effect. If the group is actually chasing her, the visual narrator is showing us that nobody is willing to take the threat seriously. If Liz is only hallucinating, the narrator on the visual track has conformed to her perception. Normally, such a conformation occurs by means of subjective shots or by means of shots that highlight the distorted perspective with optical effects. In the fragment from *Dressed to Kill*, the scene develops rather conventionally and has only a few shots that can be characterized as internal focalization. The camera predominantly operates outside of Liz's perspective. If we want to maintain the option of a hallucination, we are required to say that the external focalizor has taken on the guise of a hierarchically inferior internal focalizor. The position of the visual narrator would be strictly subservient in that case: 'I am looking along with this character, but my perspective is far from superior to hers.'

From Eyeline Match to Fantasy Shot

Whereas the status of the fragment from *Dressed to Kill* is uncertain in its entirety, the status of the shots in one and the same scene can shift from the perception of a character to fantasy. In *Vertigo* (Alfred Hitchcock, 1958), Scottie Ferguson has been assigned to trail the supposedly suicidal Madeleine Elster. He has been told that Madeleine dines in a certain restaurant and we see him spying on her from a barstool; she is sitting with her back turned to him. We see some eyeline matches, but that changes when Madeleine gets up and starts walking in Scottie's direction. In fear of being looked in the eye, he turns his head away. As Scottie is keeping his eyes down, we see a shot in which Madeleine's face, in profile, is exactly in the middle of the frame. The music swells and the red background flashes extra bright. Although the shot is filmed from Scottie's position, it is external focalization instead of an eyeline match. After all, the shot cannot be Scottie's perception since he is not looking at Madeleine. Because of Madeleine's theatrical pose, the overly present music, and the flashing red background, however, it seems that the external focalization here is a representation of Scottie's fantasy about her outward appearance.[14] In the form of an external focalization, the 'picture' of Madeleine is charged with Scottie's fantasy about how she looks (or should look). Here, the visual narrator turns itself into a medium for the dream image of a character.

The Complicit Visual Narrator

Precisely this option of a subservient position for the visual narrator is crucial in *Fight Club* (David Fincher, 1999). The film shows us an insurance agent, who uses different aliases but is known mainly as Jack, and a certain Tyler Durden as two separate characters. A narrative twist occurs when the subdued Jack, whose voice-over we keep hearing, realizes that Tyler does not exist: he is only a boisterous alter ego, sprung from his own imagination. The visual narrator, in his role as external focalizor, has consequently conformed its vision to the (distorted) perception of the insurance agent up until this point. *Fight Club* contains a meaningful scene that exposes the role of the visual narrator as 'double agent.' In a parking garage, Jack has become caught up in a fierce but strictly speaking impossible fight with Tyler. Next, we see shots made by surveillance cameras that show how Jack is beating himself up. The scene in the garage itself demonstrates how Jack experiences the fight; the shots of the cameras in the building show how an outsider would perceive it. For the scenes in which both Jack and Tyler are present, we can now definitely say that the narrator on the visual track has 'descended' to the level of the character: the visual narrator has its perspective coincide with that of Jack. The shots of the security cameras, however, 'correct' this faulty perception. External focalization now disconnects from internal focalization: we see a 'factual' registration of the fight between Jack and the non-existent Tyler. Jack is violently dragging himself through the garage.

In *Fight Club*, the visual narrator has mainly taken on the guise of one of the characters. Shots we would normally classify as external focalization now get a strictly subjective content. This makes Fincher's film narratologically split. On the one hand, Jack is the character we continually see on screen; he is the object of focalization of the visual narrator. On the other hand, we are watching the entire film through the eyes of Jack; Tyler can be visible only as Jack's projection.[15] In short we perceive both the character and his imaginary alter ego on the same level. The security camera shots finally take the two apart again. This does not mean, however, that all the ambiguity is now solved. At the end, Jack is trying to prevent the group around Tyler from blowing up the offices of credit card companies. Jack succeeds in neutralizing his alter ego, yet the buildings start to shake. The status of this final shot before the title crawl is not explained in Fincher's film. Are the buildings really collapsing, or are we again seeing both the subject (Jack) and the object of projection (Tyler's ultimate act, namely the exploding buildings) together in the same frame?

If we assume that the buildings are indeed shaking, we are dealing with a 'purely' external focalization. The scene is interpreted by the visual narrator, who shows us what is 'actually' happening. In the case of projection, the external focalization is again 'impure.' What we are seeing corresponds to the vision of a character that is *in* the frame at the same time. External focalization in *Fight Club* turns out to have been largely 'impure,' but the final shot of the film cannot be clearly classified.

Ambiguous Focalization

Where ambiguity is concerned, the final shot of Fincher's film can be compared to the famous shot from *Il Deserto Rosso* (1964), Michelangelo Antonioni's first colour film, although the comparison is not immediately obvious. *Il Deserto Rosso* can productively be assessed in relation to a film by Hitchcock from the same year about the emotionally unstable title character, Marnie.[16] In *Marnie*, a red filter is now and then laid over the images for a short time to signify Marnie Edgar's anxiety syndrome. Her husband, Mark Rutland, later understands that the cause of her erratic behaviour must lie in a memory of her past. *Marnie* is partially a psychoanalytic puzzle: as soon as she is able to clear up the murky waters of her past, both her symptoms and the red haze that occasionally clouds her sight will disappear. Even though the function of the colour red in Hitchcock's film seems clear, Edward Branigan has just cause to probe into the issue somewhat further from a narratological point of view.[17] The bright flashes of lightning, for instance, are red in a strict perception shot that shows only the content of Marnie's look. At other times, the red haze appears as a full-frame superimposition across her face, for instance when she perceives red gladiolas or spills red ink on her white blouse. In the first case, the flashes of lightning cause her such fear that they take on the colour connected to the traumatic event of her childhood. A phenomenon that causes distress, in other words, is hallucinated as being red by means of internal focalization. The red filter that distorts her vision as a superimposition is caused by something red that comes into view. The colour red as screen-filling filter is an external focalization that indicates that her perception has been (temporarily) disabled.

Despite the difference between the internally and externally focalized instances of red haze, it is clear that the optical effect can be exclusively attributed to Marnie. This clarity is lacking in Antonioni's *Il Deserto Rosso*. Like Marnie, the protagonist, Giuliana, is a psychologically unstable woman. Together with her uncommunicative husband and her son, she lives in the industrial city of Ravenna. Not much is known about her past, but we do learn that she tried to take her own life a few weeks ago. The causes of her moods remain a mystery, however: has she become

neurotic because of the modern-looking grey factories spewing toxi-
cally yellow smoke plumes out of their pipes, or is it simply not in her
nature to adapt easily to new surroundings?[18]

A shot in which Giuliana is sitting next to a cart full of grey fruit is
famous, partially because Antonioni actually had his crew paint every
piece of fruit grey instead of using a photographic trick. (The photograph on the cover of this book shows the scene, but I will not involve
Corrado, the man standing to Giuliana's right, in my analysis.) Antonioni does not care much for the rules of classic cinema in the first
place; the shot/reverse shot principle, for instance, is employed only
rarely. The shot of the fruit cart can be an example of the compression
of this principle into a single image. We see a long shot of both Giuliana
and the grey fruit. Is this discolouration the visual narrator's way of
commenting on the dreariness of Ravenna, or can it be attributed to
Giuliana's misery? The shot lacks any other optical effects that might
have provided us with clues: we see a woman next to a cart with grey
fruit; that is all.

It may be productive to analyse the status of the shot from Antonioni's film by means of a literary transcription. In a novel, there might
have been a sentence such as, 'Giuliana sat down next to a cart with
grey fruit in it.' If I leave any other characters out of consideration, Giuliana is the object of focalization of the narrator: it is she who is sitting
down. In this sentence, the colour grey can be explained in at least two
ways. If the text had said 'green,' 'red,' 'orange,' or any other colour,
we might have been able to identify the fruit as, for example, grapes,
strawberries, oranges, and so on. 'Grey,' however, might cause a frown:
how did the fruit get that colour? Are we dealing with some kind of
distorted perception, and if so, whose perception is it and what exactly
does it distort?

To illustrate the mechanism of 'distorted perception,' I will use an
example that has nothing to do with the foregoing: 'Peggy saw the
bride and groom dancing elegantly.' This hypothetical fragment has
an external narrator, and Peggy is the focalizing character according
to the narratological formula 'A says what B sees.' The dancing couple
is the object of her embedded focalization; their dance is the act being
carried out (in the formula I mentioned earlier, 'that C is doing'). This
formula, however, leaves one word unaccounted for: 'elegantly.' This
word is the subjective assessment of the act, since there is obviously no
objective standard by which one could measure the elegance of a dance.
The word 'elegantly' here signifies a benign assessment of the scene.

This assessment might be made by the narrator: this agent believes that the bride and groom are dancing elegantly. It can also be unanimously carried by the other characters who are present: all the guests agree. In both cases, the first part of the sentence ('Peggy saw') is no more than an indication that Peggy is watching the newlyweds. 'Peggy saw,' however, can also carry a different meaning. The reference to her as a spectator can possibly be important because she is the only one who interprets the dance as elegant. The external narrator might have characterized the couple's dance as graceless, but that does not matter: the narrator simply decides to represent the events through Peggy's eyes. Perhaps Peggy herself is a character without any sense of rhythm and as she already admires the couple for taking to the floor in the first place, she mistakes the clumsy hopping for an elegant dance. An equivalent sentence might run as follows: 'The bride and groom moved clumsily over the floor [according to the narrator], but to Peggy's eyes the dance seemed elegant beyond compare.'

Narratologically speaking, a difference between 'dancing elegantly' and 'grey fruit' is that 'dancing elegantly' automatically presupposes a value judgment whereas the alienating 'grey fruit' seems far more neutral.[19] By juxtaposing the fragments, I want to indicate that 'grey fruit' might just as well be a subjective perception. A further difference between the examples is that the sentence about the dancing couple contains the verb 'saw,' which is an explicit sign of focalization. The sentence about Giuliana could, however, be rewritten to include such a sign: 'Giuliana sat down next to a fruit cart. The fruit looked grey.' The following sentence would be even more explicit: 'Giuliana was so depressed that even the fruit seemed to look grey.'

Each of these transcriptions (from a 'cart with grey fruit in it' to 'seemed to look grey') lessens the ambiguity, and therefore reverses the argumentative structure of this paragraph. The scene from *Ja Zuster, Nee Zuster* made use of the shot/reverse shot principle, which makes it possible to identify Boordevol as an internal focalizor. Moreover, the painting of the winking queen contained a recognizable optical effect that indicated a hallucination. Finally, that hallucination was also motivated on the level of the plot: the angry neighbour had just taken one of those suspicious pills. In the case of *Il Deserto Rosso*, all three of these techniques have been ignored, which makes the final status of the shot impossible to ascertain. Giuliana is not identified as a focalizor because she appears in the same shot as the fruit. Unlike in *Marnie*, no optical effects are explicitly shown. (The optical effect in Antonioni's film of actually painting the fruit grey has been created before the shoot.) Is there any narrative motivation for the colour of the fruit, then? Giuliana is in a strange but also somewhat enigmatic state of mind, but one can doubt whether that is sufficient motivation for the fruit's greyness. The unusual colour can also be a comment on the condition of modern society from which Giuliana seems to have alienated herself. A combination might even be more plausible: the grey is both an expression of the woman's despondency and a visual translation of the visual narrator's worldview. As a result, this scene from *Il Deserto Rosso* is based on ambiguous focalization. The visual narrator shows and focalizes Giuliana sitting next to a car laden with grey fruit. Focalization is always also interpretation, but whether the visual narrator focalizes the fruit as grey or whether the visual narrator conforms itself to Giuliana's focalization remains structurally unclear. If the latter is the case, internal focalization takes on the guise of external focalization.

Focalization Shifting from Character to Character

The scenes just discussed are on a sliding scale from internal focalization, as in *Ja Zuster, Nee Zuster*, to ambiguous focalization, as in *Il Deserto Rosso*. In the case of ambiguous focalization, the imaginary perception can be attributed to both the visual narrator and to a particular character. As well, focalization can shift from character to character. The structure of *The Parallax View* (Alan J. Pakula, 1974) is based on this option. Joe Frady, an investigative journalist who operates on his own, has discovered clues leading him to a covert organization. To the viewer as well, it seems that Joe has indeed uncovered evidence for a conspiracy, and we are therefore fully prepared to identify with him. At a certain moment, the camera follows Joe as he trails an individual he believes to be suspicious. When the camera makes a slight motion to the left, we see suspicious-looking men standing in hallways and watching Joe. Joe is tracking a man, his own object of focalization, but he is unaware that he has simultaneously become the object of focalization of some kind of clandestine group. The camera movement changes Joe's status. He seemed to be a clever detective who was able to outsmart others. However, the revelation that he is being watched by dubious characters shows that it is in fact he who is outwitted. Since he is ignorant of all this, the covert organization will use him as the scapegoat for its next murder.

In *The Parallax View*, the subject of focalization unknowingly turns out to be the object of focalization. The inventive aspect of a specific scene from *Out of Sight* (Steven Soderbergh, 1998) is that the identity of the focalizor seems to shift during a dream sequence. After escaped prisoner Jack Foley and police officer Karen Sisco have met each other for the first time in the trunk of a car (see Chapter 4), they go their separate ways. A few scenes later, Jack tells his comrade that he is going to take a bath to wash off the mud. We see a dissolve as the tap is turned on and steam starts to develop. As Jack stands in front of the mirror, we also see shots of Karen approaching with her gun drawn. Stealthily, she sneaks into the bathroom, apparently about to arrest Jack once he is in the bath. The scene exhibits some signs that it might be fantasized by Jack. First, the transition to this scene was a dissolve, which is the most commonly used convention to indicate a mental state. Second, the bathroom is filled with hot steam, which makes it appear somewhat dreamy. Third, Jack is reclining in the bath with closed eyes. Other clues are taken not from this scene but from the narrative within which it is embedded. Jack has already attempted to flirt with Karen, despite their conflicting interests. He wants to get to know her better in the hope that a spark will ignite between them. In terms of the plot, moreover, it is completely unrealistic that Karen should appear so soon in a house she does not know.

The sudden turn of events enhances the idea of a fantasy scenario. Karen attempts to arrest Jack, but he grabs her arm, draws her into the water, and starts to kiss her passionately. In other words, 'Casanova' Jack is daydreaming that Karen has immediately fallen for him. At the end of the scene, however, we hear a voice say, 'Karen ... Karen, honey?' We shift to a scene in which Karen is lying in bed and opens her eyes. Her father is sitting beside her and informs her that she was talking in her sleep. Karen: 'What did I say?' Father: 'Hi, yourself.' The scene that seemed to be Jack's daydream turns out to have been also the dream of the reluctant Karen all along. The suggestion that they share a parallel fantasy about the other efficiently shows that Jack and Karen are meant for each other from the first moment. *Out of Sight* shows how a fantasy can spread to several characters and make them into allies, or, in this case, into lovers. In Soderbergh's film, the status of the scene changes and 'multiplies': first, Jack just seemed to be taking a bath; then, the scene turns into his daydream; and finally, it is also (or perhaps predominantly) Karen's fantasy. There is a shift because the scene is retrospectively being focalized by two characters instead of one.

In conclusion, I would like to give two memorable examples of variations on the principle of shifting focalization. In *The Birds* (Alfred Hitchcock, 1963), we see how an evident external focalization is retrospectively revealed to be an internal focalization. In *Don't Look Now* (Nicholas Roeg, 1973), we see how a character wrongly interprets the content of his own focalization because he is unaware of his own precognitive abilities.

From God's Eye to Birds' Eyes

The scene from *The Birds* in which a gas station in Bodega Bay explodes because of the insidious actions of the gulls is famous. Initially, the scene adheres to the shot/reverse shot pattern: in the first shot, we see the location of the disaster and a man lighting a cigar near leaking gas; in the reverse shot, we see the character Melanie and other people in a diner who can see the catastrophe happening but are unable to prevent it. Their powerlessness is accentuated by the short freeze-frames of the panic-stricken face of Melanie: the stills illustrate how paralysed she is by what she is witnessing. Then, the camera goes up into the sky: from the clouds, we see the fire spreading below. Such a God's eye or bird's eye perspective presents an opportunity to examine the scene carefully and consequently has the connotation of an 'objective' panoramic shot. After about five seconds, birds glide into the frame from behind the camera (Figure 6.5). The status of the shot changes abruptly: this bird's eye perspective is literally seen through birds' eyes. The apparently 'objective' shot had been subjective all along: the camera coincided with the perspective of the birds.

6.5 *The Birds* The supposed neutrality of a God's eye perspective is problematized as soon as the birds fly into the shot from behind the camera.

It is the oscillation between supposedly objective and specifically subjective that makes the shot from the perspective of God's eye so extraordinary. This interpretation does, however, merit three further remarks. First, this scene makes every claim of 'neutrality' or 'impersonal narration' suspicious. If even a God's eye perspective cannot be straightforwardly objective, it is proven once more that every perspective entails a vision and, consequently, an interpretation. Bal's reply to Gérard Genette was that 'zero focalization' is impossible. Focalization is always 'subjectified content.'[20] Apart from the narratological dictum that the narrative is always interpreted by an external narrator or visual narrator, a shot can also unexpectedly turn out to be internal focalization. In *The Birds*, this subjective quality is specified as the looks of the birds. The heavenly shot seems to be a stock example of external focalization, but through the presence of the birds it creates the option of internal focalization.[21] In *The Comfort of Strangers*, by contrast, it remains only a suspicion that several shots are focalized by Robert.

The second brilliant aspect of the shot is that the camera is not 'flying' like a bird. Hitchcock might have chosen to let the camera glide through the air. But the shot is perfectly static and refuses to sacrifice its connotation of objectivity. Because it does not mimic the flight of birds, there is also no shift from 'objective' to subjective; they are shown as equally valid options. The status of the shot is emphatically double: objectivity is a subjective illusion and specific objectivity is always embedded within higher, external frame.

Third, the birds flying in from behind the camera cause the shot to lose every claim of inconsequentiality. The shot offers the opportunity to survey the situation, but it also forces the viewer to assume the perspective of the 'evil' birds. Being the source of all the misery on the ground, the birds may be gloating in their catastrophic triumph. Now that we as viewers must share the birds' point of view, we also need to ask ourselves what secret pleasure we take in watching the dramatic scenes taking place below.

This effect of identification demands further elaboration. During the entire film, we have invested our 'interest' in the besieged Melanie; it is an interest we will not give up so easily. Here, Nick Browne's rule concerning *Stagecoach* (see the previous chapter) applies. Even if we share the position and viewing direction of Lucy in a specific scene in Ford's Western, we do not adopt her view that Dallas and Ringo have to be excluded: the narrative context reveals that their exclusion is unjustified. In the God's eye perspective shot from *The Birds*, the viewer is invited to look along with actants that have been positioned negatively by the narrative. Because this subjective shot clashes with Melanie's interest, the viewer will feel tempted to resist this invitation. Consequently we are not forced to be as pleased with the disaster as the mischievous gulls, but we are encouraged to reflect on the sadist in ourselves.

In *Out of Sight*, the precise status of the bath/arrest/kissing scene was opaque because of the way in which the entire scene was embedded. The image of Jack bathing shifts to a fantasy about what could happen in the bath and in retrospect seems to be Karen's fantasy as well. In *The Birds*, a God's eye perspective is exposed as having a subjective content and teaches us that no shot can claim neutrality: every shot always already has a subjectified content that can be attributed to the visual narrator or the characters. The shot reminds us that ambiguous focalization is always present in cinema, even where we least expect it. Finally, the ominous aspect of *The Comfort of Strangers* resides in the option that seemingly standard establishing shots might also indicate the (indistinguishable) focalization of Robert.

Unacknowledged Second Sight

Don't Look Now is remarkable in that a character does not recognize the authority of his own focalization. At the beginning of Roeg's occult thriller, Laura Baxter is reading by the fireplace while her husband John is closely studying slides of church interiors. Outside, on the grounds of their mansion, their two children, Christine and Johnny, are playing. The editing pattern reveals striking parallels between the interior and the exterior scenes. A zoom toward a red stain above the church benches is followed by a shot of the reflection of Christine's red jacket in the water. When Laura moves her fingers near her lips, Christine immediately puts her hand in front of her mouth. When their daughter throws a ball a few moments later, John tosses a packet of cigarettes to Laura. We see the ball end up in the water, followed by a shot in which John knocks over his glass. As Christine wades into the water to retrieve the ball and her brother falls on the grass after cycling over some glass shards, John interrupts his work and looks up as if he has heard the splashing, the crunching of breaking glass, and the thump of Johnny's fall.

In the opening scene, the crucial moment occurs when John bends over with his spyglass in order to study more closely a slide he had projected on a screen earlier. We see how the stain above the church benches spreads out over the slide. Dumbfounded, John shakes his head and hurries outside. Christine has fallen into the creek and John starts to wade through the water in order to save her. An inserted shot of the slide – not focalized by John this time – shows the red stain still spreading while ominous music sets in. The red blot now seems to be a signal of the worsened condition of Christine. The rescue attempt will turn out to be futile.

I refer to this opening scene because of the close of the film. In order to deal with the loss of Christine, Laura and John go to Venice. There, they meet the blind psychic Heather and her sister. Heather has 'seen' Christine and tells Laura her daughter is happy. This encounter has a comforting influence on Laura, but John has little faith in Heather's 'mumbo jumbo.' He is unaware, however, that he has a gift similar to the blind woman's. This denial of his paranormal abilities will prove fatal. In the streets of Venice at night, he spots a small figure dressed in red running through the alleys. He pursues it because the figure reminds him of Christine in her red jacket. When he finally corners the little figure, its back is turned toward him. We see a medium close-up of John's friendly face, followed by an insert of the slide we already know. From the back, the hooded figure shows an uncanny resemblance to the red stain on the slide. After the shot of the slide, John's face looks distraught. Only then does the figure turn around and give John all the more reason to be upset. It turns out to be an ugly gnome with a dangerously large knife. The creature cuts John's throat. The inserted shot of the slide seems to have been a mental shot of John, seeing that it is framed by medium close-ups of his face.

The shift from a friendly to a disturbed expression seems to indicate that John now realizes what else the slide was trying to tell him. He had interpreted the earlier perception shot, in which he was looking through a spyglass, as a sign that Christine was in immediate danger. He had not interpreted it as a sign of his own death foretold, however, simply because he did not acknowledge his own ability to see the future. The fact that the perception shot is predominantly a foreshadowing of John's own fate is supported by the way in which blood flows from his neck after the gnome has struck, visually mimicking the spreading red stain on the slide. The fast montage sequence following John's arterial bleeding quickly revisits earlier important scenes in the film. Afterward we see a final shot of the slide, which has now become completely red. The film ends with John's funeral boat passing, an event he had already 'foreseen' earlier without the viewer knowing whose funeral was represented but that we now recognize as his own. It is of paramount importance in *Don't Look Now* to understand the narrative status of John's focalization. If he had known that he could see into the future, it might have saved him a lot of suffering.[22] If he had only recognized the red blot above the church benches on the slide as a reference to the Venetian serial killer, he might have escaped his dismal fate.

Especially in contemporary postclassic or postmodern films, the status of scenes needs to be carefully considered. In modern films, characters can be revealed as split, as we saw in *Fight Club*. The character and the product of his imagination are captured in one shot. In Fincher's film, Tyler Durden eventually reveals himself to be the alter ego of 'Jack.' Matters become even more complex in *Mulholland Drive* (David Lynch, 2002), a film that lacks any clues about the possibility of split personalities. Is the main character, Betty Elms, in fact the imaginary ideal image of Diane Selwyn, a character who is introduced only much later – and who is already dead on top of that? In that case the protagonist herself would be a dead woman's fantasy, able to feature alongside characters who are 'real' and consequently operate on a higher ontological level. In the many scenes moderated by Betty's perspective, the visual narrator then conforms to the dream world of a dead character without manifesting it. The narratological set of terms is still applicable, but one should not expect narratology to clear up the confusion of a film like *Mulholland Drive*. If the narrative structure of a film is this multilayered, narratology can only mirror the ambiguous ontological status of its scenes. It is not necessarily able to solve the riddle.[23]

chapter 7

Tension between the Visual and Auditive Narrators

'My father was a very big man. All his life he wore a black moustache. When it turned grey he used a little brush to keep it black, such as ladies use for their eyes. Mascara.' These are the first words spoken in *The Comfort of Strangers* and we hear them even before a character has been introduced. We do not yet know that it is Robert, speaking in voice-over. Later on, in the bar with Colin and Mary, he starts to speak about his father and opens with exactly the same words. In McEwan's novel, this characterization of the father is a one-time event. Only in the bar does Robert relate his experiences as the son of an authoritarian patriarch. In the film, however, the lines are spoken a third time. When the police asks Robert for his motives, he answers, 'Listen, I'll tell you this.' Once again we are told that his father was a very big man who used a brush such as ladies use for their eyes to colour his greying moustache black. After the word 'mascara,' the credits start rolling.

Robert is off-screen only during the first of the three times we hear the words; the other two times, we see him speaking on camera. The repeated use of the same phrase is already striking but is given even more emphasis by placing it at the beginning and the end of the film. The stressed repetition is a clear indication that Robert defines himself in relation to his father: 'I can only say who I am if I tell who my father was.' Even though his father uses a typically feminine attribute like mascara, its effect is hypermasculine: the son's story suggests that, apart from the father's impressive size, it is his dyed black moustache that lends him authority. Robert's self-image depends on his father to such an extent that the key to his motive must lie in his relation to this domineering old man. That is why Robert answers by telling the story of his father when asked why he committed the murder and deliberately left clues of his crime. In other words, if the policeman can rightly interpret this story, he should be able to grasp the motives of his suspect.

There is, however, yet another side to this story. Robert's narrative about his father is not visualized at any point in the film. The first and third tellings are rather short, but in the bar Robert gives the extended and complete version of the story about his father and his reason for marrying Caroline. Nothing would have been more obvious than letting Robert introduce his story and then representing it with images from his childhood. This is all the more conceivable because the events are perfectly suitable for visualization: the little Robert with his father's hand on his neck, screaming that his sisters can't wear silk stockings; the sisters and their elaborate preening rituals; the little Robert feasting on chocolate and lemonade and vomiting in his father's office. What 'logic' determines the non-visualization of these scenes that Robert so vividly describes? This chapter uses that question to examine voice-over, internal narration, and flashback. This helps us to understand that the narrative status of *The Comfort of Strangers* is more complex than it appears at first sight.

The Death of the Implied Author

The principle of 'voice' in cinema refers back to the role of explicators, the lecturers who provided commentary to accompany the images in the early days of cinema. Initially they were an attraction in addition to the images because of their unbridled enthusiasm, but around 1908 their role shifted from zealous extra to include the more functional task of explaining increasingly complex narratives.[1] The explicator, however, was not an integral part of the film, having an entirely personal impact on the (mis)interpretation of scenes and performing a function that lay beyond the control of the production companies. He was an extra aid to make an insufficiently self-evident film more understandable.[2] Title cards were useful as general guides, but they did give the impression that the film could not tell itself. Their advantage was that they were integrated into the film, but the fact that such cards consumed a lot of time was a major disadvantage. Often, we see a character speak before we can read what he or she actually says. With the advent of the sound, viewers were able to see and hear simultaneously. It also became possible to 'save time' by integrating scenes. In *Bound* (Andy and Larry Wachowski, 1996), for instance, neighbours Corky and

Violet come up with a clever scheme to steal money from the mafia. As we hear in voice-over how the plan is being developed, we also see its execution. In other words, we hear the discussion that would have preceded the action we are being shown.

In his *Coming to Terms*, Seymour Chatman has made a distinction between an auditive and a visual channel.[3] Chapter 8 specifies certain types of sound more elaborately, but here my main concern is the hierarchical relation between the auditive and visual tracks that Chatman establishes. In his discussion of a scene from *All about Eve* (Joseph Mankiewicz, 1950), he outlines how the character that introduces the rising star Eve Harrington and all the other characters by means of voice-overs dominates the visual track with his voice.[4] When Eve comes forward to collect her theatre award, we hear the voice of critic Addison DeWitt as the shot freezes. According to Chatman, Addison's voice-over is responsible for the freeze-frame. With that, he does not treat image and sound as separate tracks, but grants one track (in this case: sound, words spoken by a character) the power to intervene in the other.

In this way, Chatman creates a hierarchy that betrays the influence of an agent that is fundamental to his analysis: the implied author. The latter, however, does not equal the writer or director and cannot be equated with the external narrator. The implied author is a virtual agent constructed by the reader/viewer. He or she summons an agent into being that controls the intention of a book or film. The reader/viewer projects the textual intention on to the implied author, assigning responsibility for the meaning of the text. I would like to argue, however, that the concept of the implied author is philosophically and analytically unusable.

According to Chatman, the implied author is responsible for the total design of the film. The viewer lives under the illusion that this agent knows 'exactly what is going on' at any given moment. As overarching agent, it is by definition capable of solving all ironic tensions. Reducing ambiguity to a minimum has been the foundational thought of Wayne Booth, who 'invented' the notion of the implied author in *The Rhetoric of Fiction*. He enjoys ambiguity, but only to a certain extent. If it is not solved in the end, a meaningless void may ensue. When Booth cannot come to a stable interpretation of a text, it can only express absurdism to him. The absurd text is notoriously unstable precisely because it refuses to be understood.[5] Booth's rhetoric eventually aims at explaining away instability: when a text is absurd and pointless, the reader can appeal to the implied author in order to understand that aimlessness was intended by the text from the beginning. The implied author is the narratological guarantee that meaning, which equals intent, will be walled in.

Poststructuralists, by contrast, deny the idea that texts can form a closed whole and attach no value to the implied author. In the reader's perception, the implied author functions as the protector of the context in which a novel or film is supposed to be read. Contexts, however, cannot be limited. The meaning of a novel or film depends on the perspective that is chosen. As the context changes, so do the possible meanings.[6]

By discussing *The Straight Story* (David Lynch, 1999) we can see how impracticable it is for this hypothetical 'implied author' to mark off contexts and meanings. The narrative structure of *The Straight Story* seems clear. The disabled and short-sighted seventy-three-year-old Alvin Straight decides to visit his brother Lyle after hearing of his brother's stroke. The brothers have not spoken to each other in ten years because of a fight, the cause of which remains unclear. 'It doesn't even matter any more,' according to Alvin. He sets off on a lawnmower to cross the 500 miles to Lyle in Wisconsin. This strange journey forms the heart of *The Straight Story*. Eventually, Alvin arrives at his brother's place, where together they watch the starry sky. The film's plot is presented in chronological order without flashbacks or flashforwards. Even when one of Alvin's painful war memories resurfaces, we only see how he tells it at the bar; it is never visualized. In short, *The Straight Story* really does tell a straightforward story in which we get exactly what we see.

Despite this first impression, however, the film does breed suspicion: not because of specific scenes or shots, but because the name of the director creates a completely different expectation in the viewer. (I went to watch this film specifically because David Lynch had directed it). Lynch creates cinema that exposes the dark forces beneath the outer calm of a rural community (*Blue Velvet*) or uses grand gestures to maximum effect – think, for instance, of the extreme close-ups of lit matches in *Wild at Heart*, with Nicolas Cage heavily overacting in his role as Elvis imitator. The film preceding *The Straight Story* was the 'obscure' *Lost Highway*, a story with a schizophrenic protagonist. Many critics lamented the incomprehensible nature of that film. The irony is that it is David Lynch who comes up with something as straightforward as *The Straight Story*, as if to say, 'Here you go, critics! If *Lost Highway* was too difficult for you, then here is something even you will be able to understand.' Considering this, it becomes possible to see the serenity of *The Straight Story* as a 'provocation.' Particularly at the end of the millennium, when viewers expect apocalyptic films, the creator of *Lost Highway* – with its dark world view – comes with a seemingly calm film without any sense of pending doom. On the one hand, the film about the headstrong old man is as optimistic as it seems. On the other hand, it dares the viewer to consider whether the film raises irony to the second power. Just like the square of any negative number has a positive result, irony times irony creates an incomprehensibly transparent film.

This last option is based on a viewing attitude activated by the name of a director and not by an internal textual element. As a result, this analysis of *The Straight Story* falls outside the range of the implied author, a determining agent within the text that is nonetheless presumed to know its *actual* intention. In the case of Lynch's film, the viewing attitude is decisive: does one view the film as simply 'straightforward' or does one consider this straightforwardness a charade? Philosophically, the implied author as supposed source of meaning becomes a dead element. But even as an analytical term the implied author fails because it is employed to create hierarchies. If there is an unclear choice between possible meanings, an appeal to the implied author might make the balance shift to the 'right' option. Chatman discusses the implied author as an agent that solves 'ironic tensions.' The point, however, is precisely to resist the temptation to make a choice. *The Straight Story* is both a thoroughly conventional narrative and, at the same time, an ironic provocation addressed to the critics of Lynch's previous films. His seemingly average film is special precisely because it succeeds in simultaneously activating two interpretations that seem to exclude each other. I have used the example of *The Straight Story* to show the bankruptcy of the concept of the implied author. As a protector of meaning, it is unreliable. As an agent that is appealed to in order to ward off ambiguities and multiplicity of meanings, the implied author creates hierarchies. It is better to work without a 'lock on the door' than with one that is unreliable.

Filmic Narrator, Visual Narrator, Auditive Narrator

By casting aside agents that seek to embody textual intention, the implied author disappears from the narratological theory that I endorse. When the implied author is called upon to end the deadlock between two divergent readings, the tension between mutually exclusive theories still remains in the case of *The Straight Story*: the film cannot be pinned down on one reading or the other. And, to return to my starting point, the tension between the auditive and visual tracks remains intact without the implied author. Contrary to what Chapman implies, sound and text are not hierarchically superior to images or vice versa. To clarify the relation between image and sound/text, I propose to instate an agent that negotiates the relation between the auditive and visual tracks. This agent may resemble the implied author to a certain extent, but differs from it in two crucial aspects. First, this narrative agent has nothing to do whatsoever with textual intention. Second, I would like to refute any hierarchy between the auditive and the visual. The agent I put forward is hierarchically superior to a narrator on the auditive track or a narrator on the visual track, but both the lesser narrators essentially operate on an equal level. From now on, I will call the agent that regulates their synchronization the *filmic narrator*.

The filmic narrator is the agent responsible for the interaction of two other types of narrators. The first type controls the auditive track, which contains external and internal voice-overs, dialogue, voices, music, and all other kinds of sound. I will call this the *auditive narrator*. I already discussed the second type, the *visual narrator,* in the preceding chapter. Like the auditive narrator, the visual narrator is a subcategory of the filmic narrator. The visual narrator limits itself to the sequence of images and can be defined in relation to Gaudreault's terminology. It is Gaudreault's *monstrator*, except that the visual narrator's domain also extends to the transitions between images. It includes title cards (visual words), such as the ironic qualification 'the good' in *The Good, the Bad and the Ugly* (Sergio Leone, 1967).[7] The credits and special announcements preceding the film ('based on a true story,' for instance) also fall under the sphere of influence of the visual narrator.[8]

Once a narrative agent that regulates the interaction between words and images is defined, it becomes possible to review Chatman's discussion of the freeze-frame in *All about Eve*. According to Chatman, characters have the power to freeze images with their voice-over. I propose that the filmic narrator grants Addison only the illusion of control. The filmic narrator institutes an exchange in which the visual track is adapted to match the character's voice-over monologue. Prompted by the filmic narrator, the visual narrator freezes the image for Addison's commentary. The smug critic Addison is led to think that he can direct the narrative with his voice-over, but he can indulge in that fantasy only because the filmic narrator has determined that the visual narrator should conform itself to it. The (forced) accommodating role of the visual narrator, which shows itself particularly in the freeze-frame, magnifies Addison's vanity.

The function of the filmic narrator is to regulate the interaction between sound (in this case, the spoken word) and image. This interaction takes place on a sliding scale that runs from exact correlation between the auditive and visual tracks to the complete divergence of those tracks. In what follows I discuss this scale with reference to some examples.

A Gap between Image and Sound

The subtle clues that point forward to the surprise ending of *Fight Club* indicate the smooth interaction of the auditive and visual narrators. The plot twist was the revelation that Tyler Durden is an alter ego of the character-bound narrator Jack (see Chapter 6). In some scenes we hear Jack's voice-over, and in these scenes the visual track reveals information about Tyler's identity if we connect the text to the shots. At the beginning, Jack relates how his insomnia distorts his view of reality. While he is making copies at work, he says in voice-over, 'Everything is a copy of a copy of a copy.' As he is speaking, we see a reverse shot of his point of view. In this shot, the image of Tyler is shown in a single frame, hardly visible to the naked eye. In this way, the visual narrator gives us an early clue: Tyler is only a copy of 'Jack,' who in turn becomes a copy of the alter ego to whom he slowly gives over control as the film progresses. In a scene fifteen minutes into the film, Jack says in voice-over, 'If you wake up at a different time in a different place,' while he is being filmed at the airport. At that moment, Tyler, who still has not been properly introduced, passes on the travelator behind him. The camera turns to the left following Tyler, while we hear Jack finish his voice-over by saying, 'could you wake up as a different person?' By moving the camera from Jack to Tyler, the visual narrator suggests an answer to the question posed: yes, 'you' (Jack) can wake up as a different person (Tyler).

These two scenes from *Fight Club* show how the visual narrator can almost unnoticeably illustrate the voice-over. However similar the procedure of the two shots may seem, though, they are nonetheless different types of illustration. The shot in which we hear Jack in voice-over and see Tyler in a single frame is internal focalization. Jack sees Tyler as his copy, but this is so short-lived that he is not even aware of it. In the scene on the travelator, Tyler passes behind Jack's back. The camera movement is a clear operation of the visual narrator and is motivated by the fact that Tyler is passing. Here, Jack asks himself a question in voice-over, but the answer that is suggested visually is outside his line of sight. In the first scene, internal narration correlates to internal focalization. While Jack is speaking about copies of copies, he sees his own copy in a flash, albeit in another, dreamt-up guise. The image is hardly perceptible, thereby signifying that he is barely aware of his rebellious side. In the second scene, there is an internal narrator and external focalization. The camera movement seems to be a response to the narration, but the auditive track does not follow the visual hint. The visual narrator gives an early suggestion of how to interpret the relation between Jack and Tyler, but this suggestion is not marked auditively. In this case, there is a gap between the voice-over and the visualization: the visual narrator shows more than the character can possibly know or say.[9]

The Divergence of Text and Shot

Whereas the scene on the travelator in *Fight Club* shows a gap between the visual and auditive tracks, a scene from the Western *Johnny Guitar* (Nicholas Ray, 1954) rests on the meaningful divergence of shot and text. The title character visits the saloon Vienna, which was named after its owner, and has a drink at the bar (Figure 7.1a). The guest is welcomed by the kitchen help with the words, 'That's a lot of man you're carrying in those boots.' When these words are spoken, however, it is not Johnny whom we see, but the character Vienna, who is introduced by the visual narrator at this exact moment. Dressed in a dark outfit with tight pants and high boots, she is filmed from below, standing behind the balustrade at the top of the stairs (Figure 7.1b). The words spoken off-screen become ambiguous because of this specific shot. Strictly speaking the characterization applies to the guest, but at the same time there is another image addressing us: the low camera angle shows us a more than resolute woman, while the words accentuate her appearance since they are being spoken at the moment she is introduced. The qualification may not be meant to apply directly to her, but the connection of text and shot certainly suggests that it does. In this way, Vienna is narratively positioned through words spoken by a character who is off-screen. Johnny is the object of auditive focalization, since the kitchen help is addressing him directly. At the same time, the text characterizes an object of visual focalization who is not addressed directly, Vienna. This divergence between simultaneous shot and text creates a link: the

7.1a *Johnny Guitar* At the exact moment the hero is greeted with the words
'That's a lot of man you're carrying in those boots.'
7.1b The forceful-looking Vienna appears on the screen for the first time.

words addressed to Johnny also apply to Vienna, who is shown in the
shot. It will be no surprise to the viewer that these two will make a
formidable match.

Flashbacks Introduced through Voice-over

So far in my discussion of the interaction between the auditive and visual tracks, I have limited myself to internal voice-over and text spoken
by characters. Visualized flashbacks that are introduced by a character
form a distinct category of this interaction.[10] For an example, I will turn
to the first flashback in the Japanese murder mystery *Rashomon* (Akira
Kurosawa, 1951). A lumberjack, a priest, and a civilian take shelter from
a heavy rainfall. The lumberjack and the priest speak of a dreadful but
at the same time incomprehensible event. With the civilian as attentive listener, the lumberjack begins his story: 'It was three days ago. I
went into the hills to chop firewood.' In the shot following these words
we see the sun shining through the foliage. Even though we no longer hear the lumberjack's words, it is presumably his narration that the
shot visualizes. The introductory words immediately specify the time
(three days ago), place (a wooded mountain range), and the embedded
status of the shot (flashback). Next, we see the lumberjack making his
way through the forest, filmed from many different perspectives with a
highly mobile camera. We see him from below, from above, and we see
the back of his head and close-ups of his face in which our sight of him

is blocked by branches and leaves. On the way, he stops a few times to pick up some objects he finds: a broad-rimmed hat with a veil, male headgear, a piece of rope, a box with an amulet. Suddenly, he recoils in fear. In a medium shot, we see two rigid arms sticking up. Between those two arms, we look at the horrified expression on the face of the lumberjack (Figure 7.2a). We do not see exactly what the lumberjack sees, however; what is registered is his reaction. He rushes off, panicked by his discovery. Once again, his voice accompanies the visuals: 'I ran back as fast as I could to report it. That was three days ago.' The scene ends with a shot of the lumberjack running, followed by a wipe revealing the same lumberjack kneeling in the courtyard of the prison where he is giving his testimony (Figure 7.2b).[11]

7.2a *Rashomon* The discovery of the corpse as narrated by the lumberjack is shown to us as an external focalization.

7.2b Every witness statement, such as the one by the lumberjack, is filmed frontally. In this way, the viewer is accorded the role of the detective or judge.

In and of itself, this scene can hardly be called problematic. A lumberjack is walking through the forest and discovers strange objects. The rigid arms, together with the horrified reaction, indicate the finding of a corpse. Soon, it turns out that we are dealing with a murdered samurai. The find is not shown from the perspective of the lumberjack. That would have been logical, since the flashback we are watching was introduced as his narration, even though the greatest part of it is not accompanied by his voice-over. We have only his reaction to frame our suspicions; as viewers we do not see the dead man but only his arms sticking up. What is strictly speaking missing in this key shot, in other words, is internal focalization. The internal narration is suspended on the auditive track while the visual track offers external focalization by the visual narrator: someone is telling what he found, but we never directly see exactly what he found. It is left to the viewer to imagine this 'empty space.' Nonetheless, there is some consistency to this hiatus. The lumberjack who tells the story is not completely the same lumberjack who was in the forest three days ago. The narrative is structured as follows: 'I am telling you that I went into the hills three days ago.' Seeing that the 'selves' are not completely identical in this structure, it is justifiable to refrain from letting them coincide.[12] The scene is retold now, as a reconstruction or reliving of an earlier event. For this reason, there is a logic to limiting the number of subjective shots.

Internal Narration, External Focalization

It is quite usual to resort to the split principle of internal narration with external focalization on the visual track in flashback scenes. Even though the visual narrator in fact renders the perspective of the narrating character, the scenes shown do not coincide exactly with the character's perception. In other words, the lumberjack relates what he has seen with his own eyes, but that corresponds only *to some extent* with what we see (the visual narrator's focalization). When we hear the lumberjack's voice accompanying the images at the end of the flashback, we are once again reminded that we are in fact watching his tale. In short, the lumberjack narrates, but his focalization is embedded in the focalization of the visual narrator. The latter does not show us the lumberjack's object of focalization, the dead body of the samurai, directly, but only the startled reaction of the lumberjack. Through an external perspective, the content of the internal focalization is revealed indirectly: we have an acceptable impression of what the lumberjack stumbled upon.

Internal Narration, Ambiguous Focalization

When internal narration and external focalization diverge even further, it can become quite difficult to get a clear impression. Chatman discusses *Badlands* (Terence Malick, 1973), Holly's retrospective on her flight as a young girl with her murderous boyfriend, Kit. During the film, we hear her as voice-over, but her account is far more positive than the images warrant. Chatman suggests that she is a naïve adolescent living in a fantasy world. That is why her words are an overly romantic interpretation of their adventure. On the one hand, this hypothesis seems legitimate, but on the other, Chatman uses an invalid argument to support his analysis. Film distinguishes itself from literature because the auditive track can clash with the visual track. *Badlands* demonstrates such a conflict, which makes the narration partially unreliable. Then, Chatman argues: 'Normally, as in *Badlands,* the visual representation is the acceptable one, on the convention that seeing is believing.'[13] In other words, if there are no signs indicating the contrary, the visual track is always right: seeing is believing.

Once again, Chatman creates a hierarchy between the visual and auditive tracks. In case of an obvious visual intervention such as freeze-frame, sound may have primacy: the dominance of sound justifies the unorthodox shot. But usually, he seems to imply, it is the other way around. His hypothesis is based on the assumption that words are less truthful than images. In his view, a narrating character will exaggerate and lie sooner than will the images the visual narrator supplies. Chatman appeals to convention in order to be able to make a claim for the 'truth' of *Badlands*: the adventure has taken place as the images show. But even if you want to say something about the 'truthfulness' of *Badlands*, it is also theoretically possible that the filmic narrator permits the visual narrator to 'decolourize' Holly's words. Perhaps her story was not too rosy, but the filmic narrator may be allowing the visual narrator to create room for scepticism in order to demonstrate that Holly's account is possibly overdone. It would consequently be more correct to say that Malick's road movie concerns itself with the clash between the auditive and the visual tracks itself, without giving in to the temptation to create a hierarchy between sound and image.[14]

As was said before, Holly is a character who retrospectively relates her adventure in a voice-over commentary. At a certain point, she realizes that staying on the run will do her no good and lets herself be taken by a police squad. Kit continues his ride alone. We see him leaving the police behind by pulling a daredevil stunt with his stolen car. Nonetheless, he lets himself be captured shortly afterward. Holly wonders why. Is it because he would have been caught eventually? Is it because he was desperate? She continues: 'He claimed to have had a flat tire, but the way he carried on about it I imagine this is false.' Subsequently, we see Kit get his gun and shoot the tire of his own car on purpose. He uses stones to mark the place of his arrest.

Holly has not been present at the scene, but tells us nevertheless that she does not believe Kit's story about the flat tire – at any rate, not the simple story of the car breaking down. Her idea is that he surrendered willingly. The scene of the shot tire in *Badlands* has an ambiguous status. Either the visual narrator shows what actually happened and (coincidentally) confirms Holly's assumption that the flat tire was an excuse, or the visual narrator shows her imagined visualization of the cause of his arrest. He has shot his own tire to have the car malfunction for an excuse, or so she pictures it. The visual narrator then shows this scenario as the visualization of her thoughts.

If 'seeing is believing' is a criterion, the first option is the most believable: if we see it ourselves, it must have happened that way. When the subservient role of the visual narrator is also taken into consideration, the second option that Holly's estimation is being visualized becomes legitimate as well. Those who do not see such a subservient visual narrator as a possibility at all would consider the (in)famous flashback from *Stage Fright* (Alfred Hitchcock, 1950) 'cheating.' In the opening of the film, Jonathan Cooper tells his good friend Eve Gill why the police are after him. Jonathan has been witnessed by the chatty housekeeper in the house where the husband of his mistress was murdered. Because of this, he is the main suspect, but he tells Eve that he only came to pick up a dress for his mistress after her confession that she had killed her husband. The visual narrator delivers appropriate images to accompany Jonathan's story and corroborates his version of events. In the end, however, it turns out that Jonathan has been lying to Eve: he in fact is the murderer. This implies that the images shown earlier were straightforward deceptions. Critics who were annoyed by the plot twist spoke of a misleading film.[15] It was acceptable that a character would lie to defend his own interest, but the fact that the visual narrator perfectly visualized this lie was hard to digest.

Those who consider the compliance of the visual narrator with a narrating character a form of dubious manipulation would probably also have trouble with narrative experiments like *Rashomon*. I wrote of the lumberjack's flashback as relatively straightforward in and of itself. The rest of the film, however, contains more narrators: the bandit Tajomaru, the spirit of the deceased samurai, and his widow, Masago. Their conflicting stories about the death of the samurai are supplemented by a new story from the lumberjack, who admits that he witnessed a fight between the bandit and the samurai. In the end, it is impossible to reconstruct what happened. The civilian who has been listening to the entire story even suggests with sadistic pleasure that the lumberjack in particular has been lying about his discovery. Did he really find the corpse the way he described? Where, after all, is the precious dagger that is now missing? Has the lumberjack perhaps stolen it and decided to tell a story about a chance discovery to hide the theft? *Rashomon* remains stuck in suspicions because the visual narrator limits itself to supplying images to accompany the different statements. It takes a compliant role and does not add visual comments of its own.

The role of visual narrator can be compared to that of a police sketch artist. A witness gives a profile of a criminal, a process similar to the attempted portraiture of the infamous Keyser Söze in *The Usual Suspects,* a film I discussed earlier. The sketch artist attempts to render the witness's verbal description visually. If the witness gives a false statement, in order to protect the real perpetrator, for instance, the sketch would automatically be incorrect. The sketch artist must comply with, and depends on, the witness, just as the visual narrator depends on the narrating character. It is not necessarily the case, however, that the visual narrator functions as a police sketch artist. That is one possible role that can be accorded to the visual narrator by the filmic narrator. A potential effect of that function may be to confirm the tension between the visual and auditive tracks: if words can lie and images can comply with untruthful words, where does the true version of events reside?

To conclude, the scene with the flat tire in *Badlands* has 'internal narration and external focalization.' The question remains whether they correspond by accident or whether the visual narrator conforms itself to the ideas of the character. In other words, the hierarchy between the auditive and visual tracks cannot be decided. Where *Rashomon* is concerned, we have a similar case of 'internal narration and external focalization.' The visual narrator, however, seems to stick to its accorded role as 'police sketch artist:' it is compliant with the version of events told by the characters. A further complication of this division of roles announces itself when the object of narration focalizes, as another flashback from *Rashomon* will show.

Subjective Shots of the Object of Narration

Tied up in the courtyard of the prison, Tajomaru wholeheartedly confesses to killing the samurai after an honourable battle. The samurai's wife had incited both men to a duel by promising to give herself to the victor.[16] It is noteworthy that the visual narrator repeatedly switches from the narrating Tajomaru to the flashback. Every time the bandit speaks about what took place in the forest, he is shown in the courtyard, telling his story. We do hear Tajomaru speak in the flashback ('I have hidden weapons over there, in a safe place in the woods'), but we never hear the bandit's words in voice-over, accompanying the images of the flashback, except for one instance. The sentence following a furious reaction by Masago ('I had never seen such a passionate woman') has a different status from the sentences he speaks within the flashback. This voice-over occurs during his testimony and takes place outside the flashback, whereas all other texts are strictly part of Tajomaru's reconstruction of the past.

After the voice-over about Masago's fiery nature, we see Tajomaru overpower her despite her fierce resistance. The bandit bends over her to kiss her on the mouth. She is looking past his face, to the sky. During the kissing scene, we see four subjective shots of Masago. Within the representation of Tajomaru's flashback, in other words, we see the internal focalization of a character other than himself. This character is in fact the object of his narration. What we have here, then, is an internal narration and internal focalization of a character who does not narrate. What can be the coherence that lies behind this structure?

The crime in *Rashomon* seems simple because Tajomaru, the main suspect, immediately confesses. Later testimonies, however, cast doubt on his statement. The bandit turns out to be a braggart, above all. Masago's subjective shots reinforce the impression that he is boasting. The first three show the sun shining through the leaves of the treetops while Tajomaru molests her. In the fourth the sun is still shining, but the focus becomes blurred. The reverse shot shows that Masago closes her eyes. Then, the dagger she was holding slips from her fingers, suggesting that she has succumbed to the bandit's charms after all. Taking his smug attitude into account, it is logical to assume that the bandit is imagining how she experienced the process of being overpowered. The subjective shots are not so much Masago's as they are wishful thinking on his part: 'I, Tajomaru, imagine how she falls for me by experiencing her surrender from her own point of view.' The subjective shots are consistent in the sense that they say more about the narrating character, Tajomaru, than about the focalizing character, Masago. They bear witness to the impact he means to have on her with his overwhelming strength. Her embedded focalization is itself embedded in his wishful narrative.

The Failing Sensory Perception of the Object of Narration
The incongruent principle of flashback narration of a certain character with embedded subjective shots of a second character who is the object of narration occurs often in practice and is rarely a problem. In *Karacter* (Mike van Diem, 1996), Jacob Willem Katadreuffe is being interrogated

about his possible involvement in the death of bailiff Arend Barend Dreverhaven. Consequently, the film is a reconstruction narrated by the suspect, who turns to out to be his son. The bailiff is representative of the 'law without compassion.' By discussing two specific scenes, I want to make clear what status Dreverhaven's subjective shots have within Katadreuffe's narration.

Having got a job at a law firm, Katadreuffe is perplexed one day to encounter Dreverhaven, who is on his way to a meeting. He climbs a flight of stairs in order to be able to have a clear view of his father. When the latter finally looks up in the direction where Katadreuffe is standing, we get a subjective shot; in it, however, we see only the stairs and not Katadreuffe. Either he ran, or his father is incapable of seeing him. His son does not exist as an individual to him because all contact is prevented by the boy's mother.[17] Katadreuffe imagines that he is an abstraction to his father. In the scene following this one, Katadreuffe discovers in the archives that Dreverhaven was the acting bailiff when Katadreuffe's first business went bankrupt. 'He came to our house,' Katadreuffe realizes. After a dissolve, we see Dreverhaven visit Katadreuffe's mother, or, more accurately, how Katadreuffe imagines the visit. As Dreverhaven walks through the house, we hear the subdued conversation between Katadreuffe's mother, Joba, and the lawyer who accompanies Dreverhaven. When Dreverhaven turns to Joba, however, the music drowns out the words. Next comes a perception shot of Dreverhaven watching Joba and the lawyer. We see their lips move, but we hear no words. The wordless part of the scene lasts until Dreverhaven turns his back on them and the camera positions itself next to Joba and the lawyer. The scene implies that the bailiff is too dazed to listen to what is being said.

The subjective shots of the (now posthumous) object of narration illustrate above all how the narrating Katadreuffe views his father: Dreverhaven is incapable of adequate sensory perception. In the eyes of the son, the father is missing a certain level of sensitivity. That is why his sight is failing, his hearing worsens, and why, in a later scene, he screams without uttering a sound. The fact that Dreverhaven's perception is flawed places the first subjective shot in a different perspective. At an eviction, we get an internal focalization by Dreverhaven when he is bending over a raving woman on her sickbed. With her still on it, he drags the bed outside into the freezing cold. Immediately, she gets up from her 'sickbed' and starts swearing. We might suspect that he is capable of unmasking malingerers straight away, but later subjective shots reveal only that he lacks the ability to correctly assess situations. The first subjective shot does not show his capacity to recognize fraud but emphasizes his insensitive and heartless nature. Even if the woman had been sick, he would have acted in the same way.

Separating Text and Flashback

So far, I have discussed flashbacks introduced by an internal narrator. This did not require the complete synchronization of the images and (the tone of) the narration, as was shown in the analysis of *Badlands*. Another aspect was the internal focalization of an object of narration in both *Rashomon* and *Karacter*, but in both cases this formal technique produced a congruent meaning. What I have not discussed yet, however, is the narrative status of the flashback itself.

Visual Reconstruction by the Listener
In *Kiss of the Spider Woman* (Hector Babenco, 1985), the prisoner Luis Molina tells his cellmate Valentín Arregui about one of his favourite movies, a Nazi film about forbidden passion, betrayal, and death. The visual reconstruction of what is narrated seems to be a representation of Luis's memories of the film. In the Nazi flick, however, is an actress who also plays the part of Valentín's controversial girlfriend. She is part of the social class that Valentín and his comrades fight against. He projects his relationship with her into a film in which a singer falls in love with one of her enemies. We can assume that the film-within-a-film we see is not so much Luis's narrated recollection of it, but rather the way in which his listener and fellow prisoner visualizes it. In other words, the visual track is not necessarily controlled by the narrator's text but can also originate from the listener.[18]

In Babenco's film, the words of the narrator, Molina, conform to Valentín's hearing. The images of the visual narrator take shape in the imagination of the listener. It becomes more difficult, however, when the flashback reconstruction does not correspond to the words. *Mission: Impossible* (Brian de Palma, 1996) has often been experienced as chaotic and unintelligible. The complexity of the film is related to an undercover operation that is more than it seems, but certainly also to a very unorthodox flashback by Hollywood standards; it is this flashback that reveals the identity of a mole within the secret service.

Conflict between Word and Image

During a secret mission in Prague, an entire undercover team, led by Jim Phelps, is eliminated. The aim of the mission was to unmask a mole within the team, and since Ethan Hunt was the only one to survive the cleansing his boss, Gene Kittridge, is sure that he is the spy. Fleeing from Kittridge and his men, Ethan unexpectedly runs into his team leader, Jim. He had been shot on a bridge and plunged into the water but did not die from his injuries. Jim reveals to Ethan that Kittridge himself is the mole. Ethan, sitting opposite Jim, starts to think: 'Kittridge is the mole. My God. Of course, you're right … He was at the embassy that night … First, he took out Jack, at the elevator … Then he shot you on the bridge … He must have had back-up to take out Golitsyn and Sarah at the fence.' Ethan's considerations are interrupted by possible reconstructions: flashbacks show how Jack is taken out, how Jim is shot, and how Sarah and Golitsyn are killed by knife stabs. However, the 'he' in these reconstructions is not Kittridge, as Jim suggested, but Jim himself. Consequently, when Ethan visibly ponders how 'he' (Kittridge) led Jack to his death, a scene follows in which Jim uses his computer to sabotage the elevator in which Jack is trapped. It is possible that the flashbacks belong to Jim, thinking back on how he framed his team members, but a specific film convention endorses the assumption that the flashbacks are in fact Ethan's. We consistently see Ethan's pensive face in close-up before each flashback. In this case, we have an explicit conflict between word and image. By saying 'Of course, you're right,' Ethan seems to accept Jim's revelation that Kittridge is the mole. The viewer will be inclined to follow this suggestion. Kittridge is an entirely unsympathetic individual who has plagued Ethan to the utmost and has even arrested his parents for an insignificant reason. With the line 'Of course, you're right,' Ethan pretends to be agreeing with Jim's suggestion. While we watch Ethan acting as if he were picturing how Kittridge almost eliminated the entire team, we see scenes in which Jim plays the role of the traitor. 'He shot you at the bridge,' says Ethan, but we see Jim shoot himself. 'How did he do Hannah?' he asks, and we see Jim's wife, Claire, activating a car bomb. Then, we cut back to the pensive Ethan, who corrects himself, 'No, he could have done Hannah himself.' We see Jim crawling across the bridge to activate the explosives with his watch, reducing the previous flashback to a mere option.

The entire sequence creates confusion because the spoken text points to Kittridge as the mole, but what we see are several shots suggesting without further explanation that Ethan's friend Jim is the traitor. The confusion is even greater because the shots seem to be speculations. Ethan is only conjecturing how the team members have been taken out, which is underlined when he visualizes the murder of Hannah. It was not committed by Claire but by Jim himself. At the end of his speculations, after visualizing the murder of Hannah, Ethan asks, 'Why, Jim … why?' Jim interprets the question as, 'Why did Kittridge become a mole?' but if we take the flashbacks into consideration the question can also be read as 'Why did you [Jim] become a mole?' Jim indicates that the secret service fears it has become redundant after the end of the Cold War. Apart from that, the country is being ruled by an unworthy president. This motivation is both an answer on behalf of Kittridge and an explanation of Jim's own dubious behaviour.

Ethan's words suggest another sequence of events from that indicated by the visual reconstruction in his head. In the present, Ethan pretends with his pensive look and mumbled remarks that he believes Jim's explanation. The images that form the reconstruction imply that Jim may not be at all trustworthy. Since Jim indeed turns out to be 'false,' Ethan wisely hides a conflict between word and image from him, or perhaps fakes a conflict for the viewer. The 'he' he speaks of auditively indicates Kittridge, but in the visual reconstruction it refers to Jim. The cunning ruse of Kittridge forms the object of narration, but Jim's malicious actions are Ethan's mental object of focalization.

When analysed in isolation, the conversation of Jim and Ethan with the flashbacks owes its structure to narrative experiments like *L'année dernière à Marienbad* (Alain Resnais, 1961) and *Bad Timing: A Sensual Obsession* (Nicolas Roeg, 1980). I already discussed the film by Resnais in Chapter 1: the viewer is left to wonder whether the love story has actually taken place or whether it sprang from the supposed lover's imagination instead. In a similar way, the scenes in Nicholas Roeg's film are understandable in and of themselves, but their precise interrelations remain unclear. Carried on a stretcher, Milèna Flaherty is put on an operating table in the middle of the night; she has badly injured herself. Inspector Netusil concerns himself with the question whether her boyfriend, Alex Linden, has deliberately delayed reporting the accident. Everything seems to point to the fact that her suicide attempt was triggered by a crisis in their relationship. Has Alex raped Milèna before he alerted the hospital? Netusil discovers that the radio in Linden's car was tuned to a station that stopped broadcasting at twelve o'clock. Does this mean that he was at his girlfriend's home before midnight? The inspector will remain unable to account for the time: the temporal order continues to be distorted. This distorted quality is also an aspect of the many flashback scenes we see while Milèna is being operated upon. It is unclear whether some scenes are retrospectives by Alex, in which he contemplates his relationship, or whether they are the inspector's attempts at reconstruction. Because some flashbacks start after shots of Milèna, the retrospectives may also be induced by her narcosis. Moreover, the chronology and progress of most of these retrospectives revealing the violent love life of Alex and Milèna are not clearly marked off. The viewer is caught between story and scene, by which I mean that scenes are understandable in isolation but that it is impossible to relate them meaningfully to the larger context of the story. A clear temporal frame for the flashbacks cannot be created.

In the scene from *Mission: Impossible,* the viewer is caught between the story and visual insinuations because a logical frame for the flashbacks is initially missing. In Roeg's film, the timing is so bad that it becomes irreparably distorted. In De Palma's film, however, the narrative logic can eventually be determined, which makes *Mission: Impossible* understandable after all. Even though the story is more complex, the plot and spectacle of this cinematic remake of the late 1960s TV series are clearly inspired by the James Bond tradition. This tradition is plot driven enough to prevent the understanding of storylines from becoming a mission impossible.

Unmarked Flashforward

The point in *Mission: Impossible* is that Ethan quickly sees through Jim's treachery, as the flashbacks make clear. He is sensible enough to keep this knowledge to himself so he can set a trap for Jim. This structure is reversed in Nicolas Roeg's *Don't Look Now,* a film I discussed at the end of the previous chapter. John pejoratively terms paranormal talents 'mumbo jumbo,' an attitude that makes him impervious to his own gifts as a psychic. In Venice, he suddenly 'sees' his wife Laura on a boat with two women whom he does not trust. However, his sighting is impossible since Laura has already flown back to London. In Roeg's film, her presence on the boat is shown with a classic eyeline match. First, we see a shot of John watching the water; then, we see his point of view. He calls out Laura's name, but she does not react. What is the macabre plot twist? John unknowingly possesses the gift to see into the future, which makes the supposedly classic eyeline match an unmarked flashforward. While thinking that he is watching a boat pass by in the here and now, John in fact sees a scene that will take place a few days later, after he has been killed. The boat is carrying John's coffin, so it makes perfect sense that she does not hear him shout. Whereas Ethan in *Mission: Impossible* chose to keep silent for tactical reasons, the flashforward in *Don't Look Now* cannot be revealed as such because John does not realize what he sees. The conventional editing technique, moreover, does not provide us with any clues.

Flashback ad Infinitum

In the introduction to this chapter I indicated that the childhood memories Robert relates to the tourists are not visualized anywhere, even though his story seems particularly suitable for a flashback. *The Comfort of Strangers* is quite uncomplicated in this respect, or so it seems. Robert narrates and we keep hearing his voice, while the camera never leaves the place in which he and his listeners are located. Nevertheless, I claimed that there were reasons to complicate the status of Schrader's film in its entirety. The story about the father starts three times, but only in the café do we get the complete version. The other two times we hear only the start of the story. The words at the beginning and at the final police interrogation are identical, perhaps indicating that Robert tells the story everywhere in exactly the same fashion. This would give us all the more reason to suppose that the relationship with his father is so ingrained in his being that he has to relive it ritually time and again. But the words at the beginning and the end may also be identical because the film forms a narrative circle. At the beginning, we hear Robert's voice-over, and eventually he explains at the police station how he came to commit his crime. The opening joins up exactly with the ending and turns Schrader's entire film into a flashback. Both options – either there is no visualized flashback or the entire film is a flashback – are legitimate, which makes *The Comfort of Strangers* as ambiguous as other films made in the same period, such as *Total Recall* (Paul Verhoeven, 1990) and *The Player* (Robert Altman, 1992). Just like Schrader's film, these films could continue in an endless loop.

Total Recall ends with a dream that is more or less identical to the dream from which the protagonist wakes at the beginning. *The Player* ends with the studio boss's approval of a film that has *The Player* as a working title. On the one hand, these films end in a conventional way, but on the other you could say that they start anew at the end – ad infinitum.

chapter 8

Sound as a Narrative Force

During her first visit to the house of Robert and Caroline, Mary has a conversation with the hostess about female-only theatre groups. While Mary is walking in the direction of the camera, she says, 'We did an all-woman *Hamlet* once.' After Caroline's hesitant '*Hamlet*?' the camera shows a reverse shot. In the background we see Robert, who is calmly walking toward the women. Caroline's voice has softened, but slowly gains volume: 'I've never read it. I haven't seen a play since I was at school. Isn't it the one with the ghost?' Her words are accompanied by the clicking sound of the heels of Robert's shoes.

The volume in this scene goes down at the precise moment that the camera changes position. Because the distance from the camera to Caroline and Mary remains almost the same, it would be logical to assume that the status of the sound itself has changed. When the camera was still directed at Caroline and Mary, the rule of 'dialogue intelligibility' still applied: the viewer sees characters speaking and wants to hear what they are saying.[1] As soon as we cut to the man entering the room, however, there is a simultaneous sound cut. The sound is noticeably turned down although the camera remains within earshot of the two women. It seems most likely that we are now listening along with an internal auditor: we must be hearing what Robert hears, especially since his footsteps are clearly audible now. If the internal auditor is located at a certain distance from the speakers, we can barely hear the dialogue, and part of it may even become impossible to catch. Because Robert is walking toward the women, the words slowly become clearer.[2]

The scene in *The Comfort of Strangers* builds on a separation of image and sound. Visually, Robert is only the object of focalization: the camera shows him in a long shot as he is coming in. Auditively, however, he is an internal focalizor: the sound is a reproduction of what he is hearing. The possibility of staging such a tension between image and sound is one of the means through which the medium of film distinguishes itself from art forms such as literature and theatre. In addition, this tension is productive because it generates a narrative separation between the object and the subject of focalization that literature and theatre are incapable of generating.

The story of a film is determined by an 'audiovisual contract,'[3] or a synchronization of the auditive and the visual narrator. Michel Chion, the leading theoretician in the field of sound in cinema, has challenged the primacy of the moving image in film studies. He even teasingly claims that there is no soundtrack in cinema, by which he means to say that critics tend to assume that the visual track controls the story and sound has only some added value at most. According to Chion, the concept of 'off-screen sound,' which indicates that the source of a certain sound is somewhere outside the image, is symptomatic of this critical blind spot.[4] The concept contains the words 'screen' and 'sound,' implying an interrelation but at the same time showing that sound is made dependent on the visual in cinema. According to Chion, the function of sound is underestimated; admittedly, it has also figured marginally in this book so far. This chapter aims to broaden the function of the auditive narrator, the agent that channels sound in films. Following the customary subdivision of three categories of sound – voice/conversation, music, and noise/static – I will explore its function in depth.

Voice/Conversation

With the advent of synchronous sound in film, cinema became a 'temporal art' according to Chion. In silent cinema, shot A can occur at the same time as shot B or precede it. If shot A and B are part of an audible conversation, however, then they would have to be part of a logical temporal sequence. If not, then the conversation is incoherent or the filmmakers have chosen to use asynchronous sound. Asynchrony means that the sound we hear does not fit the moment of visual recording. Moreover, a soundless image can easily be frozen or rewound. Rewinding sound results in gibberish, whereas 'arresting' sound usually produces the typical sound called 'silence.' Sound essentially runs in one direction. Even a constant, persistent sound automatically places every static shot in a temporal sequence. Chion claims that the extent to which we are aware of temporality depends on the type of sound.

The more irregular the tones, the more emphatically we 'experience' the passing of time. Seeing that temporality is a crucial factor for a notion of narrativity, film sound has an important narrative function.

The auditive narrator is the agent that manages the auditive track. When see a character speak, the auditive narrator determines whether we also actually hear him or her. He establishes not only the volume but also the audibility. Chion asserts that cinema is predominantly focused on the voice. When we see characters engaged in conversation, we strongly want to hear what they are saying. In *Le Mépris*, the voice-oriented nature of film is parodied. The protagonists are present at an audition where very loud music is played. Every time a character speaks, the music is turned off until he or she has finished speaking. *North by Northwest* (Alfred Hitchcock, 1959) frustrates the desire to hear everything that is being said. The noise of a plane engine drowns out the discussion of a crucial plan concerning the course of action the main character is to take. In this way, the cunning strategy that is being cooked up at that moment is withheld from the viewer. Only in retrospect, when the film comes to its conclusion, do we know what was under discussion. The 'frustration' of missing the conversation is allowed to dissolve in the end.

The Focalization of Sound

In his article 'Sound Space,' Rick Altman asserts that one of the early dreams of Hollywood was to strive for an almost natural correlation between image and sound. In the films of the early 1930s, microphones were preferably placed near the camera in order to be able to locate the source of the sound easily within the frame: the closer a character was to the camera, the more audible he was. This 'dream,' however, could result in cacophony because a microphone also registers all sorts of superfluous noise.[5] Thanks to technological innovations such as the mobile microphone and tapes with multiple audiotracks, these early glitches were largely overcome. The new technological resources, however, did not lead to a more 'natural' relation between image and sound but to a more stable distribution of the relative volume on the soundtrack. The uniform starting value of the soundtrack became similar to a medium close-up. A scene in close-up was not notably louder nor was a scene in long shot essentially softer. Deviations from the medium close-up volume were not dependent on the choice of a certain type of shot. Excesses in sound volume instead accentuated the dramatic effect of words or sounds. According to Altman, the acoustic effect of sounds in certain spaces was subordinated to the *narrative* qualities of sound.[6]

As an example of the practical use of narrative sound, Altman discusses a scene from *Only Angels Have Wings* (Howard Hawks, 1939). (The example does not involve a voice, but that does not change the principle.) Geoff Carter has ordered professional pilot Joe Souther to take his small plane into the air despite an imminent storm. The camera cuts from a long shot to a medium shot twice, but the volume of the sound remains the same. When the airplane lifts off and becomes smaller and smaller, which is filmed from the rear in a long shot, the droning sound of the engine slowly becomes softer. The subsequent shot is a two-shot of Geoff and Bonnie Lee, who has only just arrived. The dropping of the volume in the previous shot can now be explained: it was focalized by Geoff and Bonnie. The softening engine sound is narratively legitimized as an explicit 'point-of-audition' shot.[7] The camera was positioned near Geoff and Bonnie. What is registered from the camera position is practically equal to what the characters hear. This method of internal focalization is reminiscent of the Hollywood dream: if one hung a microphone above the camera, the waning drone would correlate to the camera position. Image and sound coincide.

Whereas *Only Angels Have Wings* aimed merely at a 'realistic' relation between image and sound, Alfred Hitchcock had already experimented with 'controlled' or selective applications of sound. *Blackmail* (1929) contains a famous knife sequence that revolves around the distorted perception of a character. Alice White accompanies a painter, Mr Crewe, to his studio. While holding hands, they paint a female figure, and Alice later signs the painting. Then, a sexy dress catches her eye and the painter promises to draw her on the condition that she puts it on. As he helps Alice to fasten the dress and strokes her hair, he kisses her too eagerly. We see the rest of the scene first as a shadow play on the wall, and then continued behind a curtain. We only see Alice's hand reach for a knife, grab the hilt, and disappear behind the curtain once again. After some muffled sounds and no scream, a shaken Alice appears from behind the curtain with the knife still in her hand. She erases her autograph on the painting and wanders the streets in a daze.

When Alice joins her parents for breakfast the next day, a gossipy neighbour cannot keep quiet about the recently discovered murder. According to the woman, to deliver a blow to the head is one thing, but using a knife to kill someone is quite another: so 'un-British.' 'Whatever the provocation, I would never use a knife. Now mind you, a knife is a difficult thing to handle.' When Alice's father asks: 'Alice, cut a bit of bread, will you?' the neighbour's chatter turns into a single word that echoes more and more loudly: 'knife … knife … knife … knife.' At a very loud 'knife,' the knife slips from Alice's hand and falls on the floor. 'You should have been more careful. You might have cut somebody with that,' her father says.

The knife sequence is based on Alice's experience of the neighbour's babbling. Alice registers nothing, which causes the chatter to become unintelligible. Alice is focused on the word 'knife,' however, and in her perception it seems as if the neighbour repeats only that word with increasing emphasis. The scene at breakfast does not have any special optical effects and is relatively 'neutral' visually. On the auditive level, however, much more is happening. The auditive narrator conforms itself to Alice's hearing without paying any attention to camera positions. The issue here is not the spoken text of the conversation, but solely Alice's focalization of words. The neighbour does use the word 'knife' a lot, but in Alice's perception all of her words turn into 'knife.'[8]

In *Blackmail*, Hitchcock thus creates the 'auditive equivalent of visual expressionism.'[9] It is useful to distinguish between the auditive scenes in *Only Angels Have Wings*, *Blackmail*, and the scene from *The Comfort of Strangers* that I described in the introduction. In Hawks's film, the auditive position is relatively simple: the volume of the plane's drone subsides because its distance from the characters and the camera increases. In Hitchcock's film, the auditive position is predominantly the subjective experience of Alice: to her ears, the incriminating word 'knife' sounds louder and louder. Her distorted perception is demonstrated auditively, independently of the position of the visual narrator. Sound betrays how distraught she is. In Schrader's film, the visual narrator and the auditive narrator operated synchronically until the moment Robert entered. The visual narrator observes him from a distance, but the auditive narrator 'moves' and registers what Robert hears. Visually he is the object of focalization, but auditively he is an internal focalizor.

Sound Cuts

With the examples of Hawks, Hitchcock, and Schrader I have explored the most important principles of the voice in cinema, but the options are not yet exhausted. An important potential of sound is the concealed or hardly recognizable transition. Whereas visual cuts make a transition from one scene to the next easily recognizable, the auditive cut is much harder to trace. I will begin with two horrid screams, one from *Blackmail*, the other from *Blow Out* (Brian De Palma, 1981).

As Alice walks through the streets in Hitchcock's film, she encounters a homeless person. Still shaken after killing Mr Crewe, she discerns a likeness between the outstretched arm in front of her and the painter's arm. While we see the arm of the homeless person, we hear a horrid scream. At that moment, we suspect that we are hearing Alice, but any confirmation of that suspicion is withheld because there is no reverse shot. Instead, the scene changes but the scream carries on. We now see the painter's landlady scream at the discovery of her dead tenant. Theoretically, Alice and the landlady can scream in a similar way. It would be more logical, however, to assume that there was an auditive transition before the visual transition to the painter's apartment. First we hear a scream and then we can retrospectively consider the landlady as the source of the scream that began in the preceding shot.

Blow Out ends when the 'right' scream has been found. Jack is a sound engineer for a B movie. In this production, an actress is threatened with a knife in the shower but is able to produce only a very poor scream. Among other things, Jack is tasked with finding an appropriate scream. As he is recording outside, a car plunges into the water. His recordings reveal that the blowout was preceded by a gunshot. He plans to reveal the secret motive of this staged accident to a television reporter, but his plan fails and as a result a friend of his dies. He had lent his friend recording equipment and her strangulation is thus caught on tape. At home, a guilt-laden Jack listens to the tape of her screaming horridly. At the moment of the scream, we cut to a scene of the actress under the shower. It is possible that an auditive transition has also taken place, but if it has it cannot be recognized as such. First we see Jack, sombrely brooding, listening to the tape. At the moment of the visual cut, the sound recording of the previous scene could theoretically be stopped and picked up again at the same point in the next scene, the sound cut so seamless as to be unnoticeable. The fact that the original sound of an actual murder winds up being used as a suitable sound effect in a badly acted exploitation movie is of course a cruel irony. After Jack has mumbled three times that it is indeed a 'good scream,' he blocks his ears with his hands when the director plays the scream once more.

A temporally reversed sound cut can be found at the end of *The Talented Mr Ripley* (Anthony Minghella, 1999). Tom Ripley has killed rich boy Dickie Greenleaf in Italy and posed as the missing young man in order to collect money from the latter's father. His masquerade is a tricky one because he is Dickie for some but still Tom for others. He pulls it off, however, and books a passage on a large ship at the end of the film. He is travelling with Peter Smith-Kingsley, who knows him as Tom. Coincidentally, he also meets Meredith Logue, who thinks he is

Dickie. Peter has seen him in Meredith's company, so Tom now fears exposure. He is afraid that Meredith will reveal his other name and identity. Next, he tells Peter about his fear of being a nobody and asks his friend to tell him who or what Tom is. Peter starts enumerating his qualities: 'Talented, tender, beautiful, Tom is a mystery, Tom has secrets, Tom has nightmares ... Tom is crushing me.' As the sound continues, the visual track jumps forward in time. We see Tom enter his cabin on the ship, looking cautious. We hear a somewhat smothered voice saying, 'Tom ... you are really crushing me.' We have not heard an audible transition on the auditive track, so it may be possible that image and sound are separated from the point of the visual cut on: only the visual track went forward in time. It would be more logical, however, to say that a vocal cut has also taken place, so that image and sound are in fact still synchronous. Only the status of the sound has changed with the inaudible cut on the auditive track. From the moment of the visual cut onward, Peter's words are a mental reliving for Tom of the moment he strangled his friend. He replays in his head what happened in the scene that was just cut off for us.

For a final example of the interaction between visual and auditive cuts, we can refer to the famous jump cuts from À bout de souffle (Jean-Luc Godard, 1960). The camera is placed on the rear seat of Michel Poiccard's car and directed exclusively at the head of his passenger, Patricia Francini. Partially because we see the posture of her head change quite abruptly but especially because the surroundings constantly change, we notice that many frames have been cut at random from the otherwise continuous shot. In the meantime, Michel started praising Patricia's beauty and at every visual jump we hear him name another body part: a beautiful neck, beautiful knees, beautiful breasts. In their abruptness the jump cuts show that the car ride takes longer than we see here and possibly also that some words have been left out on the auditive track – Michel might have named Patricia's beautiful navel, beautiful fingertips, and so forth while we could not hear. In other words, Michel's eulogy may be a lot longer. If we assume that there is synchronicity, the auditive track must have been edited as rigorously as the images. In that case, the vocal cuts are simply less perceptible than the visually obvious jump cuts.

Eerie Voices

Chion is particularly interested in the possibly ominous dimension of the interaction between the auditive and visual tracks. In his *La voix au cinéma,* he focuses predominantly on films in which the voice creates anxiety even if it is only partially disconnected from the images.[10] The strictly external voice-over exists completely off-screen and can only have an explanatory function. The voice gains a ghostly dimension, however, when its source cannot be located but there is an internal relation to the filmic narrative, or a strong suspicion of an internal relation. Chion repeatedly uses *Psycho* (Alfred Hitchcock, 1960) as an example in his book.

In *Psycho,* Marion Crane, who is on the run with stolen money, decides to spend the night at the remote hotel managed by Norman Bates. Norman lives with his mother in a house just up the hill from the motel. Marion hears the two argue before she is herself murdered. It turns out, however, that Norman has identified with his deceased mother so strongly that he has incorporated her voice and killed Marion in the guise of his jealous mother. Once Norman has been discovered and apprehended, we see him with a blissful grin in his cell and hear the voice of an old woman (his mother) in voice-over. Perhaps he imagines how his mother would have spoken to him at this moment. In that case, the visual and auditive narrators have made a logical alliance: out loud, we hear the thoughts of the character we are seeing. During a short time, however, we see the skull of his mother's skeleton superimposed over Norman's face. This is an optical effect shown by the visual narrator, but it automatically changes the status of the sound. The voice is not simply a thought in voice-over, but seems to originate from Norman himself. It is as if the son is being ventriloquized by his mother. Her voice floats within him. *Psycho* might have a conventional ending because the criminal has been identified and provided with a psychological motive, but the film continues to be eerie because the voice still does not have an adequate physical home. It is not just that we see Norman and hear his mother. It is worse than that. Due to the superimposition, we see Norman while we hear his mother *within him.* By means of a short glimpse, the visual narrator shows us where the voice is coming from. It is this conflict between image and sound that makes the horror of *Psycho* last.

Music

Filmmakers have gratefully made use of the narrative function that music can have. This potential even brought into being an entirely new genre, the film musical, in which music is the main attraction (see

Chapter 9). In countless non-musicals, however, music carries the plot or initiates a crucial twist in the story as well. Think for instance of the famous 'Que sera, sera,' sung by Doris Day as Jo Conway in *The Man Who Knew Too Much* (Alfred Hitchcock, 1956). When she sings the song at the embassy, her kidnapped son, Hank, recognizes her singing voice and calls for his mother. His father, who is looking for him, manages to trace him in this way. In *Pillow Talk* (Michael Gordon, 1959), Doris Day plays the role of Jan Morrow. She spends a romantic weekend with a man pretending to be a Texan cowboy. Inadvertently, she plays a few notes from some sheet music her 'cowboy' has brought. The melody turns out to be the tune that the annoying man who shares her telephone line plays for his many love interests. The music not only reveals his identity to her but also determines his character: the man cannot be a Texan cowboy but must be a womanizing fraud instead.

Music can also be used to situate the story in a certain era: the compositions of Bach can be appropriate for the eighteenth century, rock 'n' roll is an option for the 1950s, and the 1970s can be evoked by using disco or punk music. The same applies to the film's geographical setting. To give the viewer an impression of an exotic location, shots can be introduced by music with an appropriate flavour. In her incisive study *Unheard Melodies*, Claudia Gorbman indicates how music can be employed to connote the irrational aspects of a certain space, as happens, for instance, in a film like *King Kong* (Merian C. Cooper and Ernest B. Schoedsack, 1933). We do not hear any background music in the film until the ship approaches the fog-ridden Skull Island. The music from that point on 'initiates us into the fantasy world, the world where giant apes are conceivable, the underside of the world of reason. It helps to hypnotize the spectator, [and] bring down defenses that could be erected against this realm of monsters, tribesman, jungles, violence.'[11]

Intradiegetic and Extradiegetic Music

In the examples above, I referred to intradiegetic music: music that is part of the story itself. It can be heard by the characters. This music can be made on the spot, whistled or played on a jukebox or radio. Intradiegetic music can also create depth in cinematic space, as Gorbman notes with reference to *The Public Enemy* (William Wellman, 1931). Two young men are standing outside the saloon, while we faintly hear a piano on the soundtrack. As the pair enters, the music becomes louder. As the camera moves to the left and right, the music gains volume until the camera finally settles on the piano player. The music 'provides temporal continuity to two spatially discontinuous shots' – from the outside into the saloon – 'acting as a seamless auditory match.' Moreover, the 'continuous progression from soft to loud means a continuous movement forward in cinematic space, toward the sound source.'[12]

A second type of music is extradiegetic music, which is added to the story by the auditive narrator and cannot be heard by the characters. Music may seem extradiegetic sometimes until the camera pans to a character who is just turning off a record player at the moment the music stops. In this case, the music was intradiegetic after all. A combination of intradiegetic and extradiegetic music is also possible. Bordwell and Thompson refer to the example of *Stagecoach* (John Ford, 1939). While the stagecoach is chased by Indians, we hear extradiegetic horns and trumpets. When the danger increases, the sound of the horns comes to the fore. Lucy's despair quickly turns to hope: 'Can you hear it? Can you hear it? It's a bugle. They're blowing the charge.' She realizes that the sound of the bugle chords announces a cavalry charge.[13] According to Chion, music in cinema is like a sidetrack. It is the only auditive element that has the privilege of moving quickly from the inside of the story to its outside and vice versa.[14]

Whether music is intradiegetic or extradiegetic makes a difference for the effect of the scene, which Gorbman illustrates with a fine example. Imagine a character dancing at a party and then suddenly receiving bad news. Logically, the cheerful music would continue, no matter how awkward the contrast. The situation would truly become shocking, however, if cheerful extradiegetic music started playing at the moment the character received the same bad news while sitting on a couch at home.[15] It is also possible to shift the scene to an internal focalization on the auditive track. This is the case when the happy music is intercut with unpleasant sounds or when it is slowed to indicate the character's shocked reaction to the news. The intradiegetic music then starts functioning as a sign for the impact the news has.

The advantage of musical intermezzos is that they can manipulate the rhythm of the story. *Once upon a Time in the West* (Sergio Leone, 1968) is famous for its sluggish rhythm and its dragged-out scenes. The preparations for a gunfight take up a lot of time, whereas the fight itself is over before you know it. The slow rhythm is acceptable because the music functions as an indication: 'Watch out, something is about to happen.' Thanks to the music, the sluggishness becomes the main strength of the film. As the preparation scenes last, the tension increases. Music can also hide the fact that nothing much is 'happening' in a film. In a film like *Easy Rider* (Dennis Hopper, 1969), the plot is held together by a motorcycle trip to Mardi Gras made by the two main characters in search of an idea of freedom. The many scenes in which 'adventurers' Wyatt and Billy tour across the roads would be rather tedious if it was not for the energetic music. Without the hippie rock on the soundtrack, some of the scenes might very well have been cut.

The example of *Easy Rider* suggests that music has a decisive influence on the rhythm of the images. A song with lyrics might slow the film's pace. According to Gorbman, 'songs require narrative to cede to spectacle, for it seems that lyrics and action compete for attention.'[16] The music has the status of an intermezzo and can be seen as a commentary on the images. Not unlike the intervention of the chorus of a Greek tragedy in the ongoing events, the progress of the story is slowed or suspended in order to allow the viewer to process what is being shown. Yet music, and extradiegetic music in particular, can also be employed to speed up the rhythm of events. Scenes can shift to another temporal or spatial point more easily because music more or less guarantees the coherence. In such a case, music can compensate for a relatively fragmented scene.

It is possible for a song text to inform us about a part of the protagonist's personal history, thereby announcing the dramatic conflict. The ballad with which *High Noon* (Fred Zinnemann, 1952) opens ('Do Not Forsake Me, Oh My Darlin''), for instance, is used to explain that Frank Miller, who has just been released from a state prison, is after the speaker and that the speaker is not planning to die a coward. At the same time, the lyrics are an appeal to the speaker's brand-new bride not to leave him while he is off fighting the released criminal. Because the auditive track has already announced the themes of the past and the dilemma between love and duty, the visual narrator can concentrate on the present time. *High Noon* is a film without flashbacks, in which the time of the story and the time of the fabula are almost entirely synchronous.

Furthermore, song lyrics can provide clues about what is going to happen to characters if the film has an open ending. In *Eternal Sunshine of the Spotless Mind* (Michel Gondry, 2004), Joel Barish and Clementine Kruczynski have had the most fantastic night of their lives together while thinking they have only just met. Later on, however, they sober up when cassette tapes reveal that they already have been in a relationship together. They both had their memories of that relationship erased by a special company. On the tapes they independently list each other's worst qualities. Eventually, they can only just stammer some apologies to each other. The final shot does not provide a clear indication what is going to happen to them. We see Joel and Clementine frolic in the snow. The running scene loops back on itself twice, making it seem as though they start running twice from the same spot. The shot is not marked temporally: it may be a moment in the past but it could also lie in the future. In the lyrics of a song we nevertheless hear a clue to interpret the ending as 'happy,' despite everything: 'Change your heart, look around you / change your heart, it will astound you / I need your lovin', like the sunshine / everybody's gotta learn sometime.' The song text seems to refer to the 'rule' of the so-called comedy of remarriage, a subgenre from the 1930s and 1940s.[17] In this subgenre each protagonist discovers that the other suffers from disappointing character flaws. After a separation, they come to the 'awful truth' that they cannot live without each other and decide to 'remarry.' The films suggest that love can only blossom in the rebound, after prejudices about the partner have been overcome. The 'change your heart' from the song's lyrics can be seen as a reference to this process. Precisely because they both immediately know what annoys them about the other, Joel can adjust to Clementine's idiosyncrasies and vice versa. According to the comedy of remarriage, that is the most promising prospect for the blossoming of love.

Music can also propel the general rhythm of a film, which seems to be the case in *Lola Rennt* (Tom Tykwer, 1998, released elsewhere as *Run Lola Run*). The story is simple: Lola has to deliver 100,000 German marks to her boyfriend, Manni, in order to save his life. Accompanied by a thumping techno beat, Lola starts sprinting. The soundtrack not only propels Lola but the film itself seems to accelerate, with flashy montage, quickly alternating photo shots, split screens, and colourful animations. In a way similar to that of the music video, the images desperately try to keep up with the music. The rhythm of the story in *Lola Rennt* is determined by the soundtrack to a large extent, as if the visual narrator were rushing to follow the hurried rhythm of the music.

Symbolic Narrative Functions of Music

No matter whether it is intradiegetic or extradiegetic, music, like voice, helps to fill in characters. A giant impresses because of his striking appearance, but if he has a high, squeaky voice or spoke softly he immediately appears more amiable. Similarly, music contributes to the way we assess characters. We would have to review our ideas about Gustav von Aschenbach in *Morte a Venezia* if he preferred heavy metal or German *schlagers* to classical music. A similar revision would be necessary if the characters in *Easy Rider* listened to Mahler rather than to Steppenwolf. This should not be taken as an essential 'rule,' of course, since there is no direct link between someone's musical taste and his identity.

Offsetting the correspondence between music and voice-overs or scenes can have an ironic effect. *Trainspotting* (Danny Boyle, 1995) opens with Iggy Pop's 'Lust for Life,' an energetic pop song. In voice-over, we hear heroine junkie Mark Renton list what life entails: a job, a career, a family, a mortgage. This definition clashes with the drift of the pop song's message to live life 'in the moment' and 'to the max.' It soon turns out that the main characters have a 'lust for life' that is diametrically opposed to bourgeois ideals. As junkies, they cannot live without drugs, and we quickly find out from one of them that an injection is the same as 'the best orgasm you ever had multiplied by thousand.' In this way, the soundtrack forms an ironic contrast to the definition of 'life' given in the voice-over. The lively music of Iggy Pop, a notorious junkie himself, justifies the logic of choosing drugs ('I chose not to choose life,' says Renton).[18]

The opening song of *Trainspotting* gives another twist to the notion of life formulated in the voice-over. A song can also overshadow an entire scene. The inclusion of an apparently light-hearted pop song has a rather vicious effect in, for example, *Reservoir Dogs* (Quentin Tarantino, 1992), a film about a well-prepared heist that fails miserably. In an attempt to find out why, psychopath Vic Vega, whose codename is Mr Blonde, threatens to cut off the ear of a police officer. Preceding this torture scene, he praises the radio station 'Supersound of the Seventies.' When he switches the radio on, we hear the middle-of-the-road track 'Stuck in the Middle with You,' by Stealer's Wheel. Then, he takes a sharp razor to the officer's ear; while the camera turns away and shows the hangar's empty wall, we hear the officer screaming through the Stealer's Wheel song. Despite its cheerfulness, the music can only partially dispel the gruesomeness of the torture taking place off-screen. The combination of carefree music with the suggestion of a horrific scene is ludicrous because of its bravura, but it also gives rise to a feeling of shame: 'This is too outrageous to be laughed about.' The song's lightheartedness also functions the other way around. Tormenting the officer was already bad enough, but the fact that the song keeps playing, 'indifferent' to his suffering, possibly makes it even worse. 'Stuck in the Middle with You' functions as a sign of a lack of consideration for the police officer. The cheerful music becomes 'complicit' with the malicious actions of Mr Blonde. In *Reservoir Dogs*, the supposedly easy-going tune loses its 'innocence' in relation to the scene.[19]

Another efficacious tactic is the introduction or characterization of the film's protagonists by means of a musical theme. No example is more famous than the melody that makes us aware of the approach of the murderous shark in *Jaws* (Steven Spielberg, 1975) without the creature actually being shown. Here, the music bears a similar relation to the images as a caption does to a news photograph. Even if we see 'nothing,' we still know that we should interpret the images as threatening. The music 'anchors the image in meaning, throws a net around the floating visual signifier.'[20] Elisabeth Weis explains how Hitchcock, in *Shadow of a Doubt* (1943), uses music not only to characterize his protagonists but also to define their relationships. Charles Oakley, a murderer of rich widows, moves to the small town of Santa Rosa in hopes of avoiding detection. His sister's family resides in the town. Charles is being picked up from the train station by his brother-in-law, two nieces, and nephews. While they eagerly await his arrival, we hear extradiegetic music proclaiming American family values. When Charles joins them and the camera gets sight of him, this music becomes interlaced with the melody of the 'Merry Widow Waltz.' In Hitchcock's film, the melody is associated with the cynical Charles, who looks down on 'ordinary little' social milieus and has appropriated the right to exploit widows. The fact that the two melodies become intermingled signifies the entrée of his corrupt views ('the world is a hell') into the provincial Santa Rosa. Charles gives his niece Charlie, who was delighted that he was coming, a ring but she immediately discovers initials in it. Charles saves himself by making up some excuse, but when the camera turns to him we see a superimposition of couples dancing to the 'waltz.' A transition takes place to a scene at breakfast, in which Charlie starts humming the melody and is unable to get it out of her head. This indicates that the young woman is actually on to something. If she succeeds in identifying the melody, she will gain insight into her uncle's true nature. When Charlie starts asking after the tune's title, Charles knocks over a glass in order to change the subject.

When Charlie realizes that Charles has torn a piece out of the newspaper, she suspects that an important piece of information has been kept under wraps. In the library she reads an article about the 'Merry Widow Murderer,' who has taken the lives of three rich widows. She looks again at the ring he gave her and walks away while the camera moves backward. At that moment, we once again see the superimposition of the couples dancing to the 'Merry Widow Waltz.' Now the superimposition and the melody that accompanies it have shifted from Charles to Charlie, and we know she has seen through his charade. The melody is stuck in her head throughout the rest of the film in order to indicate that she has lost her innocence and gained insight into Charles's corrupt worldview. She can only 'cleanse' herself when Charles, after an attempt to push her off the train, gets hit by a passing train himself. As he falls we see the superimposition with its tune for the last time, as a transition to the funeral. It is not only Charles who is buried but the waltz associated with him as well. Freed from the nagging melody in her head, she can now start a relationship with the detective who was chasing her uncle.[21]

The most important role of music in the history of cinema is the channelling and/or heightening of emotions. Think, for instance, of the very well-known convention of violin music in many a dramatic scene. In *The Desire to Desire*, a book about the rise of the so-called woman's film in the 1940s, Mary Ann Doane has mapped out the way in which music functions as a vessel for inexpressible emotions and desires. Women are bound by all sorts of conventions that limit what they are allowed to wish for. Sweet sounds set in where those desires cannot be articulated because they are excessive and fall outside conventional patterns. Women want too much, and the music on the soundtrack is an expression of their disproportionate desire. Their male opponents, however, will try to bend female demands to their own will. Doane notices that many men in 1940s films are musicians: not only can they play an instrument superbly but they also seem to attempt to control the desires that the music represents. Music is also employed in these films to substitute for the showing of romantic or erotic scenes: the sugary compositions usually indicate how the ellipses need to be interpreted. In this way, an interaction between the visual and the auditive narrator ensues. What cannot be represented visually is suggested by means of the music.

Noise/Static

Sound has a significant impact on the images we see or, rather, on the images we think we have seen. Our visual perception is strongly determined by our hearing. Marc Mancini has pointed to a striking feat in *The Empire Strikes Back* (Irvin Kershner, 1980). When the door of a spaceship is about to open, the camera is stopped. The recording continues only when the door is completely open. The shot of the closed door is immediately followed by a shot in which the door is not shown. By adding the 'whoosh' sound of a door sliding open, viewers nonetheless think they actually saw it happen.[22] The point of this example is that we are visually sensitive to what we are hearing. A second significant 'door experiment' can be found in *Les vacances de M. Hulot* (Jacques Tati, 1953). When guests push open the door to a hotel restaurant, the door automatically swings shut while we hear a sound as if a large snare drum is being played. Even though we see a full restaurant in the shot, the swinging door in the background nonetheless draws our attention.[23]

Without our realizing it, sound can make us look differently. Many beach scenes in *Les vacances de M. Hulot* offer a visually dismal picture because of the awkward behaviour of Hulot. On the auditive track, however, the sound of playing children is dominant. Chion's point is that the beach scenes become less depressing because what we hear evokes ideas of happiness; the images tell a different story from that of the sound. Our perception can easily be influenced by sounds. Directors can manipulate our viewing experience by effectively employing them. Chion gives the example of *Blade Runner* (Ridley Scott, 1982). The film is situated in a hectic Los Angeles in the year 2019. In spite of this, many shots are relatively peaceful to the eye because the rush is suggested mainly by the cacophony of city sounds. Or, as Chion argues, 'the vaster the sound, the more intimate the shots can be.'[24]

It does not directly follow from the premise that the ear can direct or deceive the sight that the ear is a more 'natural' organ than the eye. Sounds can be based more on convention than on a supposed reality. The best example is the so-called 'punch.' The sound of the blows in the boxing matches of Jake La Motta in *Raging Bull* (Martin Scorsese, 1980) do not resemble the far more muffled sound of the bashes at actual matches. The filmic sound of the punch has become convention to such an extent that it would have a surreal effect to use the actual sounds of a boxing match. Moreover, Chion argues that such a distinctive action film sound creates 'temporal elasticity': the punch makes us accept that many boxing scenes are repeated or shown in slow motion.[25] The 'abnormal' sound of the punch is such a natural point of reference that heavily stylized visuals are made believable because of it.

Whereas our hearing influences our sight, Chion indicates that the reverse is also true. We think we hear what we supposedly see because a narrative situation can drown out the acoustic qualities of sound. If we hear the sound of a watermelon being squashed while a truck drives over a boy's head, as in *La pelle* (Liliana Cavani, 1981), the watermelon sounds like a cracking skull from our perspective.[26] The sound of the squashed watermelon was not chosen accidentally in the case of Cavani's film, of course. It was especially selected because it could believably pass for the sound of a cracking skull.

The Source of Sound

A first step is to find out whether we can trace the source of a certain sound. Does it spring from within the visual frame? It is rarely shown when a character commits suicide by putting a gun to his head, but the sound of the gunshot is enough to indicate what has happened. If the source of the sound cannot be seen, does that automatically mean it is just outside the frame, 'just behind the curtain,' so that we need to anticipate its entrance? The incipient entrance can also be permanently postponed, as happens with the soprano practising her scales in *Rear Window* (Alfred Hitchcock, 1954). In this film, L.B. Jefferies spies on his neighbours. Because of the sweltering weather, all the windows are open. The customary procedure is that the visual narrator shows each window while the auditive narrator amplifies the sounds coming from that particular window in order to temporarily outdo traffic noises or the music and conversations in other apartments. The only character we occasionally hear but never see is the soprano. She has to be close considering the volume of her voice exercises, but we nevertheless do not catch a glimpse of her. Apart from this example there are more problematic categories of sound. Is the chirping we hear coming from one of the birds we see, and what should we think of the howling of the wind? Equally complex is the case of the scientist in *The Invisible Man* (James Whale, 1933). We hear him and he is in the frame, but we nonetheless do not see him.

The Status of Sound

Matters become even more complex when not only is the source of a sound hard to trace but when that sound also represents a mental process. Sound designer Walter Murch gives a good example from the work he did for *Apocalypse Now* (Francis Ford Coppola, 1979). At the beginning of the film, Captain Willard is in a hotel room in Saigon. When he looks outside, we hear all sorts of off-screen sounds: a traffic officer blowing a whistle, car horns, the buzzing of a fly. Then we hear Willard say that he cannot stand the hotel because his heart still lies in the jungle. Slowly, the earlier sounds transform into jungle noises: the police whistle becomes the chirping of crickets, the car horns start to sound like different types of birds, and the buzzing of the fly turns into the humming of mosquitoes. The auditive transition accentuates that Willard is mentally prepared to return to the jungle.[27]

Whereas sound is a relatively unambiguous underlining of the protagonist's desire in *Apocalypse Now,* the status of sound itself becomes uncertain in a film like *Blow-up* (Michelangelo Antonioni, 1966). As Thomas is taking photos in the park, we see the leaves move and hear the sound of the wind on the soundtrack. When he studies his photos later on, we again hear the rustling of the wind. Shortly afterward, we see the contours of a gun in the bushes in a blow-up of one of the photos. Do we have an auditive flashback here? By means of the photos, in which the trees do not move, we auditively return to the moment the images were made? Or alternatively, is it an internal focalization? Does Thomas hear the rustling wind in his head as he pictures the scene again, including its ambient sound? He immediately calls a friend to report his spectacular discovery. The option of internal focalization is plausible because it accords with the overall trend of the film. Has the idea that a murder has taken place not simply sprung from the photographer's imagination?

The possibility that the murder has taken place only in Thomas's head is confirmed by the closing scene, which seemingly does not have much bearing on the rest of the film. In this scene, Thomas is watching a pantomime play in which the two players act out a tennis match without a racket or ball. The onlookers join in by moving their heads from left to right as if they were actually following the match. Pretending to hit the 'ball' over the fence, one of the mime players gestures for Thomas to fetch it. After a moment of hesitation, he does what he is asked and tosses it back. Next, we see Thomas in medium close-ups as we hear the sound of a bouncing tennis ball. Because the final scene is disconnected from the plot, it functions as a commentary on the film itself. The sound of the tennis ball, which is added by the auditive narrator, can be explained in one of two ways. The auditive narrator may be ridiculing the temptation of false perceptions by means of the bouncing sound. As a general reminder, it shows we can start believing in illusions that seemed preposterous only a moment before. Alternatively, it is possible that the sound of the tennis ball is a mental experience of the character Thomas – internal focalization, in other words. This option is made more plausible because the camera remains focused on the photographer's face. Thomas is witnessing a tennis match that is no tennis match. As soon as he becomes involved in the 'game,' however, he joins in on the act and the sound of the ball becomes audible.

The auditive supplement reconnects the ending to the plot. Thomas has been looking for traces of a crime after a woman who claimed his roll of film aroused his suspicion. What follows consists of suppositions rather than certainties. We eventually see a victim, but the corpse seems unreal, as if it were made of wax. A parallel announces itself: if Thomas believes in the crime hard enough it will automatically become a murder mystery, much as he starts hearing the sound of a tennis ball without one being hit.

The sound of the tennis match can be characterized as a projection on the part of the protagonist in this interpretation. The contact between the ball and the racket exists only in his head. Sound theoreticians like Altman and Chion speak of a 'point of audition' in such a case, but caution that the idea of such an auditive standpoint is much harder to demarcate than a visual perspective. An example from *The Secret Agent* (Alfred Hitchcock, 1936) illustrates this.[28] A man who goes by the name of Richard Ashenden is ordered to eliminate a spy in Switzerland, and all the evidence points to a certain Caypor. Ashenden receives assistance from 'the General,' who takes care of the job during a hike through the mountains. Meanwhile Elsa, who was pretending to be Mrs Ashenden, is keeping the wife of the supposed spy, Caypor, company. By means of cross-cutting the filmic narrator shows that the more dangerous matters become for Caypor, the more his dog starts howling instead of barking. This does not sit well with Elsa; she suspects that the animal's instinct may be telling it what awaits its master. When the fatal push is given, the dog's howl is indeed heartrending. In the next scene, Elsa is attending a yodelling performance with Richard and the General. In addition to the singing, we hear the sound of coins spinning in a bowl. That sound fills the entire café and is heard by all who are present. It does not even matter where the characters are standing – the sound is equally audible to all. In the meantime Richard has received a telegram. When he is about to rejoin Elsa and the General, we twice hear the howling of Caypor's dog interrupt the yodelling at the moment the camera turns from Elsa to Richard. The most logical option is that the acoustic sound is temporarily mixed with a subjective sound. All the people present hear the yodellers, but only Elsa has heard the howling of Caypor's dog. We hear the dog's howling the second before Richard reveals the contents of the telegram, which indicates that Elsa has a fearful suspicion: whoever has such a loyal dog for a companion cannot possibly be a vicious spy. And indeed, the telegram reveals that the team has taken out the wrong man.

In *The Secret Agent* we hear the sound in a certain space in the same

way as all the characters in that space do. The auditive narrator inter-
mingles the auditive track with a subjective dimension. What we have
here is an external focalization of sound, the yodelling, supplemented
by internal focalization, the dog's howling. This technique has a more
ambivalent variation, too, which can be illustrated with an early scene
from *Once upon a Time in America* (Sergio Leone, 1984). The character
'Noodles' is in the Chinese theatre annex opium joint when he is startled
by a phone ringing off-screen. Equipped with an opium pipe, he calms
down again while the phone keeps ringing. The scene shifts to a flashback. During the flashback, the phone continues to ring as we see three
corpses lying on the street in the rain and the celebration of the end of
the Prohibition. A telephone appears in close-up and a hand picks it up.
As a viewer, you suspect the ringing will stop, but the sound continues.
In the next shot, we see someone pick up the receiver, at which point
the ringing stops along with the flashback: we are back with 'Noodles'
in the Chinese theatre. One possibility is that the telephone was ringing in the opium joint itself. The ringing is an external focalization by
the auditive narrator and precipitates a memory for 'Noodles.' That the
sound lasts confirms that it is his flashback, which he has while he is
still sitting in the Chinese theatre where the phone is ringing at that
moment (although it remains unclear why nobody answers). Another
possibility is that the flashback starts on the auditive track. 'Noodles'
is remembering the sound of the telephone. When the telephone rings
for the first time – in his head – he startles. The persistent ring finally
initiates the flashback visually. The ringing emphasizes the importance
of the telephone call that ends the flashback. Later, it will turn out that
this is the moment he betrays his friends. In this case, 'Noodles' has
mentally internalized the ringing sound.

The split status of sound in this specific scene from *Once upon a Time
in America* applies elsewhere to films in their entirety. In her incisive
study of sound in Hitchcock, Elizabeth Weis has argued that *Rear Window* (1954) is his most realistic film stylistically but his most asynchronous and subjective film where the soundtrack is concerned.[29] You
could say that the film shifts from auditive deep focus to a selective use
of sound as the tension increases. Auditive deep focus is a more or less
faithful representation of all the sounds heard from a certain position.
The selective usage is a consequence of the fact that the protagonist,
L.B. Jefferies, starts to connect more and more of the signals he picks up
while monitoring his neighbours. Sounds seem to conform themselves
to Jeff's perception.

His most important perception focuses on his suspicion that his neighbour, Lars Thorwald, has murdered his own wife. His suspicion is not based on much, but when he is in doubt new clues seem to present themselves: a crocodile leather bag, a dead dog, and a wedding ring. Thorwald is a distant character; unlike the other neighbours he does not play music, does not sing, and does not have any conversations with others after the disappearance of his wife. As Jeff's girlfriend, Lisa Fremont, and nurse, Stella, investigate the courtyard after already having lured Thorwald out of his apartment to look there, the noise of the traffic becomes louder than usual. Or, to confirm Weis's claim that *Rear Window* is Hitchcock's most subjective film, one should say that the traffic noise is louder in Jeff's ears. In his view, the potential danger is coming from Thorwald, who might reappear from the street where the traffic noise emanates at any moment.

Sound in *Rear Window* is deformed most strongly in a later scene, when Thorwald identifies Jeff as the one who has discovered his guilt. While Jeff waits helplessly, immobile because his leg is in a cast, he first hears the traffic, than a distant door slamming, and finally increasingly heavy footsteps. When the footsteps stop for a moment, we hear the traffic once more before the heavy tread continues. The sound here is unmistakably internal focalization and reveals that Jeff is expecting trouble. As Thorwald opens the door, Jeff tries to blind him by using the flash of his camera. The visual 'protection,' however, is less powerful than the 'danger' of sound. Thorwald overpowers Jeff, but he is arrested just in time by the police.[30]

Sinister Sounds

When we hear a character before we see him it often gives us a clue about his personality. A character who is noisy even before he enters the frame is usually querulous.[31] Depending on the nature of the film, sound can evoke an ominous feeling. This is especially true for thrillers or horror films. Hitchcock maximizes this effect by announcing Thorwald's sudden arrival with his heavy footsteps.[32] An equally chilling moment takes place in his later film *Frenzy* (1972), after Babs Milligan leaves a London café near Covent Garden because of a quarrel with her boss, who has just fired her. The cacophony dies away to complete silence while we are seeing Babs's face in close-up. Then, out of the blue, we hear the voice of Bob Rusk: 'Got a place to stay?' It turns out he was standing behind her all the time, which hid him both from Babs's sight and from the viewer's. Because of the silence, his essentially friendly offer sounds like an auditive assault. As a viewer, you imagine you already know what is going to happen: Rusk will take her home in order to strangle her. Conversely, you could say that the Harmonica Man in *Once upon a Time in the West*, about whose background we know nothing for a long time, has to be a 'good' character since he often shows up quite suddenly without making a sound.

As well as the voices of villainous characters, indeterminate sounds and strange noises are fundamental to horror films and thrillers because they scare people out of their wits without requiring any visual effects. In *Deliverance* (John Boorman, 1972), four hardened friends embark on a challenging canoe trip on the river. Their tough appearance quickly crumbles during their first night out in the woods. They hear indefinable forest sounds and Lewis, the most brazen of the four, sets off to investigate. The three who are left behind have their own opinions. 'Does he think he's Tarzan?' Bobby says. Drew confidently decides that Lewis should not think that nature is in his blood: as a city boy, all that he thinks he knows is second-hand knowledge. While the three friends are standing with their backs to the camera, Lewis walks into the foreground from the right. At the least sound, his three companions turn around and one of them yells with indignation, 'You scared the shit out of me.' Lewis has to confess that he cannot provide clarity: he heard something, but he cannot say what. The indeterminate sound turns out to be a harbinger of the unpleasant surprises that are in store for them. Visually nothing special happens in this scene, but the sound nonetheless functions as the herald of imminent danger.

Sound as (Asynchronous) Commentary
In thrillers and horror films, the visual track can remain rather sober, or stylistically realistic, because the suspense is created on the auditive track by means of asynchronicity and subjectivity, according to Weis with reference to *Rear Window*. These films are not exciting because of a cutting edge visual style but mainly because the soundtrack continually claims our attention. The effective use of sound, however, does not occur only in suspenseful films. Earlier, I referred to Jacques Tati for the way which he tapped into the comic potential of sound. He often uses inappropriate sounds in scenes. When Monsieur Hulot accidentally steps on a rope that is being used as a ship's cable in *Les vacances de M. Hulot*, we hear the sound of a spring as he is launched into the water. Such a trajectory is clearly impossible, but the suggestion that the rope acts as a spring sufficiently legitimizes the event. When Hulot, with his strangely successful serving technique, is playing tennis in another

scene, we hear what is either a strangely high-pitched version of a tennis ball being struck or the muffled thump of a frying pan being hit. This is odd at first, but we soon get used to it because the viewer tends to spontaneously discern connections between image and sound. The noises automatically start to fit the tennis match.

Chion cautions that deviations can be taken for granted all too easily. He mentions *Prénom Carmen* (Jean-Luc Godard, 1983), in which image and sound blatantly diverge when we hear seagulls in the Parisian subway. The statement that image and sound do not correspond is one thing, but, as Chion rightly notes, the issue of the narrative surplus value of sound remains. This surplus value can reside in exaggeration, achieved by blatantly dressing up a scene with sound. A well-known convention is to add the sound of the softly rippling sea to a scene in which a couple cuddles. In *Le Mépris* (Jean-Luc Godard, 1963), which seems to be Godard's attempt at making a big-budget movie, a kiss between a man and his adulterous wife is accompanied by the sound of roaring waves. Exaggerating the convention is a way to criticize it. This is an example of a stylistic excess achieved by means of sound. The narrative consequence is to enforce the idea that *Le Mépris* is first and foremost a parody of a big-budget movie.

The added value of sound can also reside in the suggestion of a perspective that reaches beyond the images themselves. Chion is enthusiastic about a scene from *Solaris* (Andrei Tarkovski, 1972). In this self-reflexive science-fiction film, Hary – the wife of protagonist Kris Kelvin – has committed suicide by poisoning herself. During a scientific expedition in a space station, she materializes as a memory of Kris's due to the bio-energy coming from the Solaris ocean. His renewed wife becomes increasingly human to him, but astrobiologist Sartorius insists that she is only a mechanical repetition. Shortly after that realization, the rematerialized Hary takes a fatal dose of liquid oxygen, in effect committing suicide again. When Kris turns her on her back, we hear the sound like the crunching of ice cubes. The sound suggests how fragile and artificial her body actually is and thereby creates an auditive commentary to the images.[33]

Ambiguous Sound Techniques

I would like to end this chapter by discussing *The Conversation* (Francis Ford Coppola, 1974), the ultimate film about sound, in order to synthesize all the observations about the interaction between image and sound and between the visual and the auditive narrators. In the film, Harry

Caul is a professional surveillance expert. He focuses on a woman and her male colleague, who are walking around a busy square. Inevitably, parts of the conversation are inaudible because of the bustle and environmental noise. With his equipment Harry tries to filter out noise and static in hope of recording a clear conversation. When he is satisfied, he delivers the tape to his employer. Instead of the director, however, his replacement shows up to collect the tape. Harry suspects foul play and refuses to give up the tape. From that moment on, he is increasingly haunted by one of the phrases he overheard the man say and which he could reconstruct only after considerable effort: 'He'd kill *us* if he got the chance.' Usually, Harry does not care what his employers do with the tapes, but now he suffers from pangs of conscience. At a later meeting, the director and his replacement are both present and Harry has no choice but to hand over the tape as agreed. He fears that the couple he listened to will be eliminated. Eventually, however, it turns out that the director is the intended victim and not the couple. Immediately, Harry replays the tape in his head, but this time with a different stress: 'He'd *kill* us if he got the chance.'

The visual narrator has only a modest role in *The Conversation*, and visually, the film is rather sober and dreary. The strength of a good eavesdropper is the ability to go unnoticed. Harry has to edit the tape in order to clear up the conversation. While he is at work, the camera is repeatedly directed at the concentrated expression on his face, and the question arises whether what we are hearing is in fact external focalization. Are these the words as registered on the tape after Harry has polished them? Or are we dealing with internal focalization here: is the sound we hear mainly Harry's interpretation of it? Other noises make the words only barely audible, but as soon as Harry comes up with a logical context for his mission the conversation immediately becomes clearer. The secrecy of the assignment suggests a murderous conspiracy, so Harry interprets the words as such. For the sake of convenience, he assumes that the man and the woman are the targets of his client because of the stress on the word 'us.' Whether the word 'us' is actually louder on the tape (external focalization) or only to Harry's ears (internal focalization) is left undecided.

After Harry hears about the director's demise, he sees the man and the woman together with the substitute director. The phrase resonates again, but because of the denouement the emphasis shifts to the word 'kill' in his mental replay. He was right about the murder plot but wrong about the intended victim. It would be logical to interpret 'He'd *kill* us if he had the chance' as internal focalization, which retrospectively increases the chances that the earlier phrase with the stress on 'us' was also predominantly focalized by Harry. A more general point made by the conversation is that sound must always be interpreted. There is no 'pure' registration of sound. Words, sounds, and noises are constantly distorted, whether they are heard by a character or focalized by the auditive narrator. We hear what our impression of the right context dictates that we hear..We have now come full circle since this chapter started with the reverse pattern: we see what we think we hear. It is because of this that the investigation of the narrative status of sound is of crucial importance to understand the manipulative effects that the interaction between image and sound can create.

chapter 9

The Narrative Principles of Genres

The film *The Comfort of Strangers* appears to be a drama focused on the psychological journey made by a single couple; its central question seems to be how the tourist couple copes with meeting the local population. At the same time, Schrader's film exudes an ominous atmosphere. What do the inserted black-and-white shots signify? Why does Robert punch Colin in the stomach and follow the attack with a friendly wink? With the unexpected murder of Colin, however, the film shifts register. Because it contains streaks of morbidity, *The Comfort of Strangers* takes shape predominantly against the background of the horror genre and places itself in the tradition of the occult horror of *Don't Look Now*. The general similarity here lies in the cruel fate that awaits the protagonists of both films in Venice. The differences are equally striking. In Roeg's film, John is under the assumption that he is pursuing the ghost of his deceased daughter as he follows a small, mysterious figure in a red jacket. But as soon as he catches the 'ghost,' he finds himself facing a dwarf, who then slits his throat. In Schrader's film the malevolent figure has been acquainted with his intended victim for a long time. Moreover, evil takes on the guise of an elegant host rather than an ugly gnome.

A parallel between the narrative positioning of Robert and the 'monster' from traditional horror stories suggests itself. In her book *Screening Space,* Vivian Sobchack sketches how classic horror exposes the fundamental duality of human beings: deep within, we are ruled by an obsessive and bestial nature. The malice of the horror monster is not completely irrational but can be encompassed within the boundaries of human understanding. There is a frame of reference within which the dark motives of the monster become comprehensible. Usually, the monster struggles with a lack of love: he hungers for acknowledgment, which is often expressed by means of a pathetic lament. A narrative condition for this kind of structure is that we partially experience the world through the monster's eyes, so that we are able to know what it is that grieves him.[1] The monster is never simply an 'object of the look': subjective shots are common rather than rare.

The characteristics mentioned above seem to apply to Robert, if with different accents. The viewer develops the retrospective suspicion that several of the establishing shots were in fact focalized by Robert. Certainty remains an impossibility, however, because the reverse shots are lacking. We therefore have no impression of Robert's facial expressions, which might have made clear in what way he was looking at the tourists and what sort of thoughts might have been crossing his mind. But maybe we are only unconsciously watching through Robert's eyes, without identifying with his focalization. The second difference with classic horror is that whereas the monster usually has no more than an anthropomorphic shape (think, for instance, of the apelike Mr Hyde or the creature created by Frankenstein), Robert has a genuinely human appearance. This 'monster' not only *resembles* a human but actually *is* one. If horrific acts are commonly ascribed to the darker, bestial side of man, *The Comfort of Strangers* shows how aggressive frustration can lurk behind a seemingly civilized façade. Nonetheless, further nuance is appropriate here. In classic horror, the thin line dividing man and beast is fundamental. In Schrader's film, it is precisely Robert's problems with being a *man* that lead to his bestial act.

The Comfort of Strangers may not be directly recognizable as horror, but the film nevertheless makes use of the narrative structure of horror. The genre, in other words, offers a specific model for the plot. This conclusion leads us to the principle of intertextuality, which holds that no single text or film can exist within a vacuum of total originality. Every film has its 'ancestors,' by which I mean to say that meaning is constructed by its relation to earlier texts or films.[2] In this chapter I indicate how the recognition and activation of references can contribute to a better insight into the story or plot of a film. I choose genres as a starting point because the majority of genres are bound to specific narrative conditions. These narrative conditions have been formed by earlier films within the same genre. If they are violated, the film shifts its generic register or establishes a connection with another genre. Through a certain narrative operation, a Western might start to resemble a film noir, or a comedy be transformed into psychological horror. It is also possible that a violation of certain conventions leads to parody, or to persiflage.

The value of a parody, however, depends on the 'example films' it reacts to. A parody inevitably evokes the generic conventions it mocks.

I do not intend to provide an exhaustive enumeration of all sorts of genres combined with narrative analyses in this chapter. By referring to a limited number of examples, I want to argue that narratological principles are intimately intertwined with characteristics of genre. If we learn to recognize these principles, we can comprehend the narrative conventions of a genre and make the films belonging to it more readily 'readable.' First I discuss the notion of intertextuality, since it is crucial to the analysis of such narrative conventions. After that, I broadly sketch the theory of genre, and finally I examine the ways in which narrative conditions can determine the nature of specific genres.

The Notion of Intertextuality

Every film offers variations on well-known conventions of genre, mode of narration, and/or style. Generally speaking, a film's originality depends on the nature and amount of that variation. Consequently, every film is intertextually determined to a large extent. It spins threads to other texts or films by means of specific references to certain narrative models (fairy tales, genres), common cultural stereotypes (relations between men and women, clichés concerning the behaviour of certain social groups), or certain stylistic features. Because stylistic features do not form a narrative aspect on their own, they strictly speaking transcend the domain of film narratology. Since they sometimes do have a certain narrative impact, however, I discuss stylistic principles in the following chapter.

Intertextuality is a textual theory insofar as the references are manifest. The much-praised cinema of Quentin Tarantino, which is full of allusions to specific scenes from pulp films and is characterized by the purposeful casting of actors because of their past roles, is symptomatic in this case. For the viewer, recognizing all the quotations becomes a sport in its own right. Intertextuality surpasses the text as well, however: the viewer can find his own references, which may be just as relevant as the 'intended' allusions.

Intertextuality indicates that every visible filmic frame contains multiple concealed layers. When Henry Fonda read the script of the spaghetti Western *Once upon a Time in the West*, for example, he understood that he had been chosen for the role of the bad guy, which was a rather unusual role for him. He assumed a change of image was required, and therefore grew a moustache and a stubbly beard and used contact lenses to look more like a villain. For Fonda, his face was an external code: if someone looks reliable, he must be a good man and, conversely, if he looks evil, then his intentions must be likewise. In other words, the face is a mask that needs to be adapted to the identity that needs to be expressed.

When Fonda appeared on the set, director Sergio Leone immediately ordered him to shave and to remove his lenses. He wanted 'the baby blues, the Fonda face.'[3] Leone insisted that Fonda appear in the style that moviegoers were already familiar with: clean shaven and with bright blue eyes. For Leone, Fonda's face needed to be interpreted not only as an external code but as an intertextual code as well. The earlier parts Fonda had played had 'stuck' to his face. In looks, Fonda had to be an exact copy of the loyal American hero he had so often portrayed. The Westerns he acted in were based on a clear distinction between 'good' and 'evil.' Because of his looks, Fonda continually played the sturdy hero. By casting him in a role that required him to kill a boy in his first scene, Leone cast those outlined moral oppositions into doubt. This fading dividing line between 'good' and 'evil' can be indirectly translated into a European critique of American heroism. By the specific casting of Fonda, *Once upon a Time in the West* problematizes the conventional supposition that Americans assume they are able to live by stringent moral binaries based on external codes.

The use of the face as an intertextual code can be expanded into an intertextual analysis of storylines. The American independent production *Down by Law* (Jim Jarmusch, 1986) can be seen as a precursor of the narrative principle of leaving out what has already been told many times. The film focuses on the exploits of three inmates during their stay in prison and after their escape. A black screen lasting for two seconds serves as the only marker of their successful escape attempt: the film assumes that, since all prison films deal with the preparation and execution of an escape plan, this part can be skipped without any problems. The two seconds of black screen represent an invitation to fill the narrative ellipsis with a conventional narrative the viewer might know from 'standard' prison films such as *Papillon* (Franklin J. Schaffner, 1973) or *Escape from Alcatraz* (Don Siegel, 1979). In order to account for the illogical 'gap' in the structure of *Down by Law*, the viewer needs to revert to an intertextual code. This code appeals to his visual erudition and leans on prior knowledge of narrative structures that have been handed down, corresponding character types, and/or the iconography of specific films. Within cinema, this knowledge is disseminated mainly via 'typical' genre or subgenre films. These offer a firm foundation for the 'box of bricks' structure of New Hollywood films that I referred to in the introduction.[4]

The Notion of Genre

If I announce that I am going to watch a Western, you will immediately have a general idea of the type of film I am about the see. The genre label is sufficient to summon a whole range of visual scenes – a cowboy on horseback crossing the border between a small pioneer town and an inhospitable landscape – and feeds the idea that the Western is completely reliant on clichés. 'If you've seen one, you've seen them all,' is a well-known dismissive judgment. The concept of genre thus serves a categorizing function: we know what kind of action and iconography is appropriate for the Western because genres meet a certain set of conventions. Consequently, the Western is usually situated in a pioneer town, surrounded by a spacious but harsh landscape. Gangster films and films noirs habitually take place in dark, urban environments. The setting of science fiction, on the other hand, is not so heavily determined. Considering that science fiction dramatizes events in an unknown future, either close or remote, this genre has no strict spatial conventions. Science fiction can be situated in an extraterrestrial location or an environment permeated by futuristic gadgets. In *Planet of the Apes* (Franklin J. Schaffner, 1968), the protagonist believes he is on a distant planet ruled by apes. To his dismay, he eventually discovers the ruin of the Statue of Liberty, icon of the city of New York. Only then does he realize that the desolate landscape is earth itself in the far future.

The function of space is also revealed in, and given greater depth by, its interaction with the plot. In the classic Western, the cowboy is the hero because he is the only one who can survive in both the wild landscape and the pioneer town. Civilized ladies and elderly people invariably choose the towns because they cannot settle in the wilderness, whereas Indians have no choice but to make that same wilderness their home: 'civilization' would be the death of their way of life. The classic gangster film takes place in an urban setting in which a small-time crook attempts to become the big boss but is punished by death for his ambition. In short, we associate genres with predictable plot structures and characteristic protagonists, all linked to specific locales. Even if a film attempts to radically depart from the conventions of a certain genre, it must demonstrate an intimate familiarity with its rules.[5]

However simple the notion of 'genre' may seem at first sight, it becomes infinitely more complex if studied closely. When and why does a film become a 'Western' or a 'melodrama?' Every label is ruled by a certain arbitrariness. There is no Western, horror, melodrama, or gangster film that can pass for the 'original' of that particular genre. And even if such an 'original' could be said to exist, that hypothetical film would be a completely uninteresting and downright boring product: it would show exclusively that which we already know and would consequently be quickly forgotten. The early genre critics of the 1950s concerned themselves primarily with the recurring characteristics said to form the basis of genres. They were looking for standards by which a genre could be measured. The problem of the notion of 'genre,' however, is that it consists of conventions rather than universal and transhistorical rules. The crux of conventions is that they are based on consensus. Unlike universal rules, the consensus can alter relatively easily. Conventions are open to change. This mutability makes genres elastic: they have a 'more or less' stable foundation that is constantly shifting nonetheless.

From the 1970s onward, critics showed increasing interest in the variable nature of genres. They realized that it was impossible to determine a standard for each genre. What a film shares with another film from its genre is partially definable, but partially consists of an 'indefinable X.'[6] The common contours of these films can be traced but not exhaustively or precisely. Consequently, these critics focused on the differences between films and required a general idea of the kind of matching patterns subsumed under that 'indefinable X.' An idea of the X is necessary to outline the differences and anomalies when comparing various films with one another. Genres thus result from the interplay between repetitive elements and variable conventions.

The Detective Genre

The generic interaction between recurring patterns and changeable elements can pertain directly to narratological issues. The detective film plot, for instance, revolves around the reconstruction of the fabula that preceded a murder case, in order that the crime is allocated a place within a sequence of causes and consequences. The story involves the attempts of the investigator to complete the fabula of the crime: what events have led to the murder? In short, the aim of the investigator is to incorporate the crime into a more or less causal and coherent context.

The case is closed as soon as the fabula of the crime has become clear within the course of the investigation. From a group of suspects with a possible motive, the detective points out the actual perpetrator – end of story.[7] Usually the perpetrator is an unexpected candidate, a device that has become so much of a cliché that it would nowadays be surprising to reveal that the initial suspect actually committed the murder.

This standard pattern of the detective genre is suitable for many shrewd variations, but I will limit myself to examples I discussed earlier in this book. *Rashomon* (see Chapter 6) is a smart narrative experiment. Kurosawa's film does not have a character who fulfils the role of detective. Within a frame story we hear four 'witnesses,' who are all positioned directly in front of the camera, each of whom delivers a statement about the murder of the samurai. This positioning of the characters invites the viewer to take the place of the detective. Nevertheless, the testimonies are contradictory, so the fabula of the investigation cannot end properly – the story of the film is over before the fabula of the crime can be closed.

Rear Window (see Chapter 8) is fascinating because of the way in which the wheelchair-bound photographer comes up with a wild scenario of murder by connecting seemingly unrelated facts: his neighbour might have murdered his own wife. A police investigator light-heartedly rejects the suggestions of the peeping Tom, but surprisingly, the photographer has picked up a trail that leads to an actual crime.

Blow-up (see Chapter 8), on the contrary, remains purposefully vague and only hints at the possibility of a real crime. A photographer is taking pictures in a park, but only when an unknown woman urges him to hand over his film does he suspect that he might have captured something out of the ordinary with his camera. A close examination of some blow-ups initiates some guesses, but these are never sufficiently substantiated. Like the mimes imitating a tennis match without rackets or a ball at the end of *Blow-up*, the film itself might be a detective story in which the murder mystery is only simulated. It does not revolve around a dead body, a murderer, or a group of suspects but around the willingness to participate in an (imaginary) game.

The Musical

In the detective genre, the central question is whether it is possible to ascertain the fabula of the crime within the limits of the fabula of the investigation. A specific narratological issue is also at stake in musicals. Although films of this genre have a main plotline, it is secondary to

the central element of musicals: intermezzos for song and/or dance.
When watching a musical, we expect to see the characters burst into
song or dance at some point (even when it's raining cats and dogs)
while the storyline is temporarily suspended. It follows that the story is
often primarily a showcase or even a bad excuse for the ultimate end of
the spectacular intermissions. This leads to the narratological question
how the story and the spectacle relate to one another in the genre. In the
Warner Brothers productions from the early 1930s, such as *Gold Diggers
of 1933* (Mervyn LeRoy, 1933), the story and the showstoppers are separate entities. The primary diegesis focuses on the social problems of its
characters, who experience the concretely miserable circumstances of
the Great Depression and are all penniless. Despite these misfortunes
they nonetheless prepare a show that had been cancelled earlier due to
financial difficulties.[8] The final performance creates a powerful contrast
with the poverty of daily life, with song and dance numbers choreo-
graphed by Busby Berkeley and glitzy costumes. The spectacle is accentuated by fluent camera movements and impossible high-angle shots.
By placing a camera directly above the dancers, some shots border on
abstract figuration.[9]

In *Gold Diggers of 1933*, the spectacle is an end in itself and functions
as a utopian diversion. Other musicals attempt to integrate story and
spectacle. That integration is prefigured by 'soft' transitions between
reality and show: specific background noises 'automatically' transform
into the sound of tap-dancing characters. Another possibility is that the
songs spring from the (dream) thoughts of one of the characters. When
a conflict arises in the character's reality, its solution announces itself in
a spectacular performance. In *An American in Paris* (Vincente Minnelli,
1951), painter Jerry Mulligan is forced to watch his beloved Lise Bou-
vier leave with her husband-to-be. Then, the wind blows the torn pieces
of one of his sketches back together. All of a sudden Jerry finds himself
in the middle of his own sketch, which has transformed into an actual
stage, on which he dances the grand finale with Lise, the woman of his
dreams. The duet dreamed by Jerry serves as a catalyst for Lise's decision to leave the car and return to Jerry. In a musical, that which takes
place in a dance intermission can be carried over to 'real' life.[10] It is a
convention of the 'integrating' musical that utopian fantasies brought
about by song and dance finally become reality.

The redemptive effect of the songs strengthens the idea that the actual story is of only minor importance and amounts to no more than a
necessary warm up. The conflict on the level of the plot has been creat-

ed only to legitimate shows of song and dance as utopian outcome. In a ground-breaking study of the musical, Rick Altman confirms the comparative irrelevance of the plot. In his book *The American Film Musical*, he posits the idea of the 'dual-focus narrative.'[11] A classic Hollywood film shows a chronological progress of carefully sequenced causal events; the story is carried on by psychological developments. The plot of a musical, on the other hand, is constructed much less tightly, which gives the impression that the story is less important than the spectacle of dance and music. By referring to *Gigi* (Vincente Minnelli, 1958), Altman claims that the musical is often constructed around oppositions, in this case the beautiful, playful young woman and the rich, standoffish gentleman. In order to show that the carefree woman and the older man are made for each other, the musical employs parallel scenes. According to Altman, every female aspect is connected to a male aspect: she is obliged to take etiquette lessons; he is 'obliged' to attend tea-time gatherings. She lives under the care of her grandmother; he lives under the care of his uncle. She is annoyed by her aunt; he is just generally bored. These parallels can continue in the montage sequences. Altman also gives a clear example from *New Moon* (Robert Z. Leonard, 1940). After the female character has sung two lines in long shot, she sings four lines while being filmed in a medium shot. From the seventh line on, we see her face in close-up. When her male counterpart is singing his song, precisely the same shot pattern is used.[12]

In film musicals with a dual-focus story, psychological developments are secondary to the identical series of acts and gestures conducted by both the male and the female lead in separate shots. In *Gigi*, the fact that Gaston sits and sings on the same bench in the park as the young heroine has done suffices to indicate that they will eventually be a couple. These parallels start the progressive development of the levelling of contrasts. The childish Gigi starts showing mature behaviour: she drinks champagne and gets more interested in the *beau monde* of which Gaston is a part. Gaston, in his turn, begins to exhibit youthful enthusiasm. He stuffs himself with caramel and engages in a game of leapfrog. A musical with a dual-focus structure works toward a utopian solution in which seemingly mutually exclusive opposites meet. This solution is not psychologically motivated but is instead mediated through parallels that even extend into the song and dance numbers.[13]

Horror versus Science Fiction

In the introduction to this chapter, I noted that classic horror can be characterized by the thin line between man and monster. This weakening of boundaries on the level of the plot also manifests itself in the focalizations. Classic horror contains scenes in which the monster figures as the subject of the look. By means of focalization through the eyes of the monster, films attempt to generate sympathy for its vision or tragic fate. If a monster becomes the subject of focalization, we might see the reasonable aspects of its point of view. As an internal focalizor, one of the possible effects is that it comes to resemble humans more than we would probably like. At such a moment, if the monster shows human characteristics, we need to consider our own possibly monstrous nature.

Vivian Sobchack has contrasted this effect of classic horror with the working of science fiction. She articulates a distinction between the science-fiction creature and the science-fiction monster. A creature is a living organism that leaves destruction in its wake and inspires fear. It could be a giant insect, a colossal sea monster, or a prehistoric dinosaur. It is the product of mutation, the consequence of the urge to discover the unknown depths of the earth, or perhaps an organism that has re-emerged from ancient masses of ice after an atomic explosion. The creature appears as a punishment for the human drive toward scientific progress.[14] In horror films, human moral dilemmas were at stake. In these science-fiction films, by contrast, nature strikes back at the human race. By showing the creature only as an 'it,' the film demonstrates nature's moral indifference. The creature is an avenger without a psyche and acts without any human considerations. For this reason, the creature is always the object, and never the subject, of focalization. The same applies roughly to the science-fiction monster, with the difference that we are now dealing with a deformed human being. This deformity is usually caused by an accident: exposure to radiation, for instance. The science-fiction monster does not fight the evil possibly lurking in his own soul, unlike the monster in a horror film. In science fiction, the focus shifts from the psychological aspects of horror to the physical effects of the deforming transformation. Horror revolves around the question of what the monster *is*, whereas science fiction centres on what it *does* and the evil it brings about. Because sinfulness and guilt are hardly ever featured, identification with the science-fiction monster is unnecessary. For that reason, the science-fiction creature or monster is represented as object of the look: it remains a 'scary thing' at a distance and is only rarely shown in close-up.[15]

Sobchack's distinction between horror and science fiction illustrates how effective the decision to permit or avoid having the monster or creature focalize can be. If a monster focalizes now and then, moral dilemmas are emphasized. In science fiction, emphasis is given to the indifferent nature of the creature or the physical repulsiveness of the monster. The inhuman nature of the science-fiction creature is enhanced by not allowing it to become a subject of focalization.

Science fiction entered a more modern phase when such subjective shots did become a part of its narrative structure. In *2001: A Space Odyssey* (Stanley Kubrick, 1968), for example, science has advanced to such an extent that a supercomputer endowed with human capacities and characteristics has become possible. To signify this, we are presented with many subjective shots from the viewpoint of the all-seeing Hal 9000. The shadow side of this development is that the computer also shares emotions like shame and vengefulness with humans, which has dire consequences. Since that time, point-of-view shots to show the human side of robots and cyborgs have become almost conventional in science-fiction films.[16] With this procedure, modern science fiction indicates that man himself has become a technological entity: the more human a cyborg, the more mechanical the human becomes.

The examples of horror and science fiction show that an analysis of the levels of focalization can be a pointer for specific genre thematics. Every genre has its own narrative conditions and limitations, its do's and don'ts, and for that reason it is advisable to explore narrative techniques when studying genre. Kubrick's *2001: A Space Odyssey* proves that the modification of such procedures can anticipate a new tendency in the genre. By means of narratological research, genres can be positioned in relation to each other.

The Western

In the myriad studies concerning Westerns, the figure of the cowboy is naturally the primary focus of critical interest. How is he constructed? What are the characteristics of the typical cowboy? Why does he exert such attraction? In order to understand the structure of Westerns, however, it is crucial to consider the cowboy as an eye catcher. Essentially, he is only a manifestation to which internal focalizors attribute characteristics. He is an empty screen on to which they project positive qualities. In Western novels, we find this structure expressed in observations and assumptions such as 'He has a sun-burnt face [he must have spent many hours riding], but he nonetheless manages to descend from his horse quite nimbly in the eyes of a certain onlooker [he must possess a lot of stamina].' Whoever watches him move immediately assumes what the boy in *Shane* (George Stevens, 1953) makes explicit: 'I bet you can shoot.' The cowboy, in short, is seen with the eyes of the imagination: with one look, you steadfastly believe he is a heroic and masculine sharpshooter.

This plot model in Westerns leads to two-way traffic where causal relations are concerned. The cowboy is the hero and proves this in the grand finale. A second track runs in the opposing direction beneath this narrative trail, however. Characters believe in the cowboy's heroism first; only then can he confirm the trust reposed in him by ultimately defeating his opponent(s). The way in which he is viewed allows him to become a hero. The so-called 'resurrection scenes,' in which a heavily wounded cowboy is nursed by a woman, are noteworthy in this regard. Now she has the chance to look at him extensively, she believes she can spot the strength that is undiminished despite his injuries. It is not primarily her nursing skills that cure him but her unbroken faith in his abilities – he now becomes the hero he has been all along.

Narratologically, it is of great importance that this pattern turns a flashback narrated by the cowboy into a structural impossibility. As soon as a cowboy starts to narrate his heroic deeds, he will soon bite the dust, like Sheriff Bill in *Unforgiven* (Clint Eastwood, 1992), or disappear completely into anonymity, like Tom Doniphon in *The Man Who Shot Liberty Valance* (John Ford, 1962). The cowboy does not brag about his celebrated past because his reputation rests on the stories that other tell about him. Films like Eastwood's and Ford's are exceptions that reveal a distinct rule: a classic cowboy does not operate on the level of narration or focalization but exclusively on the level of the action. Since we are never presented with a perspective from 'within,' we can cherish the illusion that the classic cowboy is not burdened with events in his past or with a guilt complex. At most, the past provides him with a motive for vengeance.

The cowboy owes his status as hero without psychological ballast to his narrative positioning. In the formula mentioned in the introduction, 'A says what B sees that C does,' the cowboy is C. He is the object of narration, the object of focalization, and the subject of the action. This narrative condition characterizes the classic Western and is compactly illustrated in a striking scene from the relatively minor Western *The Tin Star* (Anthony Mann, 1957). The inexperienced Sheriff Ben Owens draws his gun to arrest Bart Bogardus for murder. Bogardus has his hands in the air, takes off his hat, and moves it in the direction of his right hip. In a low-angle close-up shot from behind Bogardus's back, we see that he is secretly reaching for his gun. This action is so devious that the sheriff cannot possibly see what the murderer is up to. In the same shot filmed from behind Bogardus's back, however, we also see Morgan Hickman, a former sheriff turned bounty hunter, in the background. He apparently sees through Bogardus's ruse and shoots the gun out of the murderer's hand from a great distance. Technically speaking, this is an 'impossible' scene. The sly action is visible only from the privileged position behind Bogardus's back. This low-angle close-up, however, is external focalization. Morgan does not share its position and viewing direction and yet he sees what Bogardus is doing. On the basis of this scene you could say that the cowboy is a classic superhero who can see through every trick without ever focalizing.

When the cowboy is emphatically represented as a focalizor, the genre is transformed or shifts registers in the direction of another genre. *High Noon* (Fred Zinnemann, 1952) is such a metamorphosed Western. Criminal Frank Miller and his three shady friends will arrive on the midday train to seek out Marshal Will Kane, the man who had brought Miller to justice. Kane, who is entitled to 'retire' because of his recent marriage, regards it as his duty to do his job one more time. Just as before, he wants to find a group of brave citizens to combat Miller and company. All the citizens, however, have their own cowardly reasons to desert the Marshal; in the end, Kane is on his own. Whereas the classic cowboy always remains impervious, Kane's growing doubt is shown because the Western hero himself is the primary subject of focalization here. In *High Noon*, Kane occupies the B position more than the usual C position, which causes the Western to become more psychological. The finale, however, in which Kane defeats the quartet with the unexpected help of his pacifistic fiancée, once again adheres to the conventional pattern to such an extent that the metamorphosis cannot be called truly radical.

A film like *Pursued* (Raoul Walsh, 1947) is somewhat more irregular. Cowboy Jeb Rand is plagued by images from the past about bright flashes of light and spurred boots. As he is hiding from the gang led by Grant Callum, he tells the story of his life to his stepsister, who has become his wife. The images play a central part, but they are initially narratively incoherent. Only after his narration, when the gang has already surrounded him, can Jeb place the flashes and the spurs. Suddenly, it comes to him that he witnessed the assassination of his father. This realization has such paralysing effect that he unexpectedly surrenders to

Grant's gang. Now he has provided his childhood memories with a narrative frame, Jeb can no longer undertake any action himself. He is saved only by the intervention of his adoptive mother, who used to be in love with his father. *Pursued* is consistent where genre conventions are concerned. As long as the flashbacks in Walsh's film remain enigmatic and fragmentary, they are no more than a nuisance. They hinder Jeb but they do not hamper his capacity for action in any critical way. Only when the fragments are made to occupy their place in a larger whole does he become mentally incapable of doing anything. In terms of the genre, the significance of the flashback makes him so passive that he becomes an anti-hero.

That the reliving of a childhood trauma through a flashback does not necessarily render the cowboy powerless is proven by *Once upon a Time in the West*. Only at the end of the film, as a prelude to the final shootout, we see a flashback of the Harmonica Man. The flashback seems to arise out of a meditation, after the camera has shown his eyes in extreme close-ups. By means of the retroversion, we understand why he is targeting Frank. This reliving is not a sign of inner doubt but of conviction. The flashback reveals that this is the moment that accounts will be settled. His opponent, Frank, however, is still wondering what grudge the Harmonica Man bears him. Crucial here is that the taciturn avenger does not tell anything because this would subvert the heroism of the cowboy as established by genre conventions. Only after a shot that seriously wounds Frank does the Harmonica Man provide his rival with a clue as to his identity. He puts a harmonica between Frank's teeth, repeating what Frank once did to him. We see a close-up of Frank's face, followed by a fragment of the flashback we saw earlier: it now dawns on Frank who he is dealing with. Through his instrument, the Harmonica Man has transposed the flashback on to his opponent, who dies shortly afterward.

The mentally burdened avenger from *Once upon a Time in the West* can have his victory because his flashback is crystal clear to him. The events of the past seem to have been so traumatic that he no longer speaks or narrates but communicates only by means of his harmonica. Moreover, the Harmonica Man seems to consciously summon the flashback in order to give himself a boost before fighting Frank. In *Pursued*, in contrast, the cowboy is in the process of interpreting his fragmentary memories. An earlier event remains obscure until its truth hits him with too great a shock. Its significance overpowers him to such an extent that he is temporarily immobilized and forced to surrender. This application of the flashback is abnormal for the Western but characteristic of film noir, which is why *Pursued* has been characterized as a Western noir by some.

Film Noir

A repetitive structure within various films noirs is that a narrating character, who may or may not be a private detective, indicates how he got involved in solving a mysterious crime. This mystery unravels visually by means of flashbacks. These retroversions are, characteristically, somewhat odd for two reasons. First, in some film noirs the narration is meant as a defence; the protagonist explains himself. This happens in a film such as *Double Indemnity* (Billy Wilder, 1944), in which the ongoing narration brings the narrator's imminent death closer and closer. Strictly speaking, of course, the life force is flowing out of him because of the injuries caused by a gunshot wound, but there also is the suggestion that the progression of the story matches the stages of dying. This is also the case in *D.O.A.* (Rudolph Maté, 1950), in which a dying man in a police station reveals who has poisoned him and why.

Second, the flashbacks in films noirs are permeated by an aura of mystery because the role of the femme fatale is never truly clarified. The alluring woman who feeds the protagonist's imagination remains notoriously dubious. Narratologically speaking, she fulfils the same role as the cowboy: she is an empty screen on to which the protagonist projects characteristics. In the eyes of her male admirer, her state of mind fluctuates: she can threaten and manipulate but she can also seem vulnerable or innocent. Žižek argues that the man generally reacts to the 'hysterical breakdown' of the femme fatale at the end of the film noir in one of two ways.[17] Either he foregoes his desire and rejects her in order to safeguard his male ego, which happens in *The Maltese Falcon* (John Huston, 1941), or he identifies with her and allows himself to be dragged down with her. In *Out of the Past* (Jacques Tourneur, 1947), the hero is continually seduced and deceived by the femme fatale. At the end of the film, he seems to give in once again and agrees to flee with her. After informing the police, he heads straight for his doom – fully conscious, apparently. A torrent of police bullets finally causes their car to crash into a tree.

At first sight, the Western and the film noir appear antithetical: flashbacks narrated by the hero are all but impossible in the first genre, whereas they are a conventional requirement in the second. This difference partially explains the contrast between the one-dimensional

Western and the dark complexity of film noir. In the classic Western, the distinction between good and evil is relatively clear cut because the psychological motivation of the hero seems rather straightforward from the point of view of the focalizors: if common sense dictates that the community would do well to get rid of a certain figure, the cowboy will fight this person. This makes the cowboy into a positive character. As the flashback plot thickens in film noir, by contrast, the narrating protagonist becomes more and more entangled in its complex web of mysteries. Whether he should regard the femme fatale as a positive or a negative character becomes increasingly unclear. When she is indeed a negative influence, moreover, the question remains open whether she is in fact 'evil' or whether the 'danger' of her presence simply resides in the fact that the protagonist cannot cope with having found her irresistible.

In this chapter, I have explained how narrative choices depend on genre conventions. If the Harmonica Man from *Once upon a Time in the West* had narrated the flashback in his own words – 'Frank, this is what you have done to me' – the spaghetti Western by Leone would have had a dissonant ending. Similarly, *Out of the Past* could never have been an exemplary film noir if Jeff had seriously planned to elope with his femme fatale or if the flight had succeeded. The strength of these films is determined by the way in which they take into account the narrative principles of their respective genres. The use of flashbacks in Westerns has certain conditions; the options for the ending of a film noir are limited. Films in which echoes of these genres resonate should always relate to generic prerequisites in order to retain their credibility. A good example is offered by the neo-films noirs in which the femme fatale becomes the evident protagonist. See, for instance, *The Last Seduction* (John Dahl, 1994). Whereas the femme fatale was traditionally shrouded in mystery, Dahl's film portrays her 'from within.' We see her consciously set traps for her own financial benefit. It would have been fatal for the film if the role of the femme fatale as manifest manipulator had caused her enigmatic quality to disappear. In *The Last Seduction*, however, the mystery shifts because the effect of the woman on the men that surround her does not differ radically from that in the classic noir. The classic femme fatale usually pretended to be a seductive woman who was simply misunderstood. At this, the protagonist wondered whether he should feel sorry for her or whether she was attempting to double-cross him. Conversely, the neo-noir femme fatale acts out the role of conniving trickster so openly that the man starts to believe her behaviour is nothing more than outright bluff. Even if the strategy is completely different, the riddle surrounding the femme fatale in *The Last Seduction* remains intact for the men that surround her.[18]

The modification of old genre formulas can be fortuitous as long as the narrative conditions are appropriately readjusted. Like Sharon Willis's claims about Quentin Tarantino's 'pulp fiction' films, this procedure creates the potential to turn 'shit' into gold.[19] By recycling B movies that have largely fallen into obscurity, he creates new work that is both critically praised and commercially successful. In order to achieve this, Tarantino has meticulously studied the films he cites. This chapter has touched mainly on narrative procedures such as flashback, focalization, and the relation between story and spectacle. The final chapter specifically addresses stylistic features such as camera operations, the use of colour, and the careful composition of shots.

chapter 10

Filmic Excess: When Style Drowns the Plot

The opening shots of *The Comfort of Strangers* consist of lengthy forward camera movements past various artworks as the view traverses the rooms of a monumental palazzo for more than three minutes. Because the forward movements are constantly interrupted and picked up elsewhere in the building, the palazzo is made to seem extra spacious. The stately music of composer Angelo Badalamenti accompanies these shots. Furthermore, we hear an anglophone voice-over with a slight Italian accent talk about what kind of man his father was. The sequence in which the camera moves through the palazzo recalls the rigorous opening of *L'année dernière à Marienbad* (1961), in which the camera glides past the empty hallways, salons, and Baroque ceilings of an immense hotel for an even longer time. In Resnais' film we also hear a voice-over, this time mumbling repetitive phrases.

The stately music associated with the elegant house of Robert and Caroline in *The Comfort of Strangers* can be taken as a reference to *Morte a Venezia* (1971), a film constructed around the compositions of Gustav Mahler. In Visconti's film, the music is not tied to an inhabitant of Venice but to a tourist in the city of the doge: composer Gustav von Aschenbach. In contrast to the character Robert in McEwan's novel, the Robert of the film dresses in an impeccable white suit. This way of dressing apparently alludes to the white costume worn by the character of the composer in *Morte a Venezia,* notably in his death scene at the beach.

These stylistic references serve to situate *The Comfort of Strangers* in the tradition of European art films: a tradition in which style is considered more important than 'content.' Where *L'année dernière à Marienbad* is concerned, the allusion is relatively arbitrary. Whereas the status of both the images and the ghostly characters in the film by Resnais is ambiguous, Schrader's film has a traceable plot with well-profiled characters. In *Morte a Venezia*, the references turn out to be a dead end. Van Aschenbach, like Colin, will meet a fateful end, but the differences in narrative technique are far more remarkable. The level of focalization is the most crucial one in Visconti's film. The composer becomes obsessed with the beauty of the young boy Tadzio. His gaze continually searches for it. *The Comfort of Strangers* appears to offer the reverse of this perspective: the young man who is object of the look in Visconti's film (Tadzio) seems to become the focalizor of the story in Schrader's (Colin). Robert's white suit gives the impression, moreover, that his role is going to be analogous to that of Von Aschenbach. The dead end that fools us in Schrader's film is that the suggested parallels between the observed young men Tadzio and Colin on the one hand and the voyeurs Von Aschenbach and Robert on the other are in fact unfounded. Robert's voyeurism is not the primary focus of *The Comfort of Strangers*. He is not interested in Colin as a homoerotic viewing object: his interest is embedded in the repetitive narration about his childhood trauma. Within the frame of Robert's fantasies, Colin figures as a rival. As I indicated in Chapter 2, it is only when we recognize the importance of the recurring narration that we can understand the morbid turn of events that will cost Colin his life.

In the previous chapter I claimed that the horror genre functions as a plot model for Schrader's film. There, I was referring to the conventions of the genre and its mode of narration. Stylistic conventions were left out of the discussion because strictly speaking they transcend the field of narratology. I would, however, like to propose that stylistic procedures belong to the domain of narrative theory in a broader and more practical sense, even when they do not seem to propel the story.

Chapter 1 introduced the concept of 'filmic excess.' This surplus is created when the style becomes autoreferential to such an extent that it overloads the 'content.' If narrative aspects concern temporal developments, style can be called excessive when it becomes so prominent that it interrupts or freezes those developments. When a certain style does not serve the plot, or even pushes it to the background, we can speak of 'overkill.' My point in the first chapter was that every film knows a certain degree of excess simply because stylistic elements always distort the content or build-up of the story and are, to certain extent, autonomous. I postulated as well that a firm narrative logic absorbed the stylistic effects and their excess. In a film with an intricately wrought plot, in other words, the stylistic elements may seem so 'functionally' applied that the formal distortion of the content can largely be neutralized.

I have explained earlier that narratology is not a wonder theory in the sense that it offers an all-encompassing model for analysis. An interpretation does not end with a solely narratological discussion; interpretation remains 'narratology plus X.' Excess does not hold the exclusive right to the position of this X, but it can lead to a crucial broadening of our perspective.[1] First, I want to illustrate the process of the neutralizing of excess, which transforms seemingly unwarranted stylistic manoeuvres into functional elements of the story. It appears that excess can only truly exist if a film situates itself in the margins of the narrative tradition. With the example of melodrama, I want to refute this hypothesis. An apparently classic story can become secondary to style on the condition that stylistic elements no longer support the story but become built-in guides for 'reading' or watching. Keeping this modification of the hypothesis in mind, I want to come back to the stylistic imitations of European art films in *The Comfort of Strangers*.

Functional Compensation for Excess

The difficulty of 'excess' is that it is not a well-defined characteristic but a matter of interpretation. A first logical step in the tracing of excess is of course gaining awareness of unorthodox stylistic elements: sharp-edged transitions or an extremely low number of cuts, shaky or very steady camera operations, illogical transitions in time or space, a bizarre choice of actors, quaint music or sounds, and so forth. A second step is checking whether the story legitimates unorthodox stylistic means. In other words, is the style functional and does it propel the plot? The notion of excess is predicated upon the interaction between form and content. Horror films sometimes take liberties with causal relations. If the monster does not operate according to human logic, the common sequence of causes and consequences need not be adhered to. Since they find themselves threatened by an irrational monster, the characters hardly realize what they are dealing with and causal relations can be dispensed with. In addition, horror films also make relatively little use of the shot/reverse shot structure. These stylistic characteristics are motivated by the fact that horror is based on the fear of unknown threats: the reverse shot is withheld in order to ensure that the monster will long remain mysterious.

If a character has a distorted notion of time, like the protagonist in

Don't Look Now (Nicolas Roeg, 1973), or is spatially disoriented, like the alien creature in *The Man Who Fell to Earth* (Nicholas Roeg, 1976), illogical transitions in time or space are, in a sense, logical. They represent the experience of the main character. A distinct category is also formed by genres that offer 'attractions' rather than a story. A good example is the musical, in which songs occasion intermezzos with lavish mise en scène consisting of, for instance, grandiose decors, bright colours, and theatrical gestures made by the actors. These excessive stylistic elements are consistent with the representation of extravagant spectacle that is presented separately from the actual plot. A spectacle may point to the dreamy mood of characters who 'lose themselves' in song and dance, or it can take place on a specially prepared stage. In these cases, the music and dance scenes mark a separate world. Their deviating and patently artificial nature is heightened by the superfluous styling. Because the excessive style in musicals serves to represent the utopian world, stylistic overkill is motivated by the content and the tendency toward excess is mitigated.

If excess in musicals resides in the representation of a world that is separated from the main storyline, the modern action film is excessive because of its representation of the male hero. The naked torsos of actors like Sylvester Stallone and Arnold Schwarzenegger in the action cinema of the 1980s were so inflated that they have come to represent a 'hysterical image' of masculinity. According to Yvonne Tasker in her book *Spectacular Bodies,* the modern action heroes overdo the virile display of their muscled chests to such an extent that they have become male pin-ups.[2] By blatantly showing themselves off, they take over the position that Laura Mulvey has identified as exclusively female within the Hollywood tradition: 'Look at me and acknowledge the attractiveness of my body.'[3] Although casting heavily muscled actors – an element of the mise en scène, and consequently a stylistic element – makes the representation of the action hero excessive, his physical appearance is functional for the firm actions he undertakes. The feats of the action hero (on the level of the fabula) compensate for his showy appearance (on the level of the story).

The examples mentioned above, which could easily be added to, illustrate that excess can in principle be found in all types of films. In these examples, however, excess is only a starting point because stylistic elements are at the same time neutralized by the content or plot.[4] Excess as defined by Kristin Thompson manifests itself only when the style remains self-directed and is emphatically *not* compensated for by the content.[5] Such is the case when metaphoric connections obscure insight into the temporal developments, which happens in the abstract *Ballet mécanique*. This also occurs when the plot all but disappears, as I claimed was the case with *L'avventura* in Chapter 1. The narrative rhythm of this film is extremely sluggish and crucial events are overlooked. What remains is a film with exceptionally steady shots in which characters are reduced to elements in desolate surroundings. We see them as 'extras' against the backdrop of modern architecture. The meticulous compositions implicitly tell the 'story' of the alienation of the modern human condition.

Because of their neglect of tightly structured plots, these films function in the margins of the narrative traditions. Since there is so little content, an excess of style cannot be compensated for: the first condition of excess. The forgotten search and the slow rhythm lend *L'avventura* almost the same level of stillness as a painting. The question remains whether excess can also manifest itself in films that are not just stylistic exercises but that have a particularly narrative character instead.

Ostentatious Film Styles

The European immigrant Douglas Sirk (born as Detlev Sierck) is known as the master of 1950s Hollywood melodrama. Sirk's plot are relatively tight, psychologically comprehensible, and have a bitter, sentimental subtext. In *All That Heaven Allows* (1955), a widow from a well-to-do background has an affair with her young gardener, to horror of her two children and gossipy neighbours (see Chapter 3). In *Imitation of Life* (1959), a daughter is frustrated with the frequent absences of her career-minded mother, while a friend of the daughter is aiming for a career in the showbiz and has to disavow her own black mother in order to achieve it.

It does not take much effort to analyse the classic, potentially tear-jerking storylines of these melodramas because there is much logically structured 'content' to be analysed. Melodramas are usually situated in a rather restrictive social milieu. The story takes place in a wealthy middle-class setting in which it is inappropriate to settle conflicts by means of direct, forceful action.[6] The outlet often chosen in melodramas – and this was Sirk's strong point – is to embellish the plot with syrupy stylistic features. The colours are bright and exuberant to draw attention to the role of outward display within provincial milieus with rock-solid social codes. The music is sentimental and underlines the emotions that are sometimes held back by these codes and that, at other times, are expressed in the most theatrical of ways. The characters operate within kitschy decors and are carefully framed behind windows, the lattice work of stairways, or bedposts, or among mirrors in order to emphasize the lack of human contact (Figure 10.1).

10.1 *Imitation of Life* The banisters between Lora (on the left) and Sarah Jane accentuate their disagreement.

In a Sirk melodrama, the emphatically present stylistic procedures result in an ultra-kitsch approach. The storylines themselves already strike a maudlin tone, but the stylistic features create an even more hyper-sentimental effect. The filmic style manifests itself so ostentatiously that it draws attention to itself and outshines the story – which is the defining characteristic of excess. Form outweighs classic plot construction. The story, in other words, is told first and foremost by means of the excessive filmic form.[7]

Generally speaking, there are two options for Sirk's melodramas. On the one hand, the viewer could choose to see them as 'simply' sentimental because of their classic narrative structures. On the other hand, he could also adopt an ironic stance in the face of melodramas and label them as *overly* sentimental by focusing on the form imbued with pathos. Such an attitude would lead the viewer to consider the stylistic features to be straining after effect to such an extent that the dramatic context can no longer be taken seriously. Instead of an identification with the events the characters get caught up in, irony creates a buffer between the viewer and the emotions displayed on the screen. The viewer will watch Sirk's cinema with some critical distance and not be carried away by the tear-jerking content.

In earlier chapters, I have argued that excess occurs when style and form are not functional because of a lack of content and plot. This claim is concurrent with the spirit of Bordwell's *Narration in Fiction Film* and

Thompson's essay on filmic excess. Nevertheless, Sirk's melodramas also prompt a re-evaluation of this claim. It could be said that the stylistic features of his films are in fact overly functional. The colours, shot compositions, framing, and music magnify the story's sentimentality so strongly that a paradoxically inverted effect takes place. Excess is created here by emphatically underlining the formal features.

The consequences of an ironic viewing attitude can spread like an oil stain. Films such as *All That Heaven Allows* and *Imitation of Life* are acknowledged melodramas; once you decide to read such a melodrama ironically, it becomes almost impossible to cast off this stance completely. As soon as you are unable to see melodrama unironically, the genre as a whole becomes automatically tainted by the excess it generates. Melodrama itself turns out to be infected by sentimental overkill, as is shown by the remakes of Sirk's cinema.

The plot of *Angst Essen Seele Auf* (Rainer Werner Fassbinder, 1974) is based on Sirk's *All That Heaven Allows* (1954). In the earlier film, a widow is rejected by her quasi-chic but in fact provincial social peers after entering a relationship with a young gardener. Fassbinder changes the setting, the class, and the ethnic background: to the dismay of those around her, an elderly German woman Emmi, a housecleaner, has an affair with a Moroccan migrant worker whom she has dubbed 'Ali.' The form of *Angst Essen Seele Auf* is also completely different. Instead of lavish interiors, there are barren ones; the pathetic music is replaced mainly by songs from a jukebox; the characters are down to earth and do not show any signs of theatricality. Every trace of excess where music, colour, or acting styles are concerned seems to have disappeared in *Angst Essen Seele Auf*. Fassbinder's 'melodrama' looks like a social-realist docudrama. On the level of the framing, however, the excessive nature of melodrama has been preserved.

One of Sirk's trademarks is to show the characters in their surroundings. As I noted before, they are 'imprisoned' in the reflection of the television screen, amid a sea of flowers, or behind the lattice work of stairways. Fassbinder copies this trademark and even exaggerates it in some scenes. When her colleagues turn away from Emmi, we see her eating her lunch behind the balusters of a staircase. Later on, this shot repeats itself structurally when Emmi and her fellow housecleaners reject a new Yugoslavian colleague during their lunch break. The repetitive structure makes this shot doubly framed since it shows both the exclusion of the new employee and Emmi's own hypocrisy. In another scene, in which 'Ali' feels depressed and misunderstood, we see him sitting on a bed. Sirk might make do with a shot framed by the doorway, but in Fassbinder's film the camera is also positioned at the other end of a corridor (Figure 10.2). The excess in Fassbinder's film resides in the amplification of such shot compositions.[8] At the same time, the framing of *Angst Essen Seele Auf* can also be taken figuratively. By transposing an American genre to a tragic German social reality, Fassbinder reframes Sirk's melodrama. In a self-reflexive way, Fassbinder situates the narrative skeleton of *All That Heaven Allows* in a new, poignant social context.

10.2 *Angst Essen Seele Auf* Not only is 'Ali' caught in the frame of the doorway, but the camera is also positioned at the other end of the hall to achieve an increased effect of isolation.

Style as an In-built Guide for Reading/Viewing

Unlike Fassbinder's film, *Breaking the Waves* (Lars von Trier, 1996) rewrites Sirk's method by means of erratic camera operations. In Chapter 6, I presented an overview of the plot of this film about Bess, who 'suffers' from goodness and who is doing penance because she thinks herself guilty of the fate of her paralysed husband. Every attempt at retelling the story gives the impression that the plot is ridiculously romantic and pathetic. Because of the blatantly sentimental nature of the plot, Von Trier has chosen to cast the unbridled emotions in a jerky, sloppy form (handheld cameras, discontinuous editing methods) completed by greyish tones. This is what Von Trier himself has said about his approach:

What we've done is to take a style and put it over the story like a filter. Like encoding a television signal, when you pay in order to see a film: here we are encoding a signal for the film, which the viewer will later ensure they decode. The raw, documentary style which I've laid over the film and which actually annuls and contests it, means that we accept the story as it is.[9]

In *Breaking the Waves,* the story itself is excessive. The only thing that makes the overkill of pathos acceptable is the contrasting form. Because of the raw style and its quasi-realistic effect, the near impossible content is toned down and neutralized. The style dresses the story in such a way that we are prepared to accept that we indeed witnessed the miracle the film's tagline promised.

Opposite the formal excess of Sirk's melodrama, which makes the story pathetic, Von Trier's film places a neutralizing style, which lends the excessive story credibility. Whereas the style is overly functional and outdoes the plot in the first case – and, *nota bene,* this is the defining characteristic of excess as filmic concept – the style is functionally manipulative in the service of the plot in the second. Von Trier has rewritten melodrama in such a way that the excess seems to have dissolved. Since I decided earlier that melodrama was the genre of excess, I should ask whether *Breaking the Waves* can still be called a melodrama. If the answer to this question is 'yes,' it must be related to 'redundant' stylistic features I have not yet mentioned. Von Trier's film is divided into seven chapters and an epilogue: a structure that radically interrupts the plot. At the beginning of each chapter, we see a static film shot of an impressive landscape with a painterly appeal. The minimal changes we can perceive – slowly moving clouds, a rainbow that appears, lapping waves – are the only things that prove we are not actually looking at paintings. Each chapter heading is prominently accompanied by pop and rock songs from the 1960s and 1970s: Procul Harum, Elton John, and Deep Purple are a few of the featured artists. If consciously sloppy camera operations and sudden shot transitions give the impression of a documentary, the chapter headings emphasize the artificiality of the film. These chapters overshadow the functionally raw realistic style and offer the viewer an opportunity to keep a distance from the story. The intermezzos, which are reminiscent of tableaux, refer to, or perhaps provoke, the excess of form that is typical of Sirk's melodramas.

At this point I would like to reconsider Thompson's notion of excess. For her, excess resulted when a filmic style displayed itself for its own sake. On the basis of Sirk's melodramas and their remakes, I would like to extend her concept: excess can also indicate *a style that functions as an in-built guide that serves to create a distance to the content or plot*. This allows the concept to pertain to films at the heart of the narrative tradition as well. The question remains whether the viewer recognizes the style as an in-built guide and is willing to build a well-founded interpretation on it. In other words, the viewer needs to trace conspicuous stylistic elements in order to ascertain whether those elements are functional to the story or whether they have an alienating effect similar to that I detected in melodrama. In the next section I analyse three films, each of which is excessive in its own way.

Persiflage, Pompous Meta-Commentary, Parody

This Is Spinal Tap (Rob Reiner, 1984) is a 'documentary' about the British heavy metal group Spinal Tap, whose star is fading years after a big break in the late 1960s. We follow the gum-chewing, long-haired musicians on an American tour; there are interviews with the people involved and we see old television gigs. Spinal Tap fits the stereotypical image of a heavy metal group completely – except that the band did not exist. This knowledge makes *This Is Spinal Tap* turn at least ninety degrees. The film continues to uphold the guise of a rock band documentary to perfection. The trick of this 'behind the scenes' documentary is that a certain (journalistic) form is imitated so precisely that we might easily make the mistake of taking its content seriously. When we realize that *This Is Spinal Tap* is a pseudo-documentary, it could be claimed that the actual contents become inessential and that Reiner's film is predominantly concerned with form instead. The danger of persiflage like this is that a standard narratological analysis is certainly possible but completely misses the point. Persiflage is based on imitating a certain type of film as flawlessly as possible; careful replication is meant to mock the style and narrative structure of the 'example.' As the simulated nature of persiflage is recognized, one realizes that the style does not serve to convey the content transparently but to alienate the viewer from that content instead. The style forces one to not take the content literally, and the narrative status of the film thus needs to be reconsidered.[10]

A second example is the pompous book adaptation *Bram Stoker's Dracula* (Francis Ford Coppola, 1992). By incorporating the name of the original author in the film's title, Coppola's film seems to have the pretension of being an extraordinarily faithful adaptation. This pretension should perhaps be taken ironically, seeing that the film inserts a prologue not found in the novel before the opening credits. This prologue shows Dracula as a tragic figure who is turned into a vampire because he is consumed by love. Jokingly, one could say the prologue makes *Bram Stoker's Dracula* more faithful to the vampire's history than is the original novel because it is more complete.

That Coppola's film adaptation has not met with unanimous critical approval can partially be ascribed to its status as spectacle, made to show itself off. *Bram Stoker's Dracula* is full of visual fireworks and bombastic images: almost every filmic technique in the book is used. Moreover, it contains myriad intertextual references, ranging from Renaissance paintings to historical recording equipment and innumerable scenes re-created from other films. The question is whether Coppola's film seeks to impress for its own sake or whether its exhaustive fullness has an ascertainable end.

When Dracula arrives in London in 1897 in order to find Mina, whom he has recognized as a reincarnation of his dead fiancée, Elisabeta, someone is advertising in the streets for the cinema: 'See the cinematograph, the amazing new invention!' As a boy shouts this slogan, Dracula, who appears in the guise of Prince Vlad, attempts to attract Mina's attention amid the hustle and bustle of the city by whispering hypnotically, 'See me, see me now.' By their simultaneous call to be seen, *Bram Stoker's Dracula* draws a parallel between the cinema and the figure of the vampire. This analogy is strengthened in the following scene. A white wolf causes a stir in a room where films are being shown. We see how Mina, too, startles when the wolf approaches her, but Prince Vlad is apparently able to influence the beast and calms it down. After a shot of Mina's still fearful expression, however, we do not see the wolf we might expect in the countershot but instead the vampire, flanked by the projected image of a train arriving at a station.

Mina's fright can be explained in two possible ways. She might have been startled by the fact that the wolf obeys the prince. Consequently, she asks him who he is. The images taken from *L'arrivée d'un train en gare de la Ciotat* (Lumière brothers, 1896) that we see projected to Dracula's left might also be meaningful. Tradition dictates that the film's first audiences were shocked because they believed the train was actually coming directly at them. Mina's reaction thus concerns the uncanny appearance of the vampire as well as her fear of the unknown medium of film.

The surplus value of *Bram Stoker's Dracula* resides in the parallel it creates between the vampire and cinema. The vampire feeds on the blood of living women, and the analogy suggests that film as a medium is also parasitic. Cinema feeds itself by absorbing and draining other sources: the novel on which this film is based, the paintings from which it copies compositions, the many other films it references, all the stylistic procedures it cites, and so on. Rather than an adaptation of Bram Stoker's *Dracula, Bram Stoker's Dracula* is first and foremost a commentary on cinema in the 1990s. Fredric Jameson and others have claimed that postmodern films can exist only on account of their systematic propensity to cite and copy. By creating an analogy between vampires and cinema, Coppola's film incorporates a guide for viewing it: if modern cinema is naturally inclined to plunder other sources, then I am not ashamed of exaggerating that method. More than any other film, *Bram Stoker's Dracula* shows that postmodern cinema is constantly calling out, 'See me, see me now.' It suggests that it is quintessential for cinema to show off all its available tricks and techniques in their full glory in order to draw attention to itself. Coppola's film can easily be read ironically. It employs stylistic citations that are simultaneously criticized by being overdone, as if to say that modern films pride themselves on the tricks they borrow without any conditions. *Bram Stoker's Dracula* itself forms the superlative of this practice. This brings me back to the issue of excess. The bombastic style of Coppola's film is not functional in telling the story of Dracula, but it is functional as a self-reflexive critique of the contemporary film and its many (stylistic) quotations.

A third example of a narrative but nevertheless excessive film is *Adaptation.* (Spike Jonze, 2002). The success of this film is mainly due to its brilliant scenario – the best script ever, with the exception of *Casablanca*, I would say. *Adaptation.* (with a consciously placed period at the end of the title word) is a seemingly 'insane' film, both literally and figuratively: not only do the characters seem to lose their grip on reality but the viewer seems to get caught up in the spiralling story as well. Screenwriter Charlie Kaufman, unanimously praised for his witty script for *Being John Malkovich* (Spike Jonze, 1999), makes himself into the main character of this film. At the beginning, the character of film producer Valerie Thomas engages him to adapt the real non-fiction bestseller *The Orchid Thief* (1998) by Susan Orlean into a film script. Charlie enthusiastically tells her that he wants to take a different approach from the usual 'Hollywood thing': no thefts, sex, car chases, or quasi-profound life lessons but 'just a movie about flowers.' Since the book has no structure, the film should also be able to do without, or so he thinks. This consequential choice leads to a writer's block and slowly drives him mad as the film progresses.

The relation between Charlie and his twin brother, Donald, is crucial. Because of Charlie's success, Donald has become inspired to write a scenario as well and decides to take a three-day seminar with the script guru McKee. While Charlie is struggling to finish his latest assignment, Donald effortlessly pens a story of his own. Even though the result is a cross between *Silence of the Lambs* and *Psycho,* Charlie's agent is delighted with the manuscript and exhorts his protégé to ask Donald for help. After this, Charlie sets aside his scepticism and visits McKee's seminar. Jonze's film makes ample use of voice-overs. Just as Charlie is again ranting in voice-over, McKee condemns this stylistic feature as a sign of 'flaccid, sloppy writing.' In a private conversation with Charlie, the script guru adds that a deus ex machina – a saviour appearing 'out of nowhere' – is an absolute writerly sin but that a screenwriter can turn a film into a hit if he overwhelms the audience in the final act.

After Charlie visits the seminar and Donald interferes with Charlie's script, *Adaptation.* switches into a higher gear. Up until that point, Charlie's hampered attempts at writing have been interspersed with fragments that show Orlean working on her book. Other scenes show her meetings with the subject of the book, the swaggering orchid thief, John Laroche, a boorish Southerner far removed from her intellectual milieu. In the final act, however, Donald leads Charlie on a trail of sensation and spectacle. Donald finds a nude picture of Orlean on a website administered by Laroche. Subsequently, the brothers learn that the writer is a drug addict and discover her in a loving embrace with Laroche. Completely beside herself, Orlean decides to pursue and kill Charlie and his brother. This chase ends in Donald's death, and Laroche dies after an alligator attack. At the end of the film, Charlie tells us in voice-over how he plans to finish his script.

The final act of *Adaptation.* looks a lot like a B film and does indeed 'overwhelm' the audience with sentimental wisdom, sensational developments, and cheap action. As soon as Donald interferes, *Adaptation.* follows McKee's commercial Hollywood recipe to the letter. The brilliant gesture of Jonze's film is that it sins against the script guru's 'do nevers' at the same time that it identifies them: an alligator appears as a ridiculous deus ex machina and the accursed voice-overs are used throughout the movie. Jonze's film, which promises to be another instance of Charlie's 'unique voice' at the beginning, laces so many film clichés together that it becomes an abysmal rendition of an already hackneyed standard plot. It is exactly in this superlative of triteness, however, that the unique voice of the film resides. *Adaptation.* combines so many commonplaces and banal cinematic principles that oddly enough it becomes annoyingly 'original.'

A full-blooded structuralist narratologist who makes do with an analysis of the plot and dénouement of *Adaptation.* is left with nothing but a one-dimensional film. A meaningful interpretation cannot be made without taking into account that the extreme banality makes up the heart of the film. The excessive aspect of Jonze's film resides predominantly in the superfluous use of the voice-over principle, which McKee considered to be the ultimate sign of weakness of a screenwriter. In classic cinema, the voice-over conveys crucial information about the story and tells those stories that are difficult to show on-screen. In *Adaptation.* the narrating voice leads to endless reflections and hampers the progression of the 'story,' which Charlie will not allow to become a worn-out Hollywood tale. The film even ends with Charlie's voice-over as he is leaving a parking garage: 'I know how to finish my script now ... Shit, that's voice-over, McKee would not approve. How to show this thought? I don't know. Who cares what McKee says? ... I wonder who's gonna play me.' Here, the voice-over functions as a strained trick whose narrative significance remains limited to announcing the end of the film. Charlie's voice-over, however, is first and foremost an excessively overused technique that makes the film superbly banal and therefore wonderfully original. The voice-over functions as a built-in guide for interpreting *Adaptation.* as a film that largely adheres to the structure of the classic Hollywood narrations – with an introduction, main conflict, and dénouement – but at the same time turns this tripartite structure into a parody.

Exaggerated Stylistic Imitations for a Magnified Narrative

Excessive stylistic devices offer possibilities for shifting the status of the film narrative when the plot becomes secondary to persiflage, parody, and/or self-reflexive commentary. Only by recognizing the possibility of such a shift can stylistic devices such as excessive use of voice-over or pompous referencing – which seem annoying because they hamper the progression of the story – be properly evaluated. What functions, then, do the stylistic imitations of European art films serve in *The Comfort of Strangers*?

In the introduction to this chapter, I mentioned that the stylistic affinity with films like *L'année dernière à Marienbad* and *Morte a Venezia* has almost no narrative surplus value. The comparison has little narrative significance and rather puts one on the wrong track. Stylistic imitations may afford Schrader's film the 'ambiance' of an art film, but that would be a rather inconsequential argument. (It is precisely this ambiance, moreover, that leaves us unprepared for the horror-like turn of events.)

For a more well-founded argument concerning the function of stylistic citations I want to return to the difference between Schrader's film and his source, McEwan's novel. Early in *The Comfort of Strangers* is a fragment in which the text gives an indication of the disproportionate nature of its own fabula. From his hotel room window, Colin watches a scene down on the street. When he relates the miniature drama to Mary, he blows the incident up to a farce: 'He heard himself exaggerate its small pathos into vaudeville, perhaps in an attempt to gain Mary's full attention … In fact the word "incredible" suggested itself to him at every turn, perhaps because he feared that Mary did not believe him, or because he did not believe himself' (17). According to Ernst Van Alphen, the fragment functions as a reading guide for the novel as a whole. In the same way that Colin exaggerates to convey the scene lucidly and credibly, the narrator 'exaggerates' the representation of Robert's lust for power to provide a clear insight into the novel's homosocial patterns. In this manner, the novel 'confesses' its excessive nature by means of an embedded mirror text.[11]

The film contains no reference to the scene from the novel just mentioned. My point is that the excessiveness of the narrative is conveyed by means of stylistic features such as stately music, the decor of Robert and Caroline's palazzo, the repeated voice-over, and the costumes designed by Giorgio Armani. These excessive aspects on the levels of mise en scène and sound are functional insofar as we read them as portents of an excessive story. The excessive nature of the film's opening is no aim in itself. The overly present style prepares us to see the top-heavy finale as an overstated attempt to expose a certain structure, just as Colin's farcical description of the street scene functions in the same way in the novel. Large parts of the narrative developments might be 'misread' if the viewer or reader adhered to a standard of realism. The artificial style should warrant against such a reading: the venomous undertone of inter-male behaviour comes to the surface only when it is shown through a magnifying lens.[12]

The Benefits of Excess

Kristin Thompson's argument was that excess 'diminishes' when plot, style, content, and form are more evenly balanced.[13] After revising the concept of excess, however, this rule of thumb is no longer necessarily valid. The excessive aspects of style at the beginning of Schrader's film have no narrative function but on closer inspection can be seen to function as a viewing guide for the plot. The extreme style runs parallel to the excessive turn of events. This twist is necessary to make the point of both the novel and the film: under the guise of camaraderie, a man conducts a murderous competition with another man in order to construct his masculinity. This message can only be properly conveyed by means of an ostentatiously magnified narrative, just as the Colin of the novel presumed that the incident he witnessed had to be exaggerated into farce in order to merit attention. The overly accentuated references to *L'année dernière à Marienbad* and *Morte a Venezia* in Schrader's film can be interpreted as a viewing guide that invites the viewer to see the film's fabula as a magnification. The final word on the matter, however, is left to the viewer. Where stylistic devices are so emphatically present that the storylines appear ridiculous, for instance in melodramas, *Bram Stoker's Dracula, Adaptation,* or *The Comfort of Strangers,* the viewer can transcend a naïve (and consequently negative) response by considering whether the excess in fact offers a viewing guide that may serve to ascertain the film's status. It is only when the viewer recognizes melodramas as overly sentimental, *Bram Stoker's Dracula* as purposefully bombastic, *Adaptation* as overly banal, and *The Comfort of Strangers* as a magnification of inter-male behaviour that the old maxim that less is more can be reversed: excess may indeed have its benefits.

Appendix: *The Virgin Suicides* as a Test Case

I would like to recapitulate the most important aspects of this book. In order to test the usefulness of the theory under discussion, I refer to a film not yet mentioned. *The Virgin Suicides* (Sofia Coppola, 1999) may seem to be relatively transparent, but the film has sufficiently complex facets to make an interesting example. For the sake of clarity, I have chosen the somewhat dry form of an enumeration, so that this appendix can function as a checklist for future analyses.

Fabula

The fabula comprises a logical and chronological sequence of events. A reconstruction of the fabula of *The Virgin Suicides* could be as follows. The thirteen-year-old Cecilia Lisbon tries to kill herself but is discovered in time. Shortly afterward, her next suicide attempt succeeds. In the wake of Cecilia's death, her four older sisters (Lux, Bonnie, Mary, and Therese) seem to be getting on with their lives reasonably well. Their parents adopt a strict regime, but as an exception the daughters are allowed to attend the homecoming dance at their high school. When Lux gets home long past the curfew, the sisters are locked up in the house and not allowed to go to school any more. Eventually, all four girls commit suicide on the same night.

Story Time

I earlier defined the story as the way in which the events are presented. In *The Virgin Suicides*, an internal narrator looks back on the events. At the moment of narration, the temporal distance from the events is twenty-five years. As viewers, we are informed of this fact right after the opening credits, when a text appears in the frame: 'Michigan, 25 years ago.' Furniture, fashion, hair styles, and especially music by Electric Light Orchestra, 10cc, Todd Rundgren, and the Bee Gees suggest that the events are taking place in the 1970s. The stretch of time covered by the anachrony is about a year. Only the voice-over provides some clues in this case. Cecilia has slit her wrists at some time during the summer. The film ends the following summer, when the tragedy of the sisters overshadows the debutante parties.

Coppola's film tells the story chronologically and violates the overall narrative structure in only two ways. First, we hear the voice of an internal narrator who speaks about the past from the present. His retrospective voice-over joins in with the sounds of the past (the music and dialogues). This internal narrator is not shown, however, and we never see him in his 'contemporary' guise. Unlike the auditive track, the visual track conforms itself to the chronological line of events in the past. This visual policy is only diverged from once, and this is the second violation of chronological ordering. As a teenager, popular Trip Fontaine had an affair with Lux in the year of her suicide. Many years later, a visibly older Trip gives an interview about that period, but the interviewer is never seen or heard. Fragments of this conversation with the contemporary Trip have been cut into the film three times.

As well as these two violations, minor chronological disturbances occur within specific scenes. We first see Lux waking up on a football field in the early morning after the night of the homecoming dance, for instance, only to be shown later that Trip had left her there alone in the middle of the night.

The Logic of the Story

The fundamentals of classic films are time, space, and causal relations. Time is not completely transparent in *The Virgin Suicides*, but neither is it completely unclear. It can be reconstructed roughly: the film covers a time span somewhere in the middle of the 1970s, lasting from one summer to the next. The location can be pinpointed more accurately. The film takes place in a community somewhere in Michigan. There is a high school, little traffic, a factory nearby, and a lot of elm trees, some of which are sick. Within the community is a clear spatial separation that is experienced negatively by both the boys in the neighbourhood and the Lisbon girls. The Lisbon house was never accessible to just anyone, but after the homecoming dance it is completely shut off from the outside world. The neighbourhood boys, who are fascinated by the sisters, are unable to enter and the girls cannot get out.

Causal relations are much harder to establish. Why does Cecilia commit suicide? Why would the life of a thirteen-year-old be so miserable? The boys cannot provide a definite explanation and come to the conclusion that they are simply unable to fathom the girls. The narrator believes that although the boys were still merely boys, the girls were already 'women in disguise.' It would be an obvious solution to assume that the choice of the four sisters to take their own lives is a direct result of their house arrest of unknown length. At some point, we hear Lux say off-screen, 'We're suffocating ... I can't breathe in here.' Their deaths appear to be a protest against the strict regime of their parents. Nevertheless, as the mother is leaving the house with her husband, we hear her claim, 'None of my daughters lacked for any love. There was plenty of love in our house. I never understood why.'

By the insertion of a voice-over speaking about pieces of the puzzle that do not fit, the film assumes the structure of a search for the precise motivations of the sisters. Four neighbourhood boys interrogate one of their number, Paul Baldino, who claimed to have found Cecilia with her wrists cut. They also question all the boys who claim to have made out with Lux, even though they are terrible braggarts. And, finally, an interview with Trip about his relationship with Lux is conducted many years later.

Some characters are never shown to be interrogated but may have been sources of information for the curious boys. Peter Sisten was a classmate who was once invited by the father to join the Lisbons for dinner. Father Moody visits the house after Cecilia's death. Furthermore, we see television reports by journalist Lydia Perl about Cecilia's death and the protest of the other four sisters against the felling of a sick elm tree. Lydia never speaks to the sisters herself, however, and is consequently unable to provide deeper insight. This lack of insight also applies to the women of the town, who rely on gossip. Information can also come from objects, however. The boys collect all sorts of souvenirs coming from the Lisbon family: as well as finding family photos and Cecilia's diary in the trash, they even go so far as to order the same travel brochures as the family. However, the voice-over can eventually only conclude that they have gathered 'pieces of the puzzle' in every possible way, 'but however we put them together, gaps remained.'

Of all the sources of information mentioned above, Trip is characterized as the most reliable. And his influence is more extensive. It his request alone that finally persuades father Lisbon to allow his four daughters to attend the homecoming dance. At the same time, it is his fault that Lux returns home too late, and he thereby brings about the sisters' isolation. Apart from being a source of information, he also has a crucial influence on the progression of the fabula. Narratologically speaking, Trip is an actant who helps the sisters to escape from the secluded environment of their home but who also further isolates them because of his carelessness and underestimation of the strict house rules.

The Identity of the Voice-Over

The film is constructed by means of the internal narrator's memories, with the Lisbon sisters as the objects of narration. These memories are shared by others, since the narrator continually speaks in the first person plural and never uses the word 'I.' Although the narrator never names himself, it is clear that he belongs to the circle of close friends from the neighbourhood: David Barker, Chase Buell, Parker Denton, and Tim Weiner. We see them sitting on a sidewalk when the voice-over says, 'Even then, as teenagers, we tried to put the pieces together. We still can't.' There are two options: either the narrator is one of the four boys (and in that case, I would opt for Chase),[1] or the identity of the voice-over is 'the collective.' In the second case, the internal narrator is only a spokesperson for the homogeneous, harmonious quartet and represents a patchwork of memories. If the boys are about fifteen years old in the film, they will now be in their forties.

Status of the Voice-Over

The internal narrator in *The Virgin Suicides* distinguishes himself from the other characters in two ways. First, we hear only his voice and never see him as he looks 'now.' For this reason, it is possible to claim that the internal narrator is embedded in the auditive rather than in the visual narration. Second, the internal narrator has the ability to view the events in retrospect. Since he already knows the outcome, he can look back at what transpired years ago with hindsight. The only character who is also capable of retrospective narration is Trip, but he speaks about Lux only now that he has ended up in a psychiatric ward. Trip's commentary restricts itself to the realization that he lost the love of his life when Lux died. The internal narrator's ponderings have a far more reflexive nature.

Keeping these distinctions in mind, it becomes possible to claim that the voice-over is of a different order from the texts of characters. When Paul Baldino explains how he found Cecilia, his story is drowned out by the voice-over stating, 'When Paul said this, we believed him.' The voice-over is of a different order because he is capable of reacting to the text of a character, whereas Paul is unable to refute the voice-over's judgment (unless a postmodern trick were used, in which case Paul might have addressed the voice-over saying, 'You'd better!'). Nevertheless, the voice-over is not superior to any character's text: he does not determine the text of the characters and can supplement only his own observations at most. The voice of the internal narrator would be hierarchically superior only if it were to paraphrase Paul's story without letting us hear him tell it in his own words.

The Relation between Voice-Over and Flashback

In principle the voice-over operates independently of the images, by which I mean to indicate that the internal narrator has no manipulative influence on the images being shown. For this point, see also my discussion of the freeze-frame from *All about Eve* (Chapter 7). Every supposed correspondence between the voice-over and the images it accompanies is based on the interaction between the auditive narrator and the visual narrator. The filmic narrator is responsible for this interaction. A good example involves a different type of voice-over from that of the internal narrator. Lux is watching a documentary about hurricanes in a darkened classroom with her fellow students as Trip takes the empty seat next to her. Up to that point, Lux has given no indication that she is the least bit interested in him. While the camera remains directed at Lux and Trip, we hear the commentator of the documentary speak of warm air and cool air and the way in which they come into contact with one another. We see how Trip moves his arm and how Lux subtly responds to this signal. When the voice-over subsequently explains that 'a surging storm of tremendous strength that strikes with forceful determination' is the result, the links between text and image suggest that the outwardly standoffish Lux has fallen for Trip's charms.

Where the internal narrator is concerned, it is crucial to make a distinction between the scenes he witnessed and the scenes he could not possibly have witnessed. The voice-over, for example, tells us at some point, 'This was the time we began to see Lux making love on the roof with random boys and men.' At the same time, we see the boys gazing at the Lisbons' roof through a telescope. The scene could be considered the way in which the narrator remembers Lux's habit. However, when the voice-over remarks, 'The girls were taken out of school and Mrs Lisbon shut the house in maximum security isolation,' the status of the accompanying images is quite different. We see the four sisters sitting together in a melancholy way. This scene cannot possibly have been witnessed by the narrator. Furthermore, no outsider or visitor is present who might have informed the narrator about the girls' mood.[2] This leaves two options: either the visual narrator is showing us how the voice-over imagines the girls after their harsh punishment, or it is showing us the situation in the Lisbon house regardless of the internal narrator's text. In the first case, the visual narrator conforms itself to the vision and expectations of the voice-over. In the second, the correspondence of text and image would be only a coincidence. Therefore, the status of the images accompanied by the voice-over depends on the manner of focalization. Could the scenes have been observed by the internal narrator (or another outsider), or are they only the product of the narrator's imagination (because inside witnesses are lacking)?

Visual Focalization

In order to analyse focalization, we need to make some technical distinctions. First, the identity of the focalizor needs to be taken into consideration. We need to ask several questions about *The Virgin Suicides*. What events could and what events could not have been directly perceived by the four neighbourhood boys, the group that the narrator is a part of? Which scenes have been witnessed by another character able to provide the boys with crucial information, such as Trip or Peter Sisten? And what scenes have taken place within the privacy of the Lisbon house and could not have been focalized by a third party? I discussed these points in the previous section.

Second, the reliability of focalization needs to be evaluated. Are we dealing with 'pure' internal focalization? Are optical effects being used to signify a distorted perception? If so, which ones? The most conventional way of signalling focalization occurs by means of the eyeline match principle. We see a character looking at something outside the frame, after which we see a shot of what this character is looking at. The order of this procedure can also be reversed. The scene with the telescope is a good example of narratively motivated focalization. We see the boys take turns at gazing through the telescope. Each time, we see what they are directing the lens at, we see the movements they make with the instrument, we see them adjusting the focus, and we observe how they zoom in on conspicuous details, such as a hat belonging to a Burger Chalet uniform. In shots like these, we are looking directly through the telescope along with the boys.

Nevertheless, Coppola's film also contains evidently hallucinatory shots. At a certain point, Tim drowsily sits up in his bed. In a reverse shot, we see Cecilia sitting next to him. Still feeling somewhat groggy, Tim looks stunned. In the next shot, Cecilia says, 'God, you snore loud.' Again, there is a shot of Tim, who now startles as the alarm clock starts ringing. Immediately following this scene, we see Chase being brought to school by car. When he looks outside, the reverse shot reveals Cecilia lying on the branch of a tree. Rather than any optical effect, it is the narrative embedding of these shots that determines their hallucinatory nature. Since Cecilia is dead, neither of the boys can actually have seen her. The fact that they do indicates only that she is still present in the back of their minds: they are still (day)dreaming about her.

Optical effects are used in several other scenes. At the beginning of the film, the girls are introduced visually by means of freeze-frames, with the four boys watching from the side. In some scenes, the sisters are also shown in slow motion. Both procedures emphasize the magnetic impact of the sisters on the internal focalizors. Time seems to stand still as they walk by. When Alice's debutante party seems to take place in slow motion at the end of the film, the effect corresponds to the boys' experience: they are so distraught at the tragedy that they cannot bring themselves to enjoy the party.

The overwhelming impression that Lux makes on Trip is also conveyed by means of optical effects. In order to avoid getting caught cutting class, Trip sneaks into a random classroom and sits down at one of the desks. Then we see a shot that might be focalized by Trip (although the camera does not entirely coincide with his eyeline). It is completely out of focus, characterizing his mental absence after smoking marihuana. As the shot suddenly comes into focus again, Trip is sitting behind Lux. Because she turns around, we see her face shift from blurred to focused and then a sparkle appears in her left eye. This shot – from the blur to the sparkle – shows in a few seconds that Trip, the internal focalizor, is dazzled by the sudden appearance of Lux.

Third, the embedding of each instance of focalization needs to be determined. Can the internal focalizor focalize 'autonomously' or is he also (partially) visible in the frame? And is the internal focalizor not being focalized himself? The first question concerns the distinction between an eyeline match, an over-the-shoulder shot (see the analysis of *E.T.* in Chapter 6), and external focalization that conforms itself to the perception of an internal focalizor (see the example of *The Gold Rush*, also in Chapter 6). In the scenes of the telescope, the daydreams, and Trip's sudden encounter with Lux, we continually see eyeline matches, and in some cases we even have an eyeline match that coincides completely with the point of view of the focalizor (a subjective shot). As a general rule, the measure in which a character can focalize 'autonomously' indicates the development of his subjectivity in the film and determines the extent of the influence of his point of view on the story.[3] The scene in which Trip joins the Lisbons to watch television offers a good example of this principle. While mother Lisbon is sitting between him and Lux, we see a close-up of Trip as he looks to the right, in the direction of the girl. A next shot shows his eyeline match: one of Lux's bare feet is subtly moving on the table. Again, there is a close-up of Trip, who visibly gulps. The sequence of shots makes clear that he takes Lux's internally focalized gesture as an erotic signal. Then we see Trip, Lux, and her mother in a three-shot; the latter instructs her daughter to take her foot off the table, after which she puts the TV guide on it. Because we do not see an internal focalization of the mother, it remains unclear how exactly she interprets the foot on the table. Is it simply inappropriate, does she merely intend to put the TV guide on the table, or does she object to the erotic signal her daughter is giving off? Due to the eyeline match sequence, we have a much clearer idea how Trip interprets Lux's action.

In Coppola's film, we are shown what the boys (including Trip) think about the girls rather often, but the way in which the sisters regard the boys remains largely shrouded in mystery. The girls are happy that they are allowed to attend the homecoming dance, but they did not get to choose their dates. The boys have 'divided' the sisters among themselves and it remains uncertain how happy the sisters are with the partners they end up with. The only exception is Lux, who had been invited by Trip personally. As each of the girls embraces her date, the camera pans down and shows Lux's dress at the level of her hips. As in an iris shot, we are looking through a hole in her dress and see that the name 'Trip' is embroidered on her underwear. (Cecilia's diary has already made clear that Lux has done the same in the past with the name 'Kevin'). By means of an iris, the shot shows a detail that none of the characters can see. This makes the shot an exclusive external focalization of the visual narrator (the auditive track does not refer to it). At the same time, however, the iris can be seen as a mental focalization on Lux's part: it is an indication that her thoughts are completely with Trip as they are kissing and that her feelings for him are real. In this sense, the shot is symptomatic for the narrative structure of the film: the boys can focalize 'autonomously,' but Lux's perspective on Trip has to be mediated by the external focalizor.

Although some scenes in *The Virgin Suicides* do feature internal focalization by the sisters, these instances remain conditional. A scene with Dominic Palazzolo illustrates this. Dominic was madly in love with Diana Porter. We see him watching Diana as she plays tennis. The close-ups and slow-motion shots of the girl emphasize Dominic's obsession with her. When Diana goes on vacation, Dominic jumps off the roof 'to proof the validity of his love.' Before we see the actual jump in long shot, we see a shot of Cecilia and Mary, who are watching from a distance. Dominic's suicide is thus focalized by two of the Lisbon girls, but its impact on Cecilia's choice to take her own life remains tentative. The incident is part of a sequence of wild rumours, among which are ridiculous speculations such as 'she just wanted out of that decorating scheme' (referring to the Lisbon's rather dull interior design). According to the voice-over, the incident with Dominic is 'the most popular theory' within this sequence. No optical effects are used to specify the nature of the girls' focalization further. By embedding it in a series of speculations, the 'theory' about the incident with Dominic tells us more about the prevalent gossip on the block than about the possible motivations for Cecilia's choice. The focalization of Cecilia and Mary remains embedded in the fantasies of others about them.

Films always contain all sorts of characters whose only function is internal focalization. The focalization of these 'extra' characters has a supporting function and is embedded in a pre-existing point of view in order to specify it further. In order to emphasize that admiration for Lux is not just a quirk of a few adolescents, the voice-over refers to a knife sharpener: 'Almost every day ... Lux would suntan, wearing a swimsuit that caused the knife sharpener to give her a fifteen minute demonstration for free.' We see a close-up of Lux's cleavage, followed by a shot of the knife sharpener. He is not paying any attention to his work, but is blissfully staring at the Lisbon house instead. His function in the story does not lie on the level of the action but is to emphasize that the assessment of Lux's attractiveness is widely shared. The fact that the shot preceding the image of the knife sharpener was so close only indicates how much Lux is drawing attention to herself.

As Trip is introduced, his sex appeal is also accentuated, but these focalizations are of a different nature than in Lux's case. First, the voice-over reports that the assessment of Trip's beauty is shared only by women: Trip has just 'emerged from baby fat to the delight of girls and mothers alike.' We first see his boots, after which the camera gradually scans upward. Nothing indicates that Trip has any problems with being screened up close by the visual narrator. Shortly afterward, as the song 'Magic Man' by Heart starts playing,[4] Trip is filmed in slow motion as he is walking down the hall. Behind his back, we see the girls he passes turn their heads toward him with admiring glances. Since they are in the image, the girls themselves are objects of focalization (for the external visual narrator), but within the story they are focalizors. Their presence is functional to convince the viewer (and the internal narrator) that Trip's beauty is widely recognized by females.

Auditive Focalization

Internal focalization of sound takes place if that which is heard can be attributed to a specific character; such a character can nonetheless be an object of visual focalization. In a scene from *The Virgin Suicides*, we see father Lisbon in long shot as he is standing in the hallway. His posture seems to imply that he is listening. Softly, we hear a muted dialogue. Lux says, 'We're suffocating,' to which another voice replies, 'You're safe here.' Lux answers, 'I can't breathe in here.' At that point we hear the sound at a volume that implies that the microphone is hanging over the father's head; the scene is comparable to the example taken from *Only Angels Have Wings* (Chapter 8). Another example of internal auditive focalization in which image and sound correlate can be seen during the homecoming dance. When Trip and Lux hide under a stage, the volume of the music and people speaking on the stage is suddenly muted. This corresponds to the new position of the young lovers.

A character can be seen perceiving an imaginary sound in the scene in which Lux is dreamily staring out of the window after she has been locked in the house. At that moment, we hear Trip's voice whispering, just as before at one of their first meetings, 'You're a stone fox.' His voice is imaginary and turns out to be resonating in her head.

A more complex instance can be found when Cecilia starts reading passages from her own diary. In films, the principle of a writer's voice reciting his own text while a reader is reading those same lines is rather common. In this case, it is possible that the boys hear Cecilia's voice again as they are reading. Her voice is still alive in their memory, even though Cecilia is already dead. However, this option is complicated by the way in which Cecilia interrupts the boys' reading. Chase reads the passage in which Cecilia writes about Lux's love for a garbage man: 'Lux lost it over Kevin ... Is it Heines?' His three friends confirm the pronunciation. However, the posthumous voice of Cecilia corrects the wrong pronunciation of Kevin's last name: 'Lux lost it over Kevin Haines, the garbage man.' This correction of 'Heines' into 'Haines' makes clear that Cecilia, as posthumous object of narration, is speaking to us in a language disconnected from the story itself here. Her words sound as if they are out of the reach of the other characters and directed straight at us. Cecilia's position is similar to that of the voice-over, who also cannot be heard by the characters in the film; the internal narrator and the characters exist in different time frames.

Excess

In this book, I have argued that excess is 'neutralized' if stylistic aspects are motivated by the story. Excess is the result when style drowns out the plot. As a supplement to this notion, I have proposed that excess can also signify a style that contains clues concerning the attitude one should adopt while reading or viewing the (filmic) text.

'Hard' stylistic features are rare in *The Virgin Suicides,* and where they do occur they seem to be narratively motivated. We see a split screen while the boys and girls play each other music via phone calls. This abrupt effect is nevertheless functional because the shot effectively shows both the spatial distance and the mental connection between the characters. Moments in which the filmic movement is interrupted are also legitimized by the situation. The sisters are introduced by means of freeze-frames. Other frozen shots signify that a photo is being taken at the time. The most abrupt effect is the camera jumping forward from a class picture to a close-up of Lux, but this is explained by the advice given by the voice-over to be alert to danger signals (such as the possible dilation of the Lisbon girls' pupils).

When studying *The Virgin Suicides* from a stylistic angle, the film's 'soft' techniques stand out. The film abounds in warm, radiant tints, and pastel colours. The shots of sunlight splendidly shining through the foliage are symptomatic. The dissolve, which is the 'softest' shot transition imaginable, is used frequently. Intermittently, the technique of slow motion is used. When the camera moves, it does so only at a regular pace and often in a way that can be narratively legitimized. The camera glides past the houses as the teenagers travel to the homecoming dance by car, and the final shot consists of a camera tracking backward, away from the boys. This second camera movement, which is spatial, seems to be signifying a temporal distance. As they grow older, they leave the events of their adolescence behind.

Although the subject of teenage suicide is, in the final instance, a harsh one, Coppola's film has a gentle atmosphere. The logic of this contrast lies in the boys' sweet memories of the girls. The superimposition at the beginning of the film is revealing: in it, we see a shot of a beautiful sky with the image of a winking Lux superimposed, as if she greets us from the afterlife. Her image has faded, but years later her presence is still felt in the community. The deaths of the Lisbon girls seem to mark the end of an idyllic period in the lives of the boys. They have made exotic journeys with the sisters in their imagination, which are shown in imaginary shots of slides; according to the narrator, the boys were 'happier with dreams than wives.' Already at the beginning, the voice-over remarks that the Lisbon suicides marked the start of the neighbourhood's demise: 'wiped-out elms, harsh sunlight and the continuing decline of our auto industry.' It does not matter whether there actually is any demise. The point is that the internal narrator has experienced the times that followed as a decline. The reversal also translates into a shift in colours and lighting. After the deaths of the Lisbon girls, the empty house has a cold, bluish glow. At Alice's debutante party at the close of the film, somewhat awkward green lighting is dominant.[5]

When considered in this way, the film's style is an expression of the mood of the boys. However, the soft stylistic features can also be taken as a reading guide that helps solve the film's great mystery: what has driven these girls to suicide? How were they made up psychologically, and what aspect of their characters made them choose for such a desperate option? The only textual hint is given when Tim attempts to characterize Cecilia by analysing her handwriting. According to him, she is 'a dreamer, completely out of touch with reality. She probably thought she could fly.' His exclamation sounds like a wild hypothesis, a wild hypothesis, moreover, that can be viewed ironically because Tim is dubbed 'The Brain' by the voice-over. Within his circle of friends back then he might have had that status, but from the mouth of a narrator looking back the epithet sounds somewhat derisive.

Nevertheless, Cecilia's dreamy character is accentuated in the film's most pregnant scene (stylistically speaking). While we hear Cecilia read her diary, we see a sequence of matte shots. These have been subdivided into several areas. On the left, for instance, we see Cecilia reading, while the area to the right refers to a fragment from her diary. Shortly afterward, we see a passage from her diary being visualized on the left, while the boys are reading the diary on the right. The transition between shots is never as fluent as is this sequence of matte shots.

On the one hand, it is possible that the sequence is filtered by the boys' perception, which has been influenced by Tim's analysis. On the other hand, I have suggested that this scene disconnects itself from the (living) characters. Cecilia's correction of the pronunciation of the name 'Haines' marks the start of a blurry matte sequence. This sequence suggests an esoteric and unearthly character, which can be projected on to Cecilia. Because of its excessive style, this sequence transcends the boys' perspective of the Lisbon sisters. The style evokes a dreamy sense of softness that can be taken as an indication of the characters of the sisters. Because of the style, the visual narrator tells another story that seems to carry the suggestion of a cause: constrained by their overprotective parents, the sisters were too soft and too dreamy for this world.

The voice-over in *The Virgin Suicides* cannot pinpoint the exact motive for the suicides of the Lisbon girls. It could be said that the style of Coppola's film, with the many soft optic effects employed by the visual narrator, matches the pleasant memories of the narrator's group with respect to the time before the collective suicide of the Lisbon girls. At the same time, there is reason to assume that the film's style is overly soft and consequently detaches itself from the voice-over of the boys. The visual narrator could instead be adopting the perspective of Cecilia and her sisters. Whereas the text speaks about a missing piece of the puzzle, the excessive style offers a guide for the viewer to fill in this gap: above all, the sisters desired to escape from a harsh reality.

Notes

Introduction

1 At a press conference, cited in Lunenfeld, 'The Myths of Interactive Cinema,' 151.

2 A film can offer a light-hearted parody of the happy ending, as *Wild at Heart* does (David Lynch, 1990), or, alternatively, can venomously criticize this convention, as *The Player* does (Robert Altman, 1992). The main character might also fail to achieve a rather suspect aim; in *My Best Friend's Wedding* (P.J. Hogan, 1997), for instance, Julianne Potter tries to sabotage the marriage of an old friend and eventually fails.

3 In this book, I refer to the reader or viewer as 'he' for the sake of convenience. This accords with grammatical rules, but of course the reader or viewer can just as well refer to a female subject.

4 See Elsaesser 'The Pathos of Failure,' 281. In this article, which originally appeared in 1975, he posits the idea of the 'unmotivated hero.' Apart from *Five Easy Pieces, Bonnie and Clyde* (Arthur Penn, 1967), *The Graduate* (Mike Nichols, 1967), *Easy Rider* (Dennis Hopper, 1969), *The Long Goodbye* (Robert Altman, 1973), and *Taxi Driver* (Martin Scorsese, 1976) also belong to this first phase of New Hollywood Cinema.

5 Lunenfeld, 'The Myths of Interactive Cinema,' 151.

6 The term 'popcorn movie' was coined by Dean Devlin, the producer of *Godzilla*.

7 In his *Interface en cyberspace*, Jan Simons discusses the modular, 'box of bricks' structure of contemporary Hollywood films. Characters get their function and meaning according to their structural position in the story; these structural positions can be considered familiar to 'an audience that has already internalized the morphology of the action and adventure film

... The true heroes of modern day Hollywood are not the characters of a film, but its special effects, its luxurious settings ... its extravagant vehicles, its hideous and terrifying monsters ... and the awe-inspiring destructiveness of its natural disasters' (174, translated by SvdL).

8 *Nashville* (1975), a film by Robert Altman about country musicians and politicians, can be considered a precursor of the current vogue for ensemble films.

9 Žižek, *Enjoy Your Symptom!* 205–6.

10 By emphasizing the altered nature of narration in cinema, I affiliate myself with critics who draw attention to changes within the history of film. This position is in accordance with the historical discussions of an eminent film scholar such as Thomas Elsaesser. It is diametrically opposed, however, to that of Kristin Thompson (*Storytelling*) and David Bordwell (*The Way Hollywood Tells It*). In their view, contemporary (American) cinema is 'hyperclassical' and, as such, highly indebted to the film narratives of the studio era. In these studies Thompson and Bordwell claim that even the most innovative modern films still base themselves on the classical tradition. They argue that every claim that postclassic cinema has a face of its own is unfounded, asserting that it is in fact nothing more than a series of adaptations of the success formula of classic Hollywood. To quote Bordwell's catchphrase, modern films are based on an 'intensified continuity' with classic Hollywood.

11 New media are associated with digital, multimedia, and interactive features, but Jan Simons (*Interface en cyberspace*, 88) indicates that these terms are too indefinite to characterize them. In some ways, the new media do not incorporate more media than an older medium such as film. Furthermore, the prospect of interactivity is not always fully realized. Consequently, the features cannot be said to define the new media, although they can offer useful opportunities to explore the potential of the new media.

12 Bordwell, *Narration in the Fiction Film*, 62.

13 Branigan, *Narrative Comprehension and Film*, 107.

14 Bal's 1978 study was *De theorie van vertellen en verhalen*. In their *Vertelduivels*, translated as *Handbook of Narrative Analysis*, Herman and Vervaeck claim that this introduction to narratology still functions as 'the ultimate reference' in many handbooks and syllabi (17). For me, her work holds the same status. For this reason, I have reduced my interventions in the theoretical debate on narratology to a minimum; my primary interest is the practical application of the theory. Therefore, this book presents a version of a narrative theory that has been specifically adapted for film: it does not give 'a representative selection' of the many guides you can consult when

dealing with stories, as Herman and Vervaeck do in their *Handbook of Narrative Analysis* (9). Their study complements mine, but the two books can be read in whichever order the reader wishes.

15 The productiveness of Bal's work is demonstrated by several studies that transpose her theoretical terms to other forms of art, such as music (Meelberg, *New Sounds*), theatre (Bleeker, *Visuality in the Theatre*), and photography (Tops, *Fotos*). In her *Fotos met gezag* (Photographs with Authority), Ellen Tops uses a picture of a confirmation ritual to interpret the shift from perspective to focalization. The photograph was taken over the shoulder of the bishop. The perspective (or external focalization), in other words, is from behind his back. In the picture, we see the admiring gaze of a boy looking up to the bishop's face (which is invisible to us). The boy functions as an internal focalizor. By means of the boy's face, we get an impression of the trustworthy face of the bishop (166–70).

16 Sasha Vojkovic has attempted to introduce Bal in the field of film studies. Paradoxically, her 'problem' is that the stakes she raises in her dissertation 'Subjectivity in New Hollywood Cinema' are rather high. She uses narratology to map New Hollywood by means of philosophical and psychoanalytical digressions (Plato, Derrida, Deleuze and Guattari, Freud, Lacan). Consequently, her philosophical film study transcends the scope of the book I intend to write.

17 I put the term 'identity' between quotation marks because the narrator is an agent and hence not anthropomorphized.

18 Bal, *Narratology*, 5.

19 *Le Mépris* (Jean-Luc Godard, 1963) demonstrates that adapting literature to film is not an unproblematic process of transposition. In this film, producer Jeremy Prokosch bursts out in anger when he attends a test screening of a film adaptation of Homer's *Odyssey*. He is extremely disappointed at the shots of statues and the static, theatrical scenes being shown: after all, 'That's not what's in the script.' After quickly skimming through the script, he corrects himself, 'Yes, it is in the script, but that's not what you have on screen.' Director Fritz Lang wittily responds, 'That's right, because in the script, it is written and on the screen it is pictures.' By means of this sobering reply, Lang points out to the producer that word and image belong to different media and that the transformation of text into film is often attended by mistaken expectations. Nevertheless, Prokosch does attempt to produce a script that is more faithful to the canonical work of literature by hiring a different scriptwriter. This should ideally lead to the film he has in mind. His attempt will turn out to be in vain, however, since the film is continually staging flawed translations and other forms of miscom-

munication. At the end of the film, the shooting starts again with neither the screenwriter nor the producer. With their absence, *Le Mépris* distances itself from the idea that a written text can be readily copied in a film. Film needs to be judged by its own merits.

Chapter 1: Is Cinema Essentially Narrative?

1 Bal, *Narratology*, 146.
2 For this distinction, see Herman and Vervaeck, *Vertelduivels*, 52–3.
3 Bal, *Reading 'Rembrandt,'* 166–7.
4 Bal, *Quoting Caravaggio*, 177.
5 Gaudreault, 'Film, Narrative, Narration,' 71.
6 Chatman, 'What Novels Can Do,' 129.
7 Instead of the filmic term 'photo frames,' Sean Cubitt prefers the term 'pixels' from the vocabulary of digitization (Cubitt, *The Cinema Effect*). For a critique of this 'terminological back flip' of Cubitt's history, see Stewart, *Framed Time*, 12.
8 Cubitt, *The Cinema Effect*, 15.
9 The principle of 'cutting' was introduced by Georges Méliès with his stop-motion technique. By freezing the image, he let a seated woman hidden under a cloth disappear in his film *Escamotage d'une dame au théâtre Robert Houdin* (1896). He 'magically' turned her into a skeleton before bringing her back to her former place. In the early magic act films of Méliès, the image changed by stopping the recording and replacing something in the image (the skeleton suddenly turned into a woman again). Whereas in these demonstrations of illusionism the camera position remained the same, Méliès's later films featured changing camera positions.
10 Cubitt, *The Cinema Effect*, 28.
11 Gaudreault, 'Film, Narrative, Narration,' 70–1.
12 Ibid., 73.
13 Ibid.
14 The way in which films that depart from the notion of chronological time (such as time-travel films) employ specific and precise indications of time as a structuring narrative mechanism is also noteworthy. In *Donnie Darko* (Richard Kelly, 2002), Donnie is warned by a giant rabbit on 2 October 1988 that the world will end in 28 days, 6 hours, 42 minutes, and 12 seconds. The film counts down by means of title cards: 'twenty days to go,' 'four days to go,' or 'six hours to go.' Eventually, Donnie will travel back to 2 October by means of a wormhole and a jet engine and end up at the time the film started: right before the rabbit's prophecy.

15 Chatman, 'What Novels Can Do,' 130.
16 In *Baisers volés* (François Truffaut, 1968), we see how Antoine is fired from the military, how he ruins his job as night porter in a hotel, and, finally, how he attempts to get by while working as a detective.
17 Chatman, 'What Novels Can Do,' 130.
18 See Gunning, *D.W. Griffith*, 41.
19 The early cinema was promoted with slogans such as 'Visit the wonder of cinema, marvel at what can be done with this new machine.' Visitors came to see the projector rather than the film; consequently, advertising focused on the device showing the movie: the Cinématographe, the Biograph, and the Vitascope (Gunning, *D.W. Griffith*, 42).
20 Crafton, 'Pie and Chase,' 111.
21 Gunning, 'Response to "Pie and Chase,"' 121.
22 Gunning, 'The Cinema of Attractions,' 61.
23 For their discussion of *Ballet mécanique*, see Bordwell and Thompson, *Film Art*, 7th ed., 150–4.
24 A comparable argument can be made with respect to other experimental films from the 1920s – *Anémic cinéma* (Marcel Duchamp, 1926), for instance – and short-lived movements like *cinéma pur*. Bordwell and Thompson themselves also refer to *Mothlight* (Stan Brakhage, 1963), in which the wings of dead moths, twigs, and small leaves have been glued to the film strip (*Film Art*, 4th ed., 106).
25 Thompson, 'The Concept of Cinematic Excess,' 132.
26 Ibid., 132.
27 Bordwell, *Narration*, 53.
28 Bonitzer, 'The Disappearance,' 215.
29 Culler discusses this example in the chapter 'Semiotics as a Theory of Reading' in *The Pursuit of Signs*, 47–79.
30 Bal, *Narratology*, 11.
31 Žižek, *Enjoy Your Symptom!* 35–7.
32 Meijer, *In tekst gevat*, 34.
33 The French film magazine *Cahiers du cinéma* was founded in 1951 by (among others) André Bazin. Young talents like François Truffaut and Jean-Luc Godard wrote for the magazine even before they made their first films. In an inflammatory article published in 1954, Truffaut fiercely protested against so-called quality films that adhered to standard narrative conventions. According to Truffaut, a director should preferably base his film on a script he had written himself in order to give his own hallmark to the final product.
34 See Metz, *Psychoanalysis and Cinema*, 91–8.

35 Bordwell, *Narration*, 23–4.
36 Vojkovic, 'Subjectivity,' 104.
37 The early cinema of attractions consisted of sketches performed for the viewer, but this convention has gradually been exchanged for the principle of ignoring the viewer altogether. In classic cinema, a second person is consistently present precisely because of these attempts to avoid the viewer, who must not be deterred by becoming the object of the cinematic look himself. The dictum that forbids actors to look into the camera, as if to spare the viewer the feeling of being watched, is rather well known. *The Purple Rose of Cairo* (Woody Allen, 1985) exploits the feeling of shock that results from a look directed at the audience from the screen. Cecilia, a loyal moviegoer who always goes to the films of actor Tom Baxter, is suddenly addressed by her hero of the big screen. Understandably, she reacts with surprise: 'Are you talking to me?' From that moment on, the entire film in which Tom operates as a character is lost. The plot dwindles because Tom gets down off the screen to have a date with Cecilia. *The Purple Rose of Cairo* itself, however, has not become insupportable as film: it has only entered a meta-level. It is a film about a film that is lost because of a direct look aimed at its viewer. We experience the danger of becoming the object of the look through Cecilia. But as a stand-in for the viewer, she offers a necessary buffer.
38 The documentary *The Celluloid Closet* (Rob Epstein and Jeffrey Friedman, 1995), which was based on Vito Russo's eponymous study, demonstrates a similar principle. According to the directions of the Production Code, homosexuality was forbidden subject matter in Hollywood films of the 1940s and 1950s. The viewer who is determined to discover subtle hints of homosexuality, however, can find enough suggestive material in several films. A clear example is a scene from *Red River* (Howard Hawks, 1948), in which two cowboys long to feel each other's 'weapon' in their hands. In *Ben Hur* (William Wyler, 1959), furthermore, the desiring glances that Masala directs at his old friend Ben Hur tell a story of homosexual love along with the story of their close relationship.

Chapter 2: Basic Principles of Narratology

1 Bal, *Narratology*, 78.
2 See McEwan, *The Comfort*, 31–41.
3 Ibid., 108–11.
4 Martin Amis's novel *Time's Arrow* (1991) relies on a complete reversal of chronology. All events are narrated backward: 'First I stack the clean plates

in the dishwasher ... then you select a soiled dish, collect some scraps from the garbage, and settle down for a short wait. Various items get gulped up into my mouth, and after skillful massage with tongue and teeth I transfer them to the plate for additional sculpture with knife and fork and spoon' (p. 11). The question propelling this experiment is whether our assessment of morally dubious characters changes if we drastically reverse time.

5 See McEwan, *The Comfort*, 77–87.

6 Bal uses the term *anachrony* to mean a 'deviation from chronology,' by way of explaining differences between the arrangement in the story and the chronology of the fabula (*Narratology*, 83).

7 Bal calls this technique an 'iterative presentation.' There are several variations, such as singular presentation (one event, one presentation) and repetition (one event, multiple presentations). See Bal, *Narratology*, 111–14.

8 A good example of such a psychological evaluation is the sentence 'They were inhibited by a feeling that these past few days had been nothing more than a form of parasitism, an unacknowledged conspiracy of silence disguised by so much talk' (McEwan, *The Comfort*, 91).

9 The fact that Robert wants to be physically close to Colin – by walking hand in hand, for instance – can be attributed to the masculine culture of the holiday destination (McEwan, *The Comfort*, 100).

10 The idea of a homosocial motif is partially inspired by Ernst Van Alphen's analysis of McEwan's novel (*Art in Mind*, 99–119).

Chapter 3: The Narrative Impact of the Mise en Scène

1 Because this quotation starts with 'He was shorter than Colin,' it would be logical to assume that the internal focalization can be attributed to Mary. This is not necessarily so: Colin can also immediately notice that he is taller than Robert. Preceding this passage, the narrator describes how Colin had already attempted to pass by the man when the latter grabbed his wrist. He has been close enough to measure himself in relation to Robert, in other words.

2 As soon as the continuous showing is interrupted, anyone will suspect that they are dealing with a special cinematic experiment. *La jetée* (Chris Marker, 1962), for instance, consists of a sequence of photo stills and a voice-over comment and has only one second of moving images as we know them from conventional cinema.

3 See Chatman, *Coming to Terms*, 38–41.

4 Thompson and Bordwell, *Film History*, 150.

5 I have adopted this example from a paper by Franca Treur.
6 See Van Oosterhout, *'Morocco,'* 125.
7 Hall, 'Daddy Dearest,' 88.
8 Sneek, 'Een wonder,' 32, trans. SvdL.
9 The element of 'unmotivated light' is mentioned by Van Sijll, *Cinematic Storytelling,* 204. She also uses the scene from *Léon* as an example.
10 Bordwell and Thompson (*Film History,* 182) also discuss this example from *Play Time.*

Chapter 4: The Narrative Impact of Cinematography

1 Barthes, *Camera Lucida,* 96.
2 The fact that these freeze-frames are in black and white enhances a Barthesian reading. He considers black and white to be 'original' and cannot shake the feeling that colour is simply a cosmetic addition (Barthes, *Camera Lucida,* 81).
3 This example is also mentioned in Phillips, *Film,* 63.
4 The joke that we already see what is taking place behind Johnny's back because of the position of the camera in *The General* is eventually also a joke at the expense of the viewer. When Johnny is resting after his hard labour, he does not look behind him but in front of him; what he sees is not yet visible to us as viewers. A reverse shot shows that this side is also crawling with enemy troops. In other words, we may have thought that Johnny did not see the troops behind his back, but in the end, according to Gilberto Perez (*The Material Ghost,* 112), we missed the troops 'behind our own backs' as well.
5 Rack focus is used mainly when someone or something is not noticed at first, but suddenly comes into view later. In *The Graduate* (Mike Nichols, 1968), for instance, Benjamin Braddock is talking to Elaine Robinson when he suddenly discovers her mother – the famous Mrs Robinson from the Simon and Garfunkel song – standing in the doorway. Initially, her contours are vague, but the focus suddenly switches as Benjamin looks over Elaine's shoulder. Suddenly, the mother is in focus at Elaine's expense. This change of focus indicates the shocking realization that Mrs Robinson has been overhearing the conversation in which Benjamin was trying to tell Elaine about his affair with her mother.
6 A fine example of camera movement used for another effect – that of irony – can be found in the high school comedy *Election* (Alexander Payne, 1999). Three very different candidates are running for the student body presidency, for divergent reasons. The night before the elections, all three

pray to the 'dear lord Jesus.' The ambitious Tracy Flick prays for a victory so she can 'carry out Your will on earth.' Tammy Metzler is indifferent to winning the election. She is not religious, but looks at praying as practice for the convent school she will eventually be sent to. She prays mainly for expensive leather pants and friendship with Madonna. Her brother Paul, a good-natured pushover, prays that his sister will be happy and reminds us, 'You decide who's the best.' With all three prayers the camera moves upward, away from the character. That is consistent, because the camera moves in the direction of the higher entity to whom the prayers are being offered. By moving away from the characters, however, the camera also comments on the completely trivial nature of their requests.

7 In *Strangers on a Train*, the opening sequence shows Guy's legs moving from left to right. Through cross-cutting, we see Bruno's legs moving from right to left. Because the movement from left to right is more natural, this particular movement emphasizes the fact that Guy is far more 'normal' than Bruno. See Van Sijll, *Cinematic Storytelling*, 4.

8 Waardenburg, 'Lessen,' 8, trans. SvdL.

9 See Thompson and Bordwell, *Film History*, 425.

Chapter 5: Story and Fabula Disconnected through Editing

1 See Elsaesser and Barker, 'Introduction,' 296.

2 Cross-cutting can also be 'false.' In *Dressed to Kill* (Brian de Palma, 1980), Liz Blake believes she is being pursued by a blonde, manic woman who has recently committed a murder. This woman is apparently called Bobbi. The chase is intercut with what seems to be a scene taking place at the same time. In his office, Dr Robert Elliott contacts Bobbi by telephone. The manner of editing suggests that the psychiatrist is informing Bobbi while she is stalking Liz. In the end, Elliott himself turns out to be cross-dressing as Bobbi. Logically, the phone call cannot have taken place at the same time. The apparent cross-cutting sequence was a distraction to clear Elliott of suspicion.

3 For a detailed analysis of *A Corner in Wheat*, see Gunning, *D.W. Griffith*, 240–53.

4 A dissolve is often used to suggest the transition from a diegetic reality to the mental condition of a certain character. Because of the frequent use of dissolves in *Eyes Wide Shut* (Stanley Kubrick, 1999), the nightly adventures of Dr Bill Harford can be considered a product of his imagination. *Hiroshima mon amour* (Alain Resnais, 1959) also presents a functional use of dissolves. The memories that the female protagonist is trying to hold on to

are shown in scenes that cross over into each other extremely slowly; the 'old' image is still visible behind the 'new' image for a long time. Here, this technique appeals to the hope that the memories will not fade.

5 I would like to thank Frédéric Sanders for this example.

6 In the early years of cinema, a close-up did not yet create narrative continuity but was an attraction in and of itself. Tom Gunning refers to *The Gay Shoe Clerk* (Edwin S. Porter, 1903), in which the close-up of a woman's ankle in a shoe is a case of 'pure exhibitionism' without any narrative motivation (*D.W. Griffith*, 42).

7 Heath, *Questions of Cinema*, 119.

8 See Chapter 16 and 17 in Lacan, *Four Fundamental Concepts*.

9 It is almost impossible to capture the structure of shot and reverse shot in a single recording. Imagine, for instance, two burglars looking at a safe while their reflection is at the same time visible on the safe door. A film that employed this reflection trick for its entire duration would eventually become terribly exhausting.

10 Jean-Pierre Oudart, Daniel Dayan, Stephen Heath, and Kaja Silverman have either introduced or further developed the concept of suture for film studies.

11 Heath claims that narrative 'makes the join, the suture' (*Questions of Cinema*, 119).

12 For a more elaborate explanation of the Kuleshov experiment, see Peters, *Het bezielde beeld*, 38.

13 See Verstraten, *Screening Cowboys*, 70–2.

14 A film can also frustrate suture deliberately. In Chapter 4, I referred to Campion's *Portrait of a Lady* as a film with remarkably few establishing shots (if they are used, they are often askew) and relatively many close-ups. We see the lady's head more than enough from the outside, but we almost never share her point of view or her vision. We are finally unable to grasp her motives, which has a frustrating effect. Whereas *Portrait of a Lady* makes a basically sympathetic character inscrutable by neglecting the rules of suture, *Psycho* paints a sympathetic portrait of a sick mind by emphatically adhering to the same suture conventions.

15 Teresa De Lauretis has noticed that it is predominantly women who are 'linked' to the vision of other characters as objects of the look. Inanimate items are presented as objects of focalization much less frequently: only when such items are of crucial importance to the story, such as the pumps in *The Lady Vanishes*, do they become explicit objects of someone's look.

16 See Browne, 'The Spectator-in-the-Text,' 111.

17 The close shots of Mademoiselle Dufour's cheerful face eclipse the voyeur-

ism of the men. Even if 'we don't see things or even think about them from his or her literal perspective, it still makes sense to say that we share the character's point of view' (Chatman, 'What Novels Can Do,' 134).

18 According to Žižek, the new femme fatale such as Catherine Trammell is deeply enigmatic because she so obviously plays at being a conniving trickster that men refuse to believe she is actually as cold and manipulative as she appears. For them, her attitude is a defence mechanism. Consequently, the woman can best deceive men by showing exactly how vicious she is: it both makes her seductive and defies male understanding. See Žižek, 'Death and the Maiden.'

19 Pinter, 'The Comfort,' 257.

20 Ibid.

Chapter 6: The Visual Narrator and Visual Focalization

1 Žižek, *Looking Awry*, 42.

2 In Lacanian terms, on a strictly visual level, the transition from the imaginary stage (the mirror stage) to the symbolic field of meaning is lacking.

3 It is possible to make the reverse shot a point-of-view shot for another character in turn. In *Goodfellas* (Martin Scorsese, 1990), for example, Karen is sitting astride her mobster husband, Henry Hill, who is lying on his back. She is holding him at gunpoint, feeling betrayed because of his adultery. First, we see shots from Karen's perspective: the camera is positioned close to Henry's face and in such a way that we do not see the gun. Then, we see shots from Henry's perspective: the gun is now dangerously close to the camera.

4 See also Vojkovic, 'Subjectivity,' 40. Monte did not utter the name 'Mildred' because he was looking at her face but because his final thought was of her.

5 See also Copjec, 'Introduction,' vii–ix.

6 Up until this moment, we have not seen Vincent's face: a subjective camera is used, just as in *The Lady in the Lake*. After the surgery, we transcend Vincent's perspective.

7 While we observe Vincent escape, we do not get any confirmation that he is being watched by another character. That the lack or minimal use of reverse shots can also create a totally different effect is demonstrated by *Der Letzte Mann* (F.W. Murnau, 1924). In this film, the porter of a chic hotel is parading in his carefully polished uniform. The fact that he is rather pleased with himself is shown by his disregard for everything around him:

he continuously remains the object of both the look and the camera and would not have it any other way. The minimal use of reverse shot characterizes the porter's vanity: all eyes have to be on him all the time.

8 Heath, *Questions of Cinema*, 44–5.

9 Ibid.

10 When Guido acts as interpreter for the German camp officer who is explaining the strict rules to the Italian prisoners, he alters the announcements concerning obedience, labour, and execution as punishment for any failure to comply. Guido explains to his son and his fellow prisoners that crying, asking for your mother, and nagging for a sweet will cost you points. A crucial role is played by the other inmates, none of whom shatter the illusion. They only watch with compassion as Guido desperately tries to make his son believe that the camp is in fact a game. According to his father, all the other sounds Giosué hears are attempts to distract him: they would love to see Giosué withdraw because he is in the lead and might just win the tank.

11 Bal, *Narratology*, 20.

12 Like *Schindler's List*, *Rumble Fish* (Francis Ford Coppola, 1984) has been filmed in black and white for the most part. In Coppola's film, the choice of black and white is based on the fact that the protagonist, the Motorcycle Boy, is colour blind. That the fighting fish are shown in colour at the end emphasizes his fascination for these creatures.

13 See Gunning, 'Weaving a Narrative,' 344–5.

14 For this reading, see also Žižek, *Organs*: 'Precisely insofar as Madeleine's profile is *not* Scottie's point-of-view, the shot of her profile is *totally* subjectivized, depicting, in a way, not what Scottie effectively sees but what he imagines, that is, his hallucinatory inner vision' (153).

15 Whereas we are continually watching through 'Jack's' eyes in *Fight Club*, in *The Sixth Sense* (M. Night Shyamalan, 1999) we are offered only the perspective of the boy, Cole Sear, when we see child psychiatrist Malcolm Crowe. For the other characters, the latter simply does not exist. The film's narrative trick is to hide the fact that the shots of Crowe are exclusively focalized by the boy.

16 For a comparison, see Cameron and Wood, *Antonioni*, 116–22.

17 See Branigan, *Point of View*, 95.

18 See Cameron and Wood, *Antonioni*, 122.

19 In *Il Deserto Rosso*, colours are manipulated to such an extent that the film would in fact be unsuitable for the colour blind.

20 Bal, *Narratology*, 163.

21 The God's eye perspective from *The Birds* is used the other way around

in the final shot of *Breaking the Waves,* which was discussed earlier in this chapter. In Von Trier's film, Bess's 'deal' is unmasked as a subjective misrecognition. If we assume that the final shot is God's answer, however, Bess's bizarre fantasy is 'objectified.' Bess's 'psychotic' vision is not secondary to medical or religious perspectives but in fact overshadows them. Whereas the trend in *The Birds* progresses from apparently objective to subjective, the development in *Breaking the Waves* proceeds from apparently subjective to seemingly objective.

22 In fact, the time-travel film *Donnie Darko* (Richard Kelly, 2002) is also based on a flashforward. Donnie is taking medication for paranoid schizophrenia. The giant rabbit that warns him about a certain date is actually a product of his syndrome, or so he assumes. It eventually turns out, however, that the giant rabbit is a guy in a Halloween costume who fatally hits Donnie's girlfriend Gretchen with his car on the predicted date. Donnie has in fact foreseen the future. Being interested in theories of time travel, he returns to the first night he met the giant rabbit. The result of his return is that he sacrifices his own life so that Gretchen may live.

23 A separate category of ontologically problematic films are time-travel films. Characters can meet themselves in another time, which, for instance, happens when the eight-year-old James Cole witnesses his own death at the airport without realizing it in *12 Monkeys* (Terry Gilliam, 1997). Crucial in this type of film is the rule that Doc Brown tells Marty McFly in the second part of the *Back to the Future* trilogy: the identity of a time-travelling character can never be revealed to his counterpart who is living according to the standard chronology. An ontological shock would inevitably ensue.

Chapter 7: Tension between the Visual and Auditive Narrators

1 Gunning, *D.W. Griffith,* 91.
2 Ibid., 92.
3 Chatman, *Coming to Terms,* 135.
4 Ibid.
5 In *A Rhetoric of Irony,* Booth refers to the work of Samuel Beckett as the ultimate example of 'unstable irony.' See especially 258–60.
6 'Meaning is context-bound, but contexts are boundless' (Culler, *On Deconstruction,* 123).
7 The qualification 'the good,' which appears twice, is ironic because moral norms or noble actions do not determine 'Blondie's' heroism; a genre convention does instead. In American Westerns, we always know that the good cause will prevail. In *The Good, the Bad and the Ugly,* Blondie is the

one who cunningly escapes with the booty. Because of this, he must have been 'the good' (see Verstraten, *Screening Cowboys*, 192–4).

8　The dryly comical gangster film *Fargo* (Joel and Ethan Coen, 1996) starts with the announcement that what we are about to see is a true story that took place in Minnesota in 1987. A car salesman wants to have his wife abducted, which is the start of a whole sequence of bizarre events. Later on, an alert newspaper will reveal that the whole story has been fabricated. If a film is fiction above all, why can a label like 'based on a true story' not be fiction as well? It forces the audience to consider carefully the status of the images shown.

9　This gap between the visual and auditive tracks has had a few inventive uses. The denouement of the famous *Citizen Kane* is even based on this lacuna. The flashbacks in this movie offer insights into the life and times of the deceased media tycoon Charles Kane, but they do not reveal what reporter Jerry Thompson is actually looking for. He wants to understand the meaning of Kane's last word, 'Rosebud.' Will he succeed? When the final words of the film ('Throw that junk in') sound, we see various possessions of Kane being burned. The visual narrator shows the old sled that Kane owned as a child being thrown into the flames. The name of the sled slowly disappears in the heat: 'Rosebud.' On the auditive track, *Citizen Kane* does not offer the solution to the riddle. Unbeknown to the characters, only the visual track reveals what Kane's last words refer to: the sled from his youth he was playing with on the day his mother signed the contract delivering him to Mr Thatcher. In *Citizen Kane*, the visual narrator (as external focalizor) gives us the solution independently of both the auditive track and the characters.

10　Strictly speaking, the scenes from *Fight Club* I discussed earlier are a part of an extended flashback. The film starts, after all, with the scene in which Tyler threatens Jack by putting a gun in his mouth. Two hours later, we return to this moment. However, I have not discussed these scenes as part of a flashback.

11　A wipe is a transition from shot to shot in which a horizontal line glides across the screen from the left, gradually replacing the first image by the second.

12　Narratologically, the character we see in the flashback is not the same as the character who narrates about himself in the past tense. The narrating character looks back and already knows how the events the character in the flashback is still living through will turn out. The discrepancy between the flashback character and the narrating character is particularly heart rending in a film like *La Vita è Bella*. At the time of the concentration camp, the boy Giosué is too young to realize what sacrifice his father is making. At the end of the film, however, the older Giosué's voice-over shows that he fully grasps how his father tried to guide him through the incomprehensible horrors of the camp.

13 Chatman, *Coming to Terms*, 136.

14 The only example Chatman refers to that has an accurate auditive track and an unreliable visual track is *An American in Paris* (Vincente Minnelli, 1952). In a voice-over, the American painter Jerry Mulligan portrays his surroundings in Paris. Next, the camera climbs up a building to introduce him, but ends up at a window with a couple kissing. The voice-over says, 'No, not there. One flight up,' after which we see Jerry lying in bed. A similar thing happens when Jerry's friends Adam and Henri introduce themselves. Adam is a gloomy concert pianist. When his visual introduction is pending, a cheerful young man appears: 'Ah, that's not me. He's too happy.' Henri brags about his still youthful appearance, after which the camera zooms in on a young boy looking into a mirror: 'No, that's not me. I'm not that young.' I would say that the point is not that the visual narrator is ignorant here, but that he zooms in on the wrong person for the filmic joke. When Henri brags about his youthfulness, the visual narrator, faking ignorance, teases him with a shot of a character who is far too young (*Coming to Terms*, 136).

15 See Modleski, *The Women Who Knew Too Much*, 118.

16 There are reasons to assume that Tajomaru's flashback is second hand because the main fabula encompasses only the three people taking shelter near the Rashomon gate. When we return to the three men taking shelter, the civilian also knows about Tajomaru's confession. Either the priest or (more likely) the lumberjack has told him about the bandit's testimony.

17 In an earlier scene, Dreverhaven has actually misrecognized Katadreuffe. When the son, a little rascal, is arrested by police officers, he thinks he will be clever and gives Dreverhaven's name. His father is summoned immediately, but when he arrives he declares, 'I'm sorry, I've never seen this boy in my life.'

18 The claim made by several critics that *The Usual Suspects* is the enactment of a complete lie is not entirely correct. During an interrogation, Roger 'Verbal' Kint tells Detective Dave Kujan what he knows about the explosion of a supposed cocaine ship. Verbal has escaped the explosion because he was standing guard on shore. Kujan also asks about the mysterious figure Keyser Söze, who is named in connection with the explosion. At a certain point, Kujan loses his patience and starts conjecturing himself: 'I'll tell you what I know. Stop me when this sounds familiar.' The flashback

picks up where Kint left off, but now we see Kujan's version of the events. Verbal now has to listen to what was initially his retroversion. He has told the detective quite a few untruths, but Kujan, by starting his own narration, partially creates some fictions of his own. Because the style does not change after Kujan takes over, we cannot exclude the possibility that the flashbacks are a rendition of Kujan's visualization of the scenes described by Verbal. He wishes so badly to see his own assessment of what happened confirmed that he wants Verbal to tell him exactly those things that would match his own conclusions.

Chapter 8: Sound as a Narrative Force

1 Altman, 'Sound Space,' 55.
2 The workings of sound in this scene are also referred to in Forceville, 'The Conspiracy,' 131.
3 The term *audiovisual contract* has been adopted from Chion, *Audio-vision*.
4 Ibid., 40.
5 The famous musical *Singin' in the Rain* (Gene Kelly and Stanley Donen, 1952) takes this technical imperfection as a starting point. The musical is situated in 1927, during the era of the first successes of the sound film. Studio boss R.F. Simpson decides that all his films immediately need to switch to sound. The test screening of the hastily adapted film *The Dueling Cavalier* causes great hilarity in the audience. The beautiful diva Lina Lamont not only has the voice of the crow but also forgets to speak in the direction of the microphone on her shoulder. When she turns her head to the left she becomes inaudible, whereas the fingering of her pearl necklace sounds like the rumbling of a storm. Adding sound to a silent film inadvertently results in a comedy: the test audience roars with laughter at the clumsy sound effects.
6 Altman, 'Sound Space,' 56.
7 Ibid., 57, 60.
8 A scene from *Intolerable Cruelty* (Joel Coen, 2004) offers another good example. Divorce lawyer Miles Massey has drawn up a prenuptial agreement with Marilyn Rexroth and the rich Texan oil baron Howard D. Doyle. He is sure that Marilyn will deceive her new husband. When the couple divorces shortly afterward, Miles marries Marilyn under the same conditions. He supposes that the marriage will be lucrative even if it fails, since Marilyn is the wealthy party. He realizes his mistake when he sees a soap with Howard Doyle as a doctor. He is no oil baron, but an actor. Consequently, Marilyn does not own millions at all. The realization that Marilyn

has tricked him is represented in the way the words of the actor-doctor are transformed: they are distorted to such an extent that he becomes unintelligible.

9 See Weis, *The Silent Scream*, 43. In the silent film *Das Kabinett des Dr Caligari*, a highpoint of German Expressionism, the name 'Caligari' flashes across the screen many times to signify that the name is being hammered into everyone's ears.

10 Chion, *The Voice in Cinema*, 24.

11 Gorbman, *Unheard Melodies*, 79.

12 Ibid., 25.

13 Bordwell and Thompson, *Film History*, 367.

14 Chion, *Audio-vision*, 81.

15 Gorbman, *Unheard Melodies*, 23.

16 Ibid., 19.

17 The most important study of this 'comedy of remarriage' is Stanley Cavell's *Pursuits of Happiness*. Films belonging to this subgenre are, among others, *It Happened One Night* (Frank Capra, 1934), *The Awful Truth* (Leo McCarey, 1937), *Bringin' up Baby* (Howard Hawks, 1938), *The Philadelphia Story* (George Cukor, 1940), and *His Girl Friday* (Howard Hawks, 1941).

18 Half an hour into *Trainspotting*, another noteworthy ironic contrast is created. Mark suffers from cold sweats and is urgently in need of a fix. While we are hearing 'Perfect Day' by Lou Reed (also a notorious junkie), we see Mark sink to the ground and be transported to hospital, completely senseless – a 'perfect day,' indeed.

19 Whereas the light-hearted music has a painful effect in *Reservoir Dogs*, a similarly cheerful tune becomes comical at the 'painful' ending of *Life of Brian* (Terry Jones, 1979). Brian Cohen has been taken for the Messiah and erroneously crucified. When all hope for rescue has gone, one of the other crucified prisoners encourages the group to cheer up and sets in to the optimistic musical finale, 'Always Look on the Bright Side of Life.' Because *Life of Brian* has been a hilarious parody from the beginning, the 'serious' tone of the scene – in which 140 prisoners are hanging on crosses – quickly complies with the jolly melody. With the message to 'always look on the bright side of life,' no matter how bad the circumstances, the film ends on a ridiculously optimistic note. Even if the official plot ends somewhat depressingly, the sombre mood is washed away with a joke.

20 Gorbman, *Unheard Melodies*, 154.

21 Just like Hitchcock in *Shadow of a Doubt*, Sergio Leone has provided his main characters with their own themes on the soundtrack of his spaghetti Western epic *Once upon a Time in the West*. The moments when the romantic

bandit Cheyenne appears, for example, are always preceded by a tune with a banjo and an electric piano. That theme ends abruptly when he dies. Jill McBain is associated with an orchestral theme, which is appropriate because she becomes the founder of Sweetwater's future wealth. The villain, Frank, is accompanied by an ominous trumpet and an electric guitar. The unknown avenger, who speaks only when he absolutely has to, prefers to communicate with his harmonica. Most effective is that this instrument finally joins in on the wailing tune belonging to Frank. Even though Frank does not know yet who the Harmonica Man is, it is immediately made clear that their paths are destined to cross. Only during the big finale, the showdown between Frank and the Harmonica Man, does the mysterious man reveal his identity by means of his instrument. As Frank pressed a harmonica between the teeth of the young man once, so are the roles reversed now. With the harmonica in his mouth, Frank breathes his last.

22 See Mancini, 'The Sound Designer,' 367. Chion also quotes this example in *Audio-vision*, 12.

23 Bordwell and Thompson refer to this scene as well in *Film History*, 365.

24 Chion, *Audio-vision*, 151. *The Man Who Knew Too Much* (Alfred Hitchcock, 1956) also offers a clear example of a selective use of sound to create the impression of relative serenity or commotion. On holiday in Marrakech, Louis Bernard dies in the arms of Benjamin McKenna. When the camera is directed at Benjamin's face as he is trying to catch the dying man's last words, the cacophony of city sounds softens, only regaining volume when Marrakech is shown once more in the background of the reverse shot.

25 Chion, *Audio-vision*, 62.

26 Ibid., 22.

27 See the interview with Walter Murch by Frank Paine, 'Sound Mixing,' 356–7.

28 This scene is also discussed by Elisabeth Weis, *The Silent Scream*, 68–72.

29 Ibid., 108.

30 In *Rear Window*, sound also maps out Jeff's attitude toward Lisa, who wants to marry him. Jeff has his doubts and fears the commitment required of him. Every time Lisa tries to increase their intimacy, her attempt is marked auditively. A neighbour starts to play the composition 'Mona Lisa' after Lisa has invited herself over and Jeff finally agrees. As Lisa pulls down the blinds, however, Jeff is 'saved' by a horrid scream. The dog that has been sniffing around the courtyard has been murdered. Immediately, the windows are opened again. At the end of the movie, when Jeff has both his legs in a cast, we hear the complete version of 'Mona Lisa' in order to signify that Jeff has finally surrendered to Lisa.

31 *Blue Velvet* (David Lynch, 1986) offers a nice variation on the rule that characters whom we hear before we see are querulous. Jeffrey Beaumont has just left the house of a police officer when he hears a voice coming out of the darkness. The person who appears is not a troublemaker, however, but the angelic Sandy Williams, a blonde girl dressed in white.

32 Hitchcock would not be Hitchcock if he had not also reversed the convention of the auditive assault. In *The Birds* (1963), Melanie Daniels makes a pass at bachelor Mitch Brenner by secretly delivering 'love birds,' supposedly for his little sister. They are cheerfully chirping parakeets. When she returns with her rented boat, we hear the engine drone and see a gull floating in the air. The gull swoops in to pick at Melanie's head, and only then do we hear its cry. Because the danger is not announced here, the sudden attack causes total surprise. Elizabeth Weis claims in *The Silent Scream* that the bird sounds are so frightening because they remain relatively abstract (139). The sounds are artificial and have become stylized to such an extent that they would be unrecognizable without being linked to the images of birds. The seventh and final attack is an exception. The viewer has become so familiar with the evil nature of the noisy birds by now that the suggestion, made by the sound of their wings alone, that they can also act naturally and quietly makes things 'worse.'

33 Chion *Audio-vision*, 39.

Chapter 9: The Narrative Principles of Genres

1 See Sobchack, *Screening Space*, 29–35.

2 See Meijer, *In tekst gevat*, 18. In a column in *de Volkskrant*, Barber van der Pol has jokingly but very accurately remarked that a book with a 2 per cent level of absolute originality would be completely unreadable. Two per cent sounds meagre, but we would not be able to comprehend so much originality.

3 Cited in Frayling, *Spaghetti Westerns*, 41.

4 Several New Hollywood blockbusters are rehashed versions of B film genres. The film I refer to in the introduction, *Godzilla*, is for example inspired by the Japanese monster movie *Gojira* (Inoshira Honda, 1956).

5 A good example of a rigorous variation is offered by *Lonesome Cowboys* (Andy Warhol, 1969). Unlike the average cowboy, who never hesitates to act and is never consciously concerned with his looks, the protagonists in *Lonesome Cowboys* are extremely passive and restrict themselves to striking macho poses and training their hips by means of ballet exercises. Whereas the classic cowboy attempts to display his masculine identity, this film

revolves around display itself. Rather than wondering whether they *are* real men, the relevant question for Warhol's cowboys is whether they *look* the part. The matter of looks also applies to the film as a whole. *Lonesome Cowboys* looks like a Western because of its setting and costumes, but lacks the basic premise of the genre: there is no showdown whatsoever (Verstraten, *Screening Cowboys*, 223–8).

6 Tudor, 'Genre,' 3.

7 For a further narratological analysis of the detective genre, see the first two chapters of Van der Weide, *Detective en anti-detective*, 11–58.

8 Film musicals that revolve around the preparations for a show and its final performance are called 'backstage musicals.'

9 See Rubin, 'Busby Berkeley,' 60.

10 See Feuer, *The Hollywood Musical*, 75.

11 Altman, *The American Film Musical*, 16.

12 Ibid., 17.

13 Ibid., 21–7.

14 These sci-fi films are not necessarily anti-scientific, but they do display a split attitude: namely, science not only creates the creature but is also required to dispose of it. See Sobchack, *Screening Space*, 45.

15 Ibid., 52.

16 See Smelik, 'Het kannibalistische oog,' 8–9.

17 For this reading of the femme fatale, see Žižek, *Looking Awry*, 65–6.

18 For this reading of the neo-femme fatale, see Žižek, *The Art of the Ridiculous Sublime*, 20–1.

19 See Willis, *High Contrast*, 195. Willis focuses on Tarantino's fascination with toilet scenes, as shown by a character in *Reservoir Dogs* protesting that he will be nicknamed 'Mr Brown' or by the episode of the gold watch in *Pulp Fiction*, in which the precious object handed down to Butch had at one point been secreted in a character's anus for safekeeping.

Chapter 10: Filmic Excess

1 Within the field of film studies, historical, economical, and industrial contexts have been the traditional components of analysis.

2 See Tasker, *Spectacular Bodies*, 109.

3 The modern action hero poses in the vein of actual bodybuilders and offers a performance of hypermasculinity. According to Jacques Lacan, however, ostentatiously displaying masculine signs conjures feminine effects ('The Meaning of the Phallus,' 85).

4 To take up an example from the previous chapter, the extreme close-ups of   the Harmonica Man's eyes in *Once upon a Time in the West* are an excessive stylistic device. It is only after the stubborn persistence of these close-ups that we get a flashback to reveal something of this mysterious figure's inner life for the first time. We get only an impression of his thoughts, in other words, when the camera patiently attempts to look 'right through' his eyes. The excessive device is necessary to provide this main character with a history.

5 See Thompson, 'The Concept of Cinematic Excess.'

6 See Elsaesser, 'Tales of Sound and Fury,' 364–6.

7 See also Žižek, 'Death and the Maiden,' 216–17. Speaking about the usual melodramatic way of working, he claims that the 'repressed kernel of the narrative returns in the excess of the form.'

8 See also Elsaesser, *Fassbinder's Germany*, 59.

9 Quoted in Žižek, 'Death and the Maiden,' 216.

10 *Lap rouge* (Lodewijk Crijns, 1996), a portrait of two brothers living in a remote cottage on the French countryside with their domineering elderly mother, provides us with a comparable case. For the unsuspecting viewer, the film constantly gives rise to the question of whether it is a 'real' documentary or a fiction film. Extratextual information is required to reveal that everything is staged.

11 See Van Alphen, *Art in Mind*, 114–15.

12 If you disregard the finale, *The Comfort of Strangers* would have been a relationship drama in the tradition of *Viaggio in Italia* (Roberto Rossellini, 1953). In this meditative road movie, the love of a British man and a woman on holiday in Italy is severely tested. Contact with the locals and their culture does not purge the marriage of the Joyces of its deadening routine but only strengthens their mutual alienation. It is only when they decide to divorce and subsequently get caught up in the passionate bustle of a procession in honour of Mary in a town near Naples that they seem to realize they need to depend on each other. In Rossellini's film, there is no breakthrough or sudden turn of events. The film ends with an embrace, but it does not have any proper narrative closure. Do they protect each other from the passion of life (in and around Naples), or have they learned to embrace this passion and will the journey resuscitate their marriage?

13 Thompson, 'The Concept of Cinematic Excess,' 132. One could debate whether the turn of events in *The Comfort of Strangers* is so excessive that the balance between the (exaggerated) style and the (even more exaggerated) plot is upset once more. Emphasis seems to shift to the latter at the end, after all.

Appendix: *The Virgin Suicides* **as a Test Case**

1 Of the four boys, David is the least outspoken. He is often absent and is the only one whose parents are never shown. This makes him the least likely candidate for the voice-over. Parker (Parkie) and Tim (The Brain) are both mentioned by the narrator. Chase is the only one left. He has a few scenes with the sisters, and we also see him watching television at his own house.

2 Several scenes in the Lisbon house are based on the presence of a visitor: Peter Sisten, who is allowed to join the family for dinner; Trip, who watches television with them; Father Moody, who visits after Cecilia's death; or the boys who get permission to take the girls to the homecoming dance.

3 Even though we are invited to share the vision of an internal focalizor, as viewers we can also choose to ignore it. See also my discussion of Nick Browne's analysis of *Stagecoach* in Chapter 5.

4 In *The Virgin Suicides*, music nearly always has an amplifying or illustrative function. In the eyes of the girls, Trip is a 'magic man'; when Lux and Trip kiss in secret, we hear 'Crazy on You'; when the girls are locked up, a Gilbert O'Sullivan song 'Alone Again,' is played, with the lyrics, 'But in my hour of need / I surely am indeed / Alone again, naturally.'

5 Apart from being a sign of the changing mood of the main characters, the shift in colour and lighting could also be motivated 'realistically.' Because of a spill at a nearby plant, the air has been polluted. This is the reason for the cynical theme of the final party: 'Asphyxiation.'

Bibliography

Altman, Rick. *The American Film Musical*. Bloomington and Indianapolis: Indiana University Press, 1987.

–. 'Sound Space.' In *Sound Theory/ Sound Practice*, ed. Rick Altman, 46–64. London: Routledge, 1992.

Amis, Martin. *Time's Arrow, or The Nature of the Offense*. New York: Harmony Books, 1991.

Bal, Mieke. *De theorie van vertellen en verhalen*. Muiderberg: Coutinho, 1978.

–. *Narratology: Introduction to the Theory of Narrative*. Rev. ed. Toronto: University of Toronto Press, 1997.

–. *Quoting Caravaggio: Contemporary Art, Preposterous History*. Chicago: University of Chicago Press, 1999.

–. *Reading 'Rembrandt': Beyond the Word–Image Opposition*. Cambridge: Cambridge University Press, 1991.

Barthes, Roland. *Camera Lucida: Reflections on Photography*. Translated by Richard Howard. New York: Farrar, Straus and Giroux, 1981.

Bazin, André. *What Is Cinema?* Translated by Hugh Gray. Berkeley, LA: University of California Press, 1971.

Bleeker, Maaike. *Visuality in the Theatre: The Locus of Looking*. Houndmills, UK: Palgrave Macmillan, 2008.

Bonitzer, Pascal. 'The Disappearance (On Antonioni).' In *L'avventura: Michelangelo Antonioni, director*, ed. Seymour Chatman and Guido Fink, 215–18. New Brunswick, NJ: Rutgers University Press, 1989.

Booth, Wayne C. *The Rhetoric of Fiction*. Chicago: University of Chicago Press, 1961.

–. *A Rhetoric of Irony*. Chicago: University of Chicago Press, 1974.

Bordwell, David. *Narration in the Fiction Film*. London: Methuen, 1985.

–. *The Way Hollywood Tells It: Story and Style in Modern Movies*. Berkeley: University of California Press, 2006.

Bordwell, David, and Kristin Thompson. *Film Art: An Introduction*. 4th ed. New York: McGraw-Hill, 1990.

–. *Film Art: An Introduction*. 7th ed. New York: McGraw-Hill, 2004.

Branigan, Edward. *Narrative Comprehension and Film*. London: Routledge, 1992.

–. *Point of View in the Cinema: A Theory of Narrative and Subjectivity in Classical Film*. Berlin: Mouton, 1984.

Browne, Nick. 'The Spectator-in-the-Text: The Rhetoric of *Stagecoach*.' In *Narrative, Apparatus, Ideology: A Film Reader*, ed. Philip Rosen, 102–19. New York: Columbia University Press, 1986.

Cameron, Ian, and Robin Wood. *Antonioni*. New York: Praeger, 1971.

Cavell, Stanley. *Pursuits of Happiness: The Hollywood Comedy of Remarriage*. Cambridge, MA: Harvard University Press, 1981.

Chatman, Seymour. *Coming to Terms: The Rhetoric of Narrative in Fiction and Film*. Ithaca, NY: Cornell University Press, 1990.

–. 'What Novels Can Do That Films Can't (and Vice Versa).' *Critical Inquiry* 7 (Autumn 1980): 121–40

Chion, Michel. *Audio-vision: Sound on Screen*. Translated and edited by Claudia Gorbman. New York: Columbia University Press, 1994.

–. *The Voice in Cinema*. Translated by Claudia Gorbman. New York: Columbia University Press, 1999.

Copjec, Joan. 'Introduction.' In *Shades of Noir: A Reader*, ed. Joan Copjec, vii–xii. London: Verso, 1993.

Crafton, Don. 'Pie and Chase: Gag, Spectacle and Narrative in Slapstick Comedy.' In *Classical Hollywood Comedy*, ed. Kristine Brunovska Karnick and Henry Jenkins, 106–19. New York: Routledge, 1995.

Cubitt, Sean. *The Cinema Effect*. Cambridge, MA: MIT Press, 2004.

Culler, Jonathan. *On Deconstruction: Theory and Criticism after Structuralism*. London: Routledge and Kegan Paul, 1983.

–. *The Pursuit of Signs: Semiotics, Literature, Deconstruction*. Ithaca, NY: Cornell University Press, 1981.

Dayan, Daniel. 'The Tutor-Code of Classical Cinema.' *Film Quarterly* 28, no. 1 (1974): 22–31.

De Lauretis, Teresa. *Alice Doesn't: Feminism, Semiotics, Cinema*. Bloomington: Indiana University Press, 1984.

Deleyto, Celestino. 'Focalisation in Film Narrative.' *Narratology*, ed. Susana Onega, Garcia Landa, and José Angel, 217–33. London: Longman, 1996.

Doane, Mary Ann. *The Desire to Desire: The Woman's Film of the 1940s*. Bloomington and Indianapolis: Indiana University Press, 1987.

Elsaesser, Thomas. *Fassbinder's Germany: History, Identity, Subject*. Amsterdam: Amsterdam University Press, 1996.

–. 'The Pathos of Failure: American Films in the 1970s: Notes on the Unmotivated Hero.' In *The Last Great American Picture Show: New Hollywood Cinema
in the 1970s*, ed. Thomas Elsaesser, Alexander Horwath, and Noel King,
279–92. Amsterdam: Amsterdam University Press, 2004.

–. 'Tales of Sound and Fury: Observations on the Family Melodrama.' *Film
Genre: Reader II*, ed. Barry Keith Grant, 350–80. Austin: University of Texas
Press 1995.

–, ed. *Early Cinema: Space, Frame, Narrative*. London: BFI, 1997.

Elsaesser, Thomas, and Adam Barker. 'Introduction (to the Continuity Sys-
tem).' In *Early Cinema: Space, Frame, Narrative*, ed. Thomas Elsaesser, 293–
317. London: BFI, 1997.

Feuer, Jane. *The Hollywood Musical*. London: Macmillan, 1982.

Forceville, Charles. 'The Conspiracy in *The Comfort of Strangers*: Narration in
the Novel and the Film.' *Language and Literature* 11, no. 2 (2002): 119–35.

Frayling, Christopher. *Spaghetti Westerns: Cowboys and Europeans from Karl May
to Sergio Leone*. London: Routledge and Kegan Paul, 1981.

Gaudreault, André. *Du littéraire au filmique: Système du récit*. Paris: Méridiens
Klincksieck, 1988.

–. 'Film, Narrative, Narration: The Cinema of the Lumière Brothers,' trans.
Rosamund Howe. In *Early Cinema: Space, Frame, Narrative*, ed. Thomas Elsaesser, 68–75. London: BFI, 1997.

Genette, Gérard. *Narrative Discourse*. Translated by Jane E. Lewin. Foreword
Jonathan Culler. Oxford: Basil Blackwell, 1980.

Gorbman, Claudia. *Unheard Melodies: Narrative Film Music*. London: BFI, 1987.

Grant, Barry Keith, ed. *Film Genre: Reader II*. Austin: University of Texas Press,
1995.

Gunning, Tom. 'The Cinema of Attractions: Early Film, Its Spectator and
the Avant- Garde.' In *Early Cinema: Space, Frame, Narrative*, ed. Thomas
Elsaesser, 56–62. London: BFI, 1997.

–. *D.W. Griffith and the Origins of American Narrative Film: The Early Years at Biograph*. Urbana: University of Illinois Press, 1994.

–. 'Response to "Pie and Chase."' In *Classical Hollywood Comedy*, ed. Kristine
Brunovska Karnick and Henry Jenkins, 120–22. New York: Routledge, 1995.

–. 'Weaving a Narrative: Style and Economic Background in Griffith's Biograph Films.' In *Early Cinema: Space, Frame, Narrative*, ed. Thomas Elsaesser,
336–47. London: BFI, 1997.

Hall, Ann C. 'Daddy Dearest: Harold Pinter's *The Comfort of Strangers*.' *The
Films of Harold Pinter*, ed. Steven H. Gall, 87–98. Albany: State University of
New York Press, 2001.

Harries, Dan, ed. *The New Media Book*. London: BFI, 2004.

Heath, Stephen. *Questions of Cinema*. London and Basingstoke: Macmillan, 1981.

Henderson, Brian. 'Tense, Mood, and Voice in Film (Notes after Genette).' *Film Quarterly* 36, no. 4 (1983): 4–16.

Herman, Luc, and Bart Vervaeck. *Handbook of Narrative Analysis*. Lincoln: University of Nebraska Press, 2005.

–. *Vertelduivels: Handboek verhaalanalyse*. Nijmegen: Vantilt, 2005.

Jameson, Fredric. *Postmodernism, or, the Cultural Logic of Late Capitalism*. London: Verso, 1991.

Karnick, Kristine Brunovska, and Henry Jenkins, eds. *Classical Hollywood Comedy*. New York: Routledge, 1995.

Kinder, Marsha. 'Narrative Equivocations between Movies and Games.' In *The New Media Book*, ed. Dan Harries, 119–32. London: BFI, 2004.

Kozloff, Sarah. *Invisible Storytellers: Voice-over Narration in American Fiction Film*. Berkeley: University of California Press, 1988.

Lacan, Jacques. *The Four Fundamental Concepts of Psycho-analysis*. London: Penguin Books, 1994.

–. 'The Meaning of the Phallus.' In *Feminine Sexuality: Jacques Lacan and the École Freudienne*, ed. Juliet Mitchell and Jacqueline Rose, 74–85. London: Macmillan, 1982.

Lothe, Jacob. *Narrative in Fiction and Film*. Oxford: Oxford University Press, 2000.

Lunenfeld, Peter. 'The Myths of Interactive Cinema.' In *The New Media Book*, ed. Dan Harries, 145–54. London: BFI, 2004.

Maltby, Richard. '"A Brief Romantic Interlude": Dick and Jane go to 3½ Seconds of the Classical Hollywood Cinema' (1996). *Jacques Lacan: Critical Evaluations in Cultural Theory*. Volume 4, *Culture*, ed. Slavoj Žižek, 160–85. London: Routledge, 2003.

Mancini, Mark. 'The Sound Designer.' In *Film Sound: Theory and Practice*, ed. Elisabeth Weis and John Belton, 361–68. New York: Columbia University Press, 1985.

Manovich, Lev. *The Language of New Media*. Cambridge, MA: MIT Press, 2001.

McEwan, Ian. *The Comfort of Strangers*. London: Picador, 1982.

Meelberg, Vincent. *New Sounds, New Stories: Narrativity in Contemporary Music*. PhD diss. Leiden: Leiden University Press, 2006.

Meijer, Maaike. *In tekst gevat: Inleiding tot een kritiek van interpretatie*. Amsterdam: Amsterdam University Press, 1996.

Metz, Christian. *Psychoanalysis and Cinema: The Imaginary Signifier*. Translated by Celia Britton, Annwyl Williams, Ben Brewster, and Alfred Guzzetti. London: Macmillan, 1982.

Modleski, Tania. *The Women Who Knew Too Much: Hitchcock and Feminist Theory*. New York: Methuen, 1988.

Mulvey, Laura. 'Visual Pleasure and Narrative Cinema.' In *Visual and Other*

Pleasures, 14–26. Houndmills, UK: Macmillan, 1991.Murray, Janet H. *Hamlet on the Holodeck: The Future of Narrative in Cyberspace.* Cambridge, MA: MIT Press, 1997.

Onega Susana, Garcia Landa, and José Angel, eds. *Narratology.* London: Longman, 1996.

Oudart, Jean-Pierre. 'Cinema and Suture.' Translated by K. Hanet. *Screen* 18 (1978): 35–47.

Paine, Frank. 'Sound Mixing and *Apocalypse Now*: An Interview with Walter Murch.' In *Film Sound: Theory and Practice,* ed. Elisabeth Belton and John Belton, 356–60. New York: Columbia University Press, 1985.

Perez, Gilberto. *The Material Ghost: Films and Their Medium.* Baltimore: Johns Hopkins, 1998.

Peters, Jan Marie. *Het bezielde beeld: Inleiding in de filmmontage.* Amsterdam: Amsterdam University Press, 2003

Phillips, William. *Film: An Introduction.* Boston: Palgrave, 2002.

Pinter, Harold. 'The Comfort of Strangers.' *Collected Screenplays, part 3,* 244–328. London: Faber and Faber, 2000.

Pramaggiore, Maria, and Tom Wallis. *Film: A Critical Introduction.* London: Laurence King, 2005.

Rubin, Martin. 'Busby Berkeley and the Backstage Musical.' In *Hollywood Musicals: The Film Reader,* ed. Steven Cohan, 53–61. London: Routledge, 2002.

Silverman, Kaja. *The Subject of Semiotics.* New York: Oxford University Press, 1983.

Simons, Jan. *Interface en cyberspace: Inleiding in de nieuwe media.* Amsterdam: Amsterdam University Press, 2002.

Smelik, Anneke. 'Het kannibalistische oog van de cyborg: Reflecties over een hybride genre in de science-fiction film.' *Tijdschrift voor Vrouwenstudies* 69 (1997): 5–21.

Sneek, David. 'Een wonder in soberheid. Het oeuvre van Carl Theodor Dreyer (1889–1968).' *de Volkskrant* (15 April 2004): 32.

Sobchack, Vivian. *Screening Space: The American Science Fiction Film.* New Brunswick, NJ: Rutgers University Press, 1998.

Stewart, Garrett. *Framed Time: Toward a Postfilmic Cinema.* Chicago: University of Chicago Press, 2007.

Tasker, Yvonne. *Spectacular Bodies: Gender, Genre and the Action Cinema.* London: Routledge, 1995.

Thompson, Kristin. 'The Concept of Cinematic Excess.' In *Narrative, Apparatus, Ideology: A Film Reader,* ed. Philip Rosen, 130–42. New York: Columbia University Press, 1986.

–. *Storytelling in the New Hollywood: Analyzing Classical Narrative Technique.* Cambridge, MA: Harvard University Press.

Thompson, Kristin, and David Bordwell. *Film History: An Introduction*. New York: McGraw-Hill, 1994.

Tops, Ellen. *Foto's met gezag: Een semiotisch perspectief op priesterbeelden 1930– 1990*. Nijmegen: Vantilt, 2001.

Truffaut, François. *Hitchcock*. Translated by Helen G. Scott. New York: Simon and Schuster, 1967.

Tudor, Andrew. 'Genre.' *Film Genre: Reader II*, ed. Barry Keith Grant, 3–10. Austin: University of Texas Press, 1995.

Van Alphen, Ernst. *Art in Mind: How Contemporary Images Shape Thought*. Chicago: University of Chicago Press, 2005.

Van der Weide, Jack. *Detective en anti-detective: Narratologie, psychoanalyse, postmodernisme*. Nijmegen: Vantilt, 1996.

Van Oosterhout, Ambro. '*Morocco*: de rekwisieten van de omhelzing.' *Versus* 1 (1986): 116–27.

Van Sijll, Jennifer. *Cinematic Storytelling: The 100 Most Powerful Film Conventions Every Filmmaker Must Know*. Studio City, CA: Michael Wiese Productions, 2005.

Verstraten, Peter. *Screening Cowboys: Reading Masculinities in Westerns*. Nijmegen: Vantilt, 1999.

Vojkovic, Sasha. 'Subjectivity in the New Hollywood Cinema: Fathers, Sons and Other Ghosts.' PhD diss., University of Amsterdam, 2001.

Waardenburg, André. 'Lessen van de meester.' *Zine* 2 (2004): 6–8.

Weis, Elisabeth. *The Silent Scream: Alfred Hitchcock's Sound Track*. East Brunswick, NJ, and London: Associated University Presses, 1982.

Weis, Elisabeth, and John Belton, eds. *Film Sound: Theory and Practice*. New York: Columbia University Press, 1985.

Willis, Sharon. *High Contrast: Race and Gender in Contemporary Hollywood Film*. Durham and London: Duke University Press, 1997.

Žižek, Slavoj. *The Art of the Ridiculous Sublime: On David Lynch's Lost Highway*. Seattle: Walter Chapin Simpson Center for the Humanities, 2000.

–. 'Death and the Maiden.' In *The Žižek Reader*, ed. Elizabeth Wright and Edmond Wright, 206–21. Oxford: Blackwell, 1999.

–. *Enjoy Your Symptom! Jacques Lacan in Hollywood and Out*. New York: Routledge, 2001.

–. *The Fright of Real Tears: Krzysztof Kieslowski between Theory and Post-Theory*. London: BFI, 2001.

–. *Looking Awry: An Introduction to Jacques Lacan through Popular Culture*. Cambridge, MA: MIT Press, 1991.

–. *Organs without Bodies: Deleuze and Consequences*. New York: Routledge, 2003.

Illustration Credits

1.1 *Forty Guns*, Sam Fuller © 1957 Twentieth Century Fox. All rights reserved.

1.2 *Back to the Future*, Robert Zemeckis © 1985 Universal City Studios, Inc.

3.1 *The Comfort of Strangers*, Paul Schrader, 1990.

3.2 *Partie de campagne*, Jean Renoir, 1944, courtesy Les films du Pantheon, Paris, France.

3.3 *The Comfort of Strangers*, Paul Schrader, 1990.

3.4 *Morocco*, Josef von Sternberg © 1930 paramount Pictures Corporation.

4.1 *The Comfort of Strangers*, Paul Schrader, 1990.

5.1 *La règle du jeu*, Jean Renoir, 1939 © Les Grands Films Classiques, Paris, France.

5.2 *Le Mépris*, Jean-Luc Godard, 1963.

5.3 *Stagecoach*, John Ford, 1939, still photographs provided by Westchester Films, Inc.

6.1 *Breaking the Waves*, Lars von Trier, 1995, Zentropa Administration ApS.

6.2 *La Vita è Bella*, Roberto Benigni, 1997.

6.3 *Amadeus*, Milos Forman, 1984, courtesy The Saul Zaentz Company.

6.4 *The Gold Rush*, Charlie Chaplin, 1925 © Roy Export Company Establishment.

6.5 *The Birds*, Alfred Hitchcock © 1963 Alfred J. Hitchcock Productions, Inc.

7.1 *Johnny Guitar*, Nicholas Ray, 1954.

7.2 *Rashomon*, Akira Kurosawa, 1951.

10.1 *Imitation of Life*, Douglas Sirk © 1959 Universal Pictures.

10.2 *Angst Essen Seele Auf*, Rainer Werner Fassbinder, 1974, courtesy Rainer Werner Fassbinder Foundation.

Index of Concepts

Index of Names and Titles